Church

Move

From Isolation to Community

Adrian Peck

British Library Cataloguing in Publication Data. A catalogue record for this
book is available from the British Library.

ISBN 978-1-78665-153-2

Designed by David Bell.
Printed in China.

Foreword

Growing up in a South American village was exciting, joyful, and full of adventure. There was never a dull moment! As children, we were not exempt from the 'talk of the town' gossip and general conversations of the adult populace. You only got into trouble if you were caught repeating what you heard or being too visible while adults were congregating. The punishment was a very swift rebuke with a threat to inform your parents of the unacceptable behaviour. Usually, the episodes would end with an angry outburst from the adult: 'Children should be seen and not heard!' Shame would follow, and the laughter of the other children did not help the humiliation. Looking back now as a father of four children, seeing how easy it is to cause distress by our spoken words, the memories of those years are still vivid today. In a culture where name calling was the acceptable norm, everyone had some sort of nickname. You were referred to rudely by references to the size (whether big or small) of your head, face, nose, or other body parts, and any mistake you made while speaking would become your label until death. One gentleman's correct name was made known only at his funeral. I grew up with shame all around me.

Jesus was very intentional in dealing with stigma and shame. Numerous examples are scattered throughout the gospels: He blessed the children (Mark 10:13-16); He set forth a child as an example of trust, servanthood, and humility (Matthew 18:1-5); He exorcised the demon of the Syrophoenician woman's daughter (Mark 7:24-30); and His loving touch healed all who were sick in Capernaum (Luke 4:40). They were ashamed to be part of society because of their disease or socio-economic status. They lacked hope and trust even in the religious system of their day.

In this book, Pastor Adrian Peck brings us face to face with a side of humanity we are often uncomfortable with, showing us, as with a mirror, how we so often treat people. He writes, 'Through complete acceptance of people in their humanness, boundaries may be broken, barriers pulled down, shame eradicated, and humanity enhanced.' The practical wisdom shared in this volume will go a long way to get us there. Blessed reading!

Dr Kirk Thomas
Evangelism, Adventist Missions, Publishing and Sabbath School Director,
British Union Conference of Seventh-day Adventists

Contents

Contents

Journey's beginning, journey's hope

From about 6 or 7 years of age, there were many times when I could not wait to get out of the church building. I used to sit there diligently ticking off the items as we made our way through the order of service as outlined in the bulletin. Sing three hymns – tick. Listen to a minimum of four prayers (opening, offering, pastoral and closing) – tick. Pay attention with a smidgen more interest to the children's story and endure the sermon – tick, and tick again. It was all about counting down first the minutes and then the seconds to the service's conclusion, because then I would be free. Church done for the week – tick.

As I advanced into my teens, there were occasions when the above was still true. However, by then I was permitted to sit with friends rather than parents. This opened up a plethora of exciting entertainment possibilities. Thinking ourselves to be as amusing as a bunch of stand-up comedians, we tried to get away with as much chatter as possible. Sometimes a witty exchange would have us unable to contain our mirth, so our shoulders shook uncontrollably and snatches of laughter escaped and betrayed us. Then we would find ourselves afflicted with the opprobrium and disapproval of the people around us. This would inevitably lead to aghast and embarrassed parents reproving us with the familiar line: 'You've let the family down with your behaviour.'

More acceptable were quieter pastimes such as hangman. Preacher's sweepstake, a game that involved estimating and then counting how often a speaker's favourite phrase was heard, brought a competitive edge to proceedings. Sometimes, as a last resort, we read the church's news magazine MESSENGER or youth magazines such as *Insight*. But, occasionally, we were gifted with a speaker with a sparky delivery, a sense of humour, and something relevant and interesting to say. Then word games, puzzles and twice-read magazines were temporarily set aside in favour of actually following along for a while. Now that I preach most weeks, I wonder if similar memories are being made as I speak . . . except most of the distractions are now found on oh-so-resource-full and ubiquitous mobile devices. Facebook, Snapchat and TikTok take the place of the more simple pleasures derived from games relying on pen and paper – and yes, I am showing my age.

But is that how church should be – something to be endured, even suffered, out of a sense of duty? Is the church-going experience intended to consist of those few hours sitting in a building, revelling in the bits that are enjoyable, and bemused and frustrated by the remainder? I am sure that some will be horrified at what church was for me: something to get through until that sweet moment of release, that freedom experienced by taking the first step out of the door and into the sunshine and fresh air. What I have described so far does not sound much like what God intended when He created the church. However, it was not all as calamitous as might seem the case thus far. Lifelong friendships have developed because of my time in church. Some of the most enjoyable social occasions have been generated in a church environment: times full of laughter, camaraderie and food. Yet similar outcomes might have been possible while involved with any club or society – so what is it about churches that makes them different?

Certainly, it is not freedom from conflict. In the church I grew up in, you quickly came to understand that there were two sorts of people – those out on the field playing the game, and the larger group warming the bench . . . 'pew fodder', as they were more disparagingly called. The active group were able to ascend to the summit of the moral high ground. They were the group that self-determinedly gave much more than their fair share, while the benchwarmers sat back and cheekily enjoyed the fruits of others' labours. We were warned against being numbered among those who had the temerity to turn up, sit there, maybe sing a verse or two of a hymn, and then shuffle off home in a blink of an eye.

Experience changes one's perspective. As you get to know congregations better, you find that some attendees have to deal with awful and challenging health conditions: either their own or those of their family members. Some people are struggling just to make it through the week. Some survive by working double shifts. Still others feel they cannot get out of a life-trap in which they are overwhelmingly caught. For this group of people, turning up to a church service, even just for an hour or two, is both an achievement and a chance for some respite – Sabbath rest indeed. Attending a church service is a chance to put difficulties on hold. The opportunity to warm a seat for a while is a gift from God. In some cases, their very presence is as generous an offering as the widow's mite was in her day. Even so, doesn't a community founded and grounded on Christ have yet more to offer?

There are times when it is tempting to become not so much pew fodder as a Christian tortoise. When I was writing the first drafts of this introduction, I had the privilege of belonging to Norwich Cathedral's theological library. For a small sum, I had access to thousands of books, many of which I would have loved to have found time to read but never did. Just the walk to get to the library was frankly inspiring and brought about a sense of calm. The approach is dominated by the cathedral's main spire, which measures ninety-six metres and demands your attention, even without the added attraction of hosting peregrine falcons. Soon after entering the building, you find yourself strolling through the magnificent fourteenth-century cloister. Again the eyes are drawn upwards: this time to the hundreds of bosses, or intricate sculptures, embedded in the ceiling. Each step has been rehearsed by ancient Benedictine monks and draws you away from the bustling city outside the walls. The door to the library is tucked out of the way in one corner, and going through it feels a little like you are stepping through a C. S. Lewis-inspired wardrobe into another world. The reading room, with its expansive table, is mostly unoccupied; so it is easy to sit there in wonderful solitude, surrounded by millions of pages of wisdom and learning – reading, taking notes, preparing studies and sermons. A busy schedule meant I had to resist the lure of this place, not to sit for too long in this ivory tower, to turn down the chance of retreating into my shell. But it was oh-so-tempting.

Such places and the mindset they represent are attractive because they allow us to feel insulated from life's complexity and problems. There are occasions when the church can be the opposite of this – full of issues and fully complicated. The church also requires commitment; it requires that we stick to an externally imposed timetable and structure: and, in the age of individualism and self-determination, for some this is off-putting. By retreating into our shells, religion can easily become mostly a private and solitary affair. Of course, part of being a disciple involves solitary practices: we should regularly pray, study the Bible and commune with God on our own. But there are people who, by circumstance and by choice, go for a long time without interacting with another Christian beyond a superficial 'Hello – how are you?' They never really share life, God or the Bible; their church service is a blip in a week of separateness. For the Christian tortoises, the vast majority of their Christianity takes place outside of a church community in quiet seclusion.[1] Church worship is almost a distraction from what is perceived as the 'real stuff'. And yet the biblical picture of the church offers a potentially richer and deeper experience than this – one that happens both despite other people and because of them.

So here's the thing: here is why I feel compelled to put pen to paper, or fingers to keyboard, once again. The more time I spend studying God's purposes for local churches, the more amazed I am at what God intends for them. They are to be places of Spirit-empowered healing and authentic community; of joy and tears; of God-encountering worship; of exciting transformation; of meaning and purpose; of defiance, justice and humanity. Sometimes a hint of these is experienced, maybe even more than a hint of these . . . but this picture is so big, so bright, so eye-catching and so amazing that it can feel out of reach because we are distracted and bogged down by 'reality'. It is the brilliant ideal – but we know we live in the real world, hindered and hampered by the mundane and the routine. But what about the mystery of faith that comes with the presence of the Spirit?

Turn on a porch light at night and moths find it irresistible. Maybe this is because they use the moon to navigate, or the sun to direct them to safety, and are confused. Perhaps the ultraviolet portion of the spectrum of light mimics the signal sent out by fertile females. But the truth is that no one knows.[2] Likewise, I think, deep down, it is a mystery why people voluntarily turn up to church services regularly, occasionally or at all. There is something that keeps us coming back, keeps us sticking at it. It does not matter that we cannot quite put our finger on what it is. But I also think it is time to ditch the dimmer switch. A moment's quiet reflection might lead us to the conclusion that attending services for an hour or two will not cut it. Upping the hours sat in a pew won't either. We need to turn towards the light and the wonders of what God is and could be about in our church communities. In doing so, our current and our potential practices will be put into stark contrast, potentially bringing about a transformation.

The past should not be regretted, of course. But I wonder what would change if I could go back and speak to myself when I was that immature and distracted young lad with his word games and attitude; if I could take the opportunity to tap him on the shoulder and tell him about all of this good stuff; if I could open his eyes to the world of possibilities that live within church communities. This book is an attempt to start that process – if not for him, then for me now, and perhaps for others later. This is a 'we' book, not a 'me' book. The focus is the church as a community, not the church as a collection of individuals. I believe that approaching the Bible from the perspective of 'we' or 'us' opens up the possibility of transforming our understanding of what it is to be a Christian. In a society that is driven by individualism, this is counterintuitive. We mainly approach the Bible by asking, 'What does it mean for *me*?' However, in the pages that follow, the question, 'What does the Bible mean for *us*?' will be prioritised.

As I have been writing, in my mind's eye, I have been going on a journey. Partly, this was encouraged by the parable of the good Samaritan – mostly because I recognise the journey I have undertaken in transitioning from thinking about 'me' to thinking about 'us' and how this has revolutionised my understanding of God and His mission.

To read this book is to take up the invitation to become a fellow traveller. The book offers movements rather than chapters to encourage a sense of being in transition. Each movement builds on the previous ones, so if you are tempted to jump ahead you may get lost along the way. As in life, there are ups and downs. Some movements take us backwards to allow the next to shift us forwards.

Movements 1 and 2 introduce the parable of the good Samaritan in the context of Jesus' encounter with the lawyer found in Luke 10:25-37. This wonderful story hovers in the background throughout the book. There is danger in becoming overly familiar with the story, but do not be lulled into a false sense of security. In telling this parable, Jesus takes the lawyer on a foundation-rattling ride. We travel with them, at first reading the story for what it says to 'me', but eventually the 'we' aspects start to get teased out. The parable is generated by questions concerning love and neighbourliness. Where Movement 1 concentrates on the latter issue, Movement 2 addresses how love can be commanded and still be authentic.

Movement 3, staying with the parable, addresses our desire for comfort and relief, but ends with understanding Christianity as being about challenge – especially in the way we relate to others. A sense of discomfort is introduced as a travel companion at this point. It hangs around for the rest of the journey as a reminder that unease and disquiet motivate change. Movement 4 looks at the sociological models for the church, but is not intended to be a dry academic exercise. Rather, there are serious practical consequences for church communities that focus either on externals and boundaries or the core and relationships. Movement 5 brings these issues to life through a parable that explores how we sometimes allow our systems to move from being well-intentioned to abusive. It demonstrates how collective behaviour can exclude others through the intentional and unintentional creation of boundaries.

Having started to highlight the importance of persons, the way churches are prone to diminish the humanity of others is the subject of Movement 6. We start to engage with Paul's letter to the Philippians for the next few movements. The resistance to a 'we' approach is highlighted in Movements 7 and 8, focusing on the potential isolation that comes with interpreting the Bible individualistically. By the close of Movement 8, we are contemplating how being part of the big story can alter our perspective and affect our Christian experience. Movement 9 explores the issue of values as they affect communities and as found in Christ. Rather than the familiar focus on individual witness, Movement 10 addresses the matter of collective witness. Behaviours that produce boundaries are explored further in Movement 11, particularly those driven by a need to keep churches pure and the underlying disgust response that is its partner. The issues raised in this movement are not resolved until Movement 12, where an advance from disgust towards mercy is seen. Here, a change of focus is in view, moving from boundary-making rules to concerns about people.

What starts to emerge in the previous two movements comes fully into the light in Movements 13 to 16 as we focus on shame. This is arguably one of the greatest drivers behind how we see ourselves and our church communities and how we treat others as a consequence. We will examine the treacherous way in which shame infects communities and foments a shame culture instead of the mercy we all so desperately need. There is an all-too-inevitable link to the disgust response that was touched upon in Movements 11 and 12. Here, however, the resolution that is explored is the biblical one of vulnerability. The book draws to a close with Movement 17, which proposes that it is through complete acceptance of people in their humanity that boundaries may be broken, barriers pulled down, shame eradicated, and humanness enhanced.

Dotted throughout the book are sections with variants called: 'Something to think about along the way'. More practical than the main text, the intention is to provoke thoughtful discussion and to bring things down to earth with a bump by looking at real-life situations. The reader may care to use these as an opportunity to pause and think awhile. Following the epilogue is an appendix that summarises the findings from each movement. This gives a glimpse into the exciting God-originated potential that lies within every local church community.

[1]It is acknowledged that to combine 'church' and 'community' makes one or the other redundant to a certain extent. However, this is done to distinguish and emphasise the church as a group of people, as opposed to the church as a building or a series of programmes.
[2]Natalie Wolchover, 'Why Are Moths Drawn to Artificial Lights?' *Livescience.com*, 2011: *https://www.livescience.com/33156-moths-drawn-artificial-lights.html* (accessed 19 April 2020)

From neighbours to communities of neighbourliness

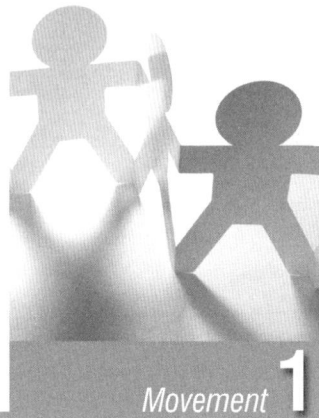

Movement 1

One of the most iconic courtroom scenes in film history occurs in the movie *A Few Good Men*, when Tom Cruise's character yells at his quarry in the stand, 'I want the truth!'[1] The witness, Jack Nicholson's colonel, responds by spitting out the immortal words, 'You can't handle the truth!' Nicholson's compellingly expressive face holds the audience captive as he sets off on a long tirade that eventually furnishes the lawyer played by Cruise with the exact answer for which he is looking: an admission of guilt. Now, good lawyers do ask questions to which they know the answers. Bad lawyers take a chance with their questions and flirt with failure. So is the lawyer that confronts Jesus in Luke 10:25-29 a good lawyer or a bad one, we might ask? He certainly knows the answer to his first question, as we shall find out, and probably *thinks* he knows the answer to the second:[2] but can he handle the truth?

The sparring commences in verse 25 as the lawyer stands, an action giving the proceedings a veneer of respect, as this is a courteous gesture in his culture. However, beneath the surface, maybe not quite fully submerged, a degree of irony is to be found, because Luke tells us that the lawyer's intention is not quite so deferential. He is standing to antagonistically test Jesus. There is hostility and aggression in the air as he seeks to put Jesus in the spotlight and catch Him out. He does this by posing the type of question most frequently found in Luke's works: 'What must I do to inherit eternal life?'[3] It is a question birthed in the cauldron of Daniel's apocalyptic writings, where resurrection is identified as leading either to everlasting life or to everlasting contempt, meaning death.[4] It is, therefore, an enquiry from the same stable as, 'What must I do to be saved?' (Acts 16:30), with a matching personal concern for making it into the ranks of the saints rather than being numbered among the damned.

It is natural to sit up and take notice as the lawyer poses this question. Ask a group of Christians whether they are concerned about being saved, and you will see a forest of arms raised in affirmation. It is not just first-century Jews who are fascinated by this subject. There is something about turning to Christianity that makes us keenly aware that our story will either continue or come to an abrupt end. We talk and debate long and hard about what it takes to be saved and how this is related to what we actually do, what we should or should not do, and in what way we must or must not do it. 'Jesus saves' may be the short answer, but that seems too easy.

We cannot be sure the lawyer is emotionally invested in the answer. He retains the dispassionate stance of an expert supervising an examination. It is Jesus and not the lawyer who is in the dock. Will he be able to tease Jesus' heretical teachings out into the open for public scrutiny? What is the basis for the question? The word 'inherit' carries legal overtones, as it refers to one named by a will or a legal provision – a natural fit for a lawyer. God's chosen people, however, were destined to inherit something far loftier than anything covered by the average will. Their inheritance was to be a new golden age when the Messiah would reign and Israel would be restored.[5] So hidden behind this question lurks another: 'What do I need to do to belong to God's people?' Get into this group and salvation will be assured. Therefore, the answer has built-in limits and boundaries that Jesus must be careful not to breach, lest He fail the examination right there in the court of public opinion.

Jesus circumnavigates the lawyer's loaded question in a customarily Jewish fashion by asking a couple of questions of His own. 'What does the law of Moses say? How do you read it?'[6] Jesus is a master tactician when it comes to debating with hostile opponents, and here He brilliantly turns the tables. Now it is His opponent who is being tested. It is the lawyer who is being forced to reveal *his* knowledge of the law . . . except his response might surprise us. It is as if we are hearing the lawyer quote his opponent, because he utters words made famous by Jesus Himself:[7] 'You shall love the Lord your God with all your heart, and with all your soul, and with all your strength, and with all your mind; and your neighbour as yourself.'[8] These are two commands found in Deuteronomy 6:5 and Leviticus 19:18 that were combined by Jesus to encapsulate godly living.[9]

Jesus' response could be seen as less than magnanimous. He was saying, in effect, 'Come on, then! Why don't you go and do what you know you should be doing anyway?' I too would have felt embarrassed at this point – caught out trying to be too clever for my own good. And, even though Jesus encourages him with: 'You have given the right answer; do this, and you will live,' the lawyer needs a time out, a sidebar. He could do with being reminded, 'This isn't supposed to be about how and why you keep the law: it's meant to be about challenging His understanding of the law. Keep your focus!' In this game of cat and mouse, the lawyer simply cannot accept Jesus' straightforward advice without losing face; so he asks his second question: 'And who is my neighbour?'[10]

It is rare for authors to reveal a character's motivations in the Bible – often, readers are left to work out what is going on based on what is said and done.[11] In this story, Luke is spoiling us and reveals that the lawyer asks this question 'to justify himself'.[12] Is he trying to prove that he is right?[13] Or is he still attempting to test Jesus, trying to snatch back the initiative? Caught off guard, has the lawyer's original hostility intensified? Is he still playing the role of a 'classic casuistic puzzler'?[14] The desire to justify oneself has a public dimension in Luke. Following the parable of the shrewd manager in Luke 16:1-13, we read of the Pharisees' love of money and their ridicule of Jesus. Jesus turns to them and responds, 'You are those who *justify* yourselves in the sight of others. . . .'[15] So, does the lawyer's self-justification similarly reveal a desire to preserve his reputation in a very public forum and appear in a good light?[16]

In Jesus' day, the question concerning your neighbour's identity was not quite so straightforward and innocent as it may seem to our modern eyes. It was weighed down with all sorts of scholarly and sectarian baggage. Most at the time would agree that the term 'neighbour' encompassed Jews and proselytes . . . but who was to be included or excluded beyond these two groups was much disputed. For example, some would exclude any non-Pharisees, while others would disqualify those they regarded as heretics from benefiting from their neighbourly attentions.[17]

It is at this point in the proceedings that the discussion slows down for a while as this question encourages Jesus to deliver one of the greatest Bible stories ever told. It's the story of a man waylaid by bandits and left half-dead on the side of the road. It is the tale of two of Judah's greatest classes of religious practitioners, a Levite and a priest, both of whom cross to the other side of that road. It's a drama dominated by a Samaritan who also crosses the road, but this time to help a victim of crime, causing him to be forever described as 'good'.

Jesus takes the lawyer on a journey to Jericho: not the Jericho of Joshua fame with formerly crumbled walls, but the Jericho of Herod the Great.[18] As the lawyer listens, does he – as some suggest – immediately identify with the 'certain man' that gets waylaid by bandits?[19] After all, he is looking to work out who the neighbour is, and it is not unreasonable to suggest that he identifies with the person in the story who is most in need. This is easily done, as Jesus offers no name for our crime victim; no ethnicity; no form of identity other than gender. He could be any man from any time, anywhere – he could be a lawyer.

If so, does the lawyer feel each winding blow to the body as the muggers get down to their task, ribs cracking and breaking like twigs underfoot in the forest? Can he feel the humiliation of being roughly and unceremoniously stripped naked, of being deprived of clothing, money, every possession he has about his person? And, as they walk away, can he appreciate the last flickers of life as it too is nearly taken from him? For he is by now 'half dead' according to Jesus.[20]

As the certain man lies there by the side of the road, unable to move, can the lawyer empathetically feel each contour of the ground beneath him, each piece of grit or stone that seems to bite into already pain-drenched flesh, adding to the discomfort that never seems complete – always more unpleasantness on the way? Can he cope with the oxygen-depriving dust kicked up by assailants' sandals as they efficiently go about their business, causing particulates to hang in the air before settling to clog up his nostrils and pores? Can he feel that dust start to mix with congealing blood that has seeped and oozed out of cuts and abrasions, leading to disturbing stains and streaks crisscrossing their way around his body, forming potential sites of infection that are the least of his worries for now? Does the local insect population kick into action, depositing eggs to be incubated in open wounds? Does he cringe as mosquitoes instinctively feed on the abundant reservoirs of crimson bodily fluids? Does the impotence of the situation hit home for the lawyer as he visualises himself in the same helpless position, his injuries disabling him, leaving him unable to swat those pesky parasites away?

Does the lawyer gasp with hope for the man as Jesus describes the passage of a priest? Does he look through slitted eyelids, only able to see a vague and blurry figure: the tassels, the hat, the robes floating into and out of focus? Does he feel gnawing disappointment as the priest moves on? Or perhaps he supports the priest's actions. Does he momentarily step out of the story, becoming coldly rational about the plight of the prostrate man lying destitute by the side of the road? Does the lawyer's face display a brief flash of approval? Because, of course, the priest must be careful not to contaminate himself – not with what must look like a dead body. Jesus has told us he's 'half dead', remember, and half dead is as good as dead in some people's eyes. Days of ritual cleansing lie ahead if the priest does not take care to avoid contact.[21] Does the lawyer go through the same mix of emotions as a Levite steps into and out of the scene with little more impact than an unpaid extra?

Is the lawyer found gasping once again, but with more negative emotions, as Jesus has a Samaritan enter stage right? Once again identifying with the man in need, does he find himself lying beside that road, feeling revulsion start to ferment in his stomach, nausea climb its way up to his throat, an unwanted metallic taste materialising in his mouth? For the Samaritan takes a different path – not to avoid the half-dead man, but this time to risk helping. Does he imagine that he would rather die than be helped by one of those Samaritans, of all people – Samaritans who have figuratively and literally gotten into bed with other nations; who have set up rival temples on rival mountains; who have desecrated the Jerusalem temple with dead men's bones;[22] who have done nothing to endear themselves to their distant cousins in a long, long time?

Is he disturbed and conflicted as he sees the look of pity and compassion on the Samaritan's face? Does he flinch at the thought of that first touch because Jews would not and could not accept ministrations from their Samaritan half-brothers? Does he feel the sting of the wine as its mildly disinfecting properties take effect on his gaping wounds? Can he appreciate the soothing, healing, comforting oil as it is applied to grazes and bruises? Does he welcome that little bit of reassurance from bandages that are carefully and skilfully applied, bringing with them a sense of security and the knowledge that he is being put back together at last?

Does he grunt with pain as his body, with as much care and consideration as possible, is laid across a donkey? As he hangs there helplessly, limp and broken, does he breathe in the musty animal odour? Does he eventually fall asleep to the gentle rise and fall of the donkey as it resumes its journey and negotiates its way forwards once more?

Waking slowly and awkwardly the next morning, does he find himself in a room he does not recognise and in a bed far softer than the last place he lay? In attempting to gain his bearings, does he spot the Samaritan who has spent the night on the floor beside him? As he lies there, still aching yet safe, board and lodging all paid for, does he think to himself, *Well, now I know what it feels like to be a neighbour. I understand that a neighbour is one who is in desperate need, bruised, battered and bleeding. A neighbour is someone who requires saving because they have nothing?*

No wonder that, over the centuries, the temptation to allegorise the story and place needy human beings by the side of the road has been too much to resist.[23] The Samaritan, despised and rejected by the Jews, readily gets identified as representing Jesus. Those potent and weighty Christian symbols – wine, representing Christ's blood, and oil, representing the Holy Spirit – get applied to a man who realises the inadequacy and poverty of his own resources: he is simply not able to save himself, and neither are we. The trip to an inn where there are plenty of rooms that are paid for is an attractive symbol of the future abode Jesus has tantalisingly put before us in John 14:2 where He tells us that in His Father's house are many rooms (NIV).

The lawyer's first question, after all, was about salvation and eternal life . . . and who would not want to experience those things? Even as an adult, at times it would be nice to experience the reassurance you had because Mum kisses your hand or knee better after a scrape. Or how about being 5 years old again, when it seemed like Dad could leap to the rescue and fix anything and everything? Never mind a guardian angel – it would be wonderful to have a good Samaritan swoop in and sweep us up in their arms, clearing up all of our messes and muddles, making everything better again. This is just what a world-weary soul needs – to be saved from ourselves and everything else; to be able to rest calmly and comfortably in the heavenly bed of salvation in a house with many rooms . . . because what a bed that would be! The mattress would be more luxuriant than anything made out of memory foam could offer, and would come with just enough give to make you feel hugged, but not so much that you do not feel supported. Opulent goose-down pillows would accommodate your head in a way that is not even experienced in Park Lane hotels. It would all be finished off with a multifunctional, highly efficient duvet that somehow seems to almost float above you to keep you cool in the summer, yet maintains a closeness that keeps you warm and snuggly in the winter. The result is garnished with a smile of satisfaction at being rescued, feeling safe and becalmed. And if the lawyer did indeed find himself identifying with the man who experienced that wonderful act of liberation, I, for one, could not blame him.

But there is something awry here, something out of kilter. We have to ask ourselves, 'Was this Jesus' intention in telling the story?' There is a familiar joke about a man falling off a cliff and grabbing hold of a branch growing from the side of it on his way down. He looks with little hope at his hands and their precarious grip, and then down to the jagged rock formations below. Crying out to God, he yells, 'Please save me!'

God's response is shocking: 'Let go!'

The man glances down nervously; then, directing his gaze heavenward once more, he shouts, 'Is anyone else there?'

What he really wanted, of course, was for a good Samaritan to appear; or for a helicopter to emerge out of the clouds to winch him to safety; or for those rocks below to be turned into nothing more threatening than piles of marshmallows. He would have welcomed a muscular arm or two to miraculously reach down with strong hands, grab his wrists with calm certainty, yank him up like a toddler, and dump him on a grassy knoll back at the top of the precipice. Hanging there, he could only dream of sitting slumped back at the top, breathing easily for the first time in ages. He yearned to be able to look down once more at those threatening granite formations with a sense of relief because they no longer represent any danger for him. He longed to have the opportunity to shed a manly tear of joy, to feel a tingling sense of happiness wash over his whole body and life, to bask in inner contentment. The last thing he wanted to do was let go.

And as our lawyer is metaphorically lying there, ruminating in his bed of salvation, luxuriating on his gorgeous mattress and delighting in his indulgent pillow-and-duvet combo, perhaps the last thing he wanted to do was to let go and leave that all behind. But Jesus asks His third question of the encounter. It is a question that rudely disturbs the lawyer's reverie. As shocking as an involuntary ice bucket challenge, the question snatches him unceremoniously out of that lovely, warm and safe environment to stand there barefoot, cold, and discomforted. Once again he is in the spotlight. 'Which of these three, do you think, was a neighbour to the man who fell into the hands of the robbers?'[24]

He has to reluctantly discount those heroes of the Jewish community, the priest and the Levite. All their societal significance, law-abiding piety and strict adherence to ceremonial and feasting requirements have come to nothing. The lawyer is left with only one qualifying candidate. It is the man who is now a little less well-off and moving forwards, who has a lighter load for his donkey to carry. It is the man who sticks with a person in need until he is sure they are safe. It is easy to imagine the lawyer frantically rehearsing the story, vainly hoping for another angle, a different outcome, a get-out clause . . . but it is all to no avail. Does he feel the revulsion in his stomach repeating on him; nausea creeping its way back up his throat; the unwanted metallic taste once again disturbing his palate? Are his teeth gritted, his jaw clenched? Can he even say, 'The Samaritan?' Famously no! Never would that word pass his lips, and the answer he gives in response to Jesus' question is not, 'The Samaritan,' but, '*The one* who showed him mercy.'[25] And so he reveals that he has much left to learn.

For a second time Jesus encourages him: 'Go and do likewise.' Except the second time arguably leaves the lawyer feeling a little battered and bruised and in need of help himself – even if he has not been waylaid by robbers. His worldview has been dismantled, and he has failed to justify himself. He has been taken on a journey that is metaphorically short in distance but deeply significant in terms of where he needs to go. It's a journey from a bed of salvation to a floor of discomfort, from the ditch to the road.

The lawyer has asked, 'Who is my neighbour?'[26] This is a matter that can be discussed dispassionately and impersonally, reducing it down to technicalities. But Jesus has turned the tables and flipped things around. Now it is not a question of identity, but of being. Instead of looking at others, Jesus has the lawyer looking at himself. It's not about him thinking about who his neighbour is: it is about him contemplating how much of a neighbour *he* is. As Paul Ricoeur suggests, what must have dawned on the lawyer was that the 'neighbour is not a social object but a behaviour in the first person'.[27] In other words, the journey, potentially, was from seeing himself in that bed as the object of another's care to being the subject offering that care – from 'neighbour' as an object to 'neighbour' as a subject.

Jesus has to mix things up because the lawyer's question is nowhere near as innocent and reasonable as it sounds. It is a question that should ring alarm bells, because behind it lies a process of objectification and limitation. By using 'neighbour' as an object, I become the focus of attention. The motivation behind identifying my 'neighbour' is so that I can keep the commandment. The focus is on rule-keeping, not the person in need. A 'neighbour' becomes an instrument through whom obedience is achieved. But it is more shocking than that. It is like asking, 'Whom should I seek not to kill?' or 'From whom should I not steal?' or 'Which wife should I not beat?' In other words, the lawyer's question could be rephrased along the lines of: 'To whom do I need to be neighbourly to comply with Scripture?' Or: 'Who can I get away with not being neighbourly to and still keep the commandment?' But the lawyer discovers through listening to Jesus telling the parable that he needs to stop making it about the rules, and start making it about people. He is to make a move away from being concerned with people as objects with and through whom to obey, and instead to become a subject – a neighbour who leads a life of compassion and concern for others. It is an absurd question, even dangerous, to ask who my neighbour is. How can I ever disqualify other people from needing my help and receiving love when I am someone who claims to love God?

There is more than a journey from object to subject in view here, if we take a step back and see how the story flows from beginning to end as the various questions are asked. The lawyer's first question was about personal participation in a *future* reality. The lawyer's second question is about how he can identify neighbours in the *present*. After the parable is told, Jesus' question has him concentrating on how to be a neighbour to others in the *present*. His focus has been realigned, and his journey, for now, is complete.

Table 1

Question	Focus
'What must I do to inherit internal life?' (vs. 25)	Personal and future
'Who is my neighbour?' (vs. 29)	Personal and present
'Which of these three, do you think, was a neighbour to the man who fell into the hands of the robbers?' (vs. 36)	Others and present

There are some uncomfortable questions we can ask ourselves at this point. Am I, too, more concerned about making it to heaven, and eventually the new earth, than I am troubled about the needs of the people around me?[28] Am I neighbourly now only because of what I can gain in the hereafter? Have I got the balance right between living for others in the present and living for me in the future?

The reality Jesus is asking the lawyer to think about being part of is awe-inspiring. Can you imagine a time and place where the whole population qualifies to have 'good' in front of their names? In a society of good Samaritans, no one will ever go hungry. No one is going to harm another creature. Going without clothing or a roof over your head is unthinkable, as shelter and suitable attire are guaranteed. People are treated with compassion and experience comfort as others instinctively come to their aid. Wounds are tended to and sores are soothed. To me, it sounds wonderful, idyllic . . . it sounds like paradise. For sure, the Bible only promises such an existence in all its rich fullness in an earth made new . . . but here's the thing: more than a hint of this is possible now, Jesus is suggesting to the lawyer. Hope for the present is to be found in the people of God who collectively know what it means to be a good neighbour; a group of people who, overcome with concern for others, purposefully and intentionally cross the road to help those in need. In such a reality, an unnamed gentleman travelling the Jerusalem-Jericho road would not be mugged and left for dead in the first place – but if he was, he would be helped by a whole team of people. This need not be pie-in-the-sky stuff. It is a glimpse of a future reality, for sure, but one that can be influencing the present nevertheless. It is made possible by individuals being transformed by their encounter with Christ, coming together in groups of like-minded people we like to call churches. Imagine Spirit-filled communities of neighbourliness . . . communities who ask themselves the right questions.

Something to ponder about along the way

Watching the blurred images race across the screen, I was trying to pick out the culprit who had kicked the church's sign to pieces. The CCTV image was a little blurred and it was all taking so long that it seemed to be an exercise in futility. But eventually there he was, time stamp 12.56am. He is walking slowly towards the church property, talking on his mobile telephone. It does not take a body language expert to spot that his conversation is not going well. His hand gestures, both despairing and aggressive, are accompanied by an increased pacing back and forth. Finally, an exasperated tilt of the head brings the exchange to a close.

Without a bit of hesitation, he approaches the aforementioned sign and proceeds to kick at it several times, leaving it in tatters like a piece of paper partly put through a shredder. As I watch, I wonder what motivates him to do this beyond frustration and anger in the moment.

Over the years that sign has often been the target of one form of attack or another, from the person who inexplicably unscrewed and then walked off with it to the far-right political group who scrawled slogans laced with expletives across it. Did we who were represented by that sign feel like we wanted to dress the attackers' wounds, feed and soothe them, wrap them up warmly and pay for a room in a local hotel for the night? Frankly, that would be a 'no.' They were vandals, aggressors, invaders of sorts, but they were not neighbours - their very unneighbourly actions had disqualified them, you see.

[1] Rob Reiner, *A Few Good Men* (Columbia Pictures Industries, Inc. and Castle Rock Entertainment, 1992)
[2] Wright suggests there were standard Rabbinic answers to these questions: Tom Wright, *Luke for Everyone* (London: SPCK, 2001), p. 128.
[3] See also Luke 18:18-30; Acts 13:46, 48. Cf. Mark 10:17 and Matthew 19:16. As Michael Green suggests, 'Luke has more to say about salvation than has the whole of the rest of the New Testament put together' (Michael Green, *Thirty Years That Changed the World: The Book of Acts for Today* [Eerdmans Publishing Company, 2004], p. 30).
[4] Daniel 12:2
[5] For more, see Wright, *Luke for Everyone*, p. 128.
[6] Luke 10:26, NLT
[7] See for example Matthew 22:34-40 and Mark 12:28-34.
[8] Luke 10:27
[9] Joseph A. Fitzmyer, *The Gospel According to Luke (X-XXIV)*, Anchor Bible (New York: Doubleday, 1985), p. 879; John Nolland, *Word Biblical Commentary: Luke 9:21-18:34* (Nashville, TN: Word Publishing, 1993), 35B, p. 585
[10] Luke 10:29
[11] Robert Alter, *The Art of Biblical Narrative* (Basic Books, 2011), p. 143ff.
[12] Luke 10:29
[13] Fitzmyer, p. 886
[14] Luke Timothy Johnson, *The Gospel of Luke* (Collegeville, MN: Liturgical Press, 1991), p. 174
[15] Luke 16:15; see also Luke 18:14.
[16] Nolland, 35B, p. 592
[17] For a discussion and further references, see Joachim Jeremias, *The Parables of Jesus*, translated by S. H. Hooke (London: SCM Press, 1972), pp. 202-203.
[18] Ehud Netzer, *Architecture of Herod, the Great Builder* (Grand Rapids, MI: Baker Academic, 2008), p. 42ff.
[19] Funk suggests there would be an assumption that the victim was a Jew, and so 'the initial perspective draws the listener into the narrative on the side of the victim in the ditch' (Robert Walter Funk, *Parables and Presence: Forms of the New Testament Tradition* [Phillipsburg, PA: Fortress Press, 1982], pp. 32, 37).
[20] Luke 10:30
[21] Numbers 19:11-13
[22] Josephus, *Antiquities*, XVIII, 2.2
[23] Particularly Augustine. See Frederick Van Fleteren and Joseph C. Schnaubelt, *Augustine: Biblical Exegete* (New York, NY: Peter Lang, 2001); Robert H. Stein, *The Method and Message of Jesus' Teachings* (Louisville, KY; London: Westminster John Knox Press, 1994), pp. 45-47.
[24] Luke 10:36
[25] Luke 10:37
[26] Luke 10:29

[27]Paul Ricoeur, *History and Truth*, translated by Charles A. Kelbley (Evanston, IL: Northwestern University Press, 1965), p. 99
[28]Revelation 21 and 22 has the saints dwelling in an earth-bound New Jerusalem.

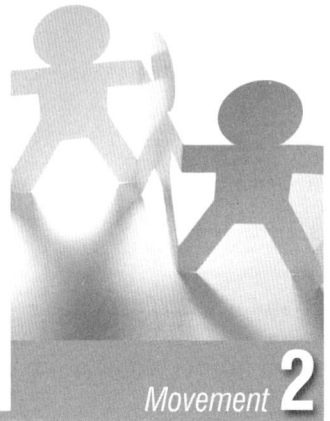

From doing to loving

Wethinkhave looked at the lawyer's questions, but what about the answer he provides? In a hurry to get to that magnificent story about a benevolent Samaritan, it is easy to skip through this part of the debate and accept his response without pause. After all, when he declares, 'You shall love the Lord your God with all your heart, and with all your soul, and with all your strength, and with all your mind; and your neighbour as yourself,' sheer logic suggests that this must be the right answer, because these words are found on Jesus' lips.[1]

This is his response to his question asking how to inherit eternal life . . . but is it possible to *do* anything to assure one's future? Doesn't the Gospel suggest a different way forward? Imagine that Paul is the lawyer's conversation partner at this point. Wouldn't Paul tell him that it is 'by grace you have been saved through faith, and this is *not your own doing*; it is the *gift* of God'?[2] And didn't Paul also say that 'the wages of sin is death, but the *free gift* of God is eternal life in Christ Jesus our Lord'?[3] Free gifts are not based on prior qualifying actions, or on the recipient doing something to earn them – that would make it a purchase. But when we listen in on the conversation between Jesus and the lawyer, Jesus does not offer a correction. In fact, Jesus wholeheartedly agrees with the lawyer's position by responding, 'You have given the right answer; *do* this, and you will live.'[4]

Some might suggest, instead of making things complicated, if God tells us to do it, we should just do it. After all, the lawyer's answers are quotes from Deuteronomy 6:5 and Leviticus 19:18, so they come to us directly from God through Moses. There is no getting away from it: God is the One who is setting these commandments in place, and the expectation is that those of us who identify as His people will comply. If God says it, just do it.

This is a challenging and yet releasing way to operate, and one I can truly appreciate. I was fortunate in that opportunities to earn money came early on in my life. I was just twelve when the first bit of legal tender – 50p from memory – crossed my palm, made sweaty with labour from mowing lawns. In due course, painting, decorating and other work followed as I continued my education. Then, one day, I became a manager. This was a paradigm shift for me. Work was no longer just about me, as such: now I had to run a team and a department. I was still being told what to do – no matter how 'high' up the ladder you get, that never stops in my experience – but now I had to plan, organise, prioritise, delegate and more. It was interesting and stimulating to finally be 'in charge' of something.

However, when experiencing periods of high-octane pressure it would have been great to go back to those moments in life when I was told what to do and when to do it; to shrug off the extra responsibility; to stop having to extricate myself or the team I managed from the effects of the latest (thankfully, metaphorical) fire that was engulfing us. You see, no matter how good a manager you are, you have days when it is necessary to don a metaphorical fireman's helmet and just get down to business. Sometimes these were exciting moments, as they generated a certain buzz; but on other occasions I would have loved a slew of instructions to descend from on high, telling me exactly how to douse those seemingly unquenchable flames, without any struggles to work out the best way forward – no risks, no worries – just 'do this, do that', problem solved.

And so I can see the attraction of the 'God-says-it-so-just-do-it' approach, because it means I can breathe easy, knowing that I have just one thing to do – obey. And who am I to question what God has commanded anyway? It seems absurd that I, a mere mortal, might even think about acting so impertinently. Who better than God understands how we should behave? Who but the Creator of the universe Himself can order and arrange things the way they should be? Questioning God, who has all the answers and the solutions, is nonsense from that point of view. So, if God says it, just do it.

However, before we get too comfortable, there are problems with this type of obedience – problems that are sneaking up on us from behind the bushes even as I write – because if my role is only to obey, my responsibility is only to obey. I am not responsible for *what* I do, *how* I do it, or the *outcomes* that are a result of my doing it. In fact, I am barely responsible at all – but God is. I am free to blame God and effectively absolve myself from being held accountable at all. I can expel a satisfying sigh of relief that I no longer have to think about consequences, because I am relying on God to sort that out. I no longer have to consider the morality of any situation, as I have given that over to God to deal with. God is, after all, the One who established the basis for morals in the first place. So, is there little accountability? No culpability? Sounds too good to be true. And when it sounds too good to be true, that is because it probably is.

Hasn't God created us as morally responsible beings? Isn't He looking to enhance and enrich human freedom rather than diminish it? This comes sharply into focus when asking 'how' questions such as, 'How am I to love God?' or 'How am I to love my neighbour?' The Bible provides many case studies from which to learn, but each moment of living challenges me to love God and my neighbour in ever-changing circumstances. As one writer notes, although Jesus spoke about divorce and marriage, 'He said nothing about birth control, large or small families, childlessness, homosexuality, masturbation, fornication or pre-marital intercourse, sterilisation, artificial insemination, abortion, sex play, petting and courtship.'[5] Even though the

Bible as whole touches on some of these matters, it also does not give guidance on social media, 5G networks or whether to use Apple or Android devices . . . so what do we do in situations not directly addressed by the words of Scripture?

Living on this planet is a complex and messy business. Navigating through what life throws at us by applying situation-specific rules is impossible because those rules just do not exist – and if they did exist, no library in the world would be big enough to house them. It would make life so much easier if God were to tell me what to do in any given situation, at a specific time and in a particular context. But the reality is that He doesn't. This means that every single one of us has to answer the 'how' questions. 'God says it; just do it' sounds fine in theory, but in practice application is not always so clear-cut.

For instance, I might evaluate my performance at the end of the day and consider myself not to have broken the Sixth Commandment because I have neither murdered someone nor committed manslaughter.[6] But then Jesus said, 'If you are angry with a brother or sister, you will be liable to judgement; and if you insult a brother or sister, you will be liable to the council; and if you say, "You fool", you will be liable to the hell of fire.'[7] Now I need to ensure that I don't get angry or curse when another driver cuts me up or a delivery is late.

But, even then, that is applying the letter and not the spirit of what Jesus is saying . . . because to do that would mean asking a more challenging question: namely, 'Have I diminished another person's life or well-being in any way?' If another's well-being is the issue, obeying the Sixth Commandment includes, but is not limited to, psychological, emotional and spiritual injury. Now it is not so easy to give myself a pass. Am I affecting my asthmatic neighbour's breathing when I release toxic gases and pollutants into the atmosphere because I have not got the catalytic converter on my car fixed? Have I used my position of authority to oppress my co-worker? What damage have I done by not giving the homeless person some money, food or shelter?

The reality is, we are making decisions on how to love God and others all of the time – and that is OK, because God has given us the tools to do that in the form of principles and values. The 'God says it; just do it' approach throws everything back at God even as He is delegating the task of loving to us. This is no trivial task: indeed, the 'command of love calls individuals to a high level of personal responsibility'.[8] We have been given the grand overview of what is required, and now we are to prioritise and make decisions as to how to achieve God's requirement to love as we live our lives. It is seductive to think that it is my duty only to obey, but in reality there is much more than that to living out these commandments.

There is a second, related issue to consider before laying the 'just do it' approach to rest. The type of unquestioning obedience being described means that, if challenged, I can claim, 'I was just following orders.' And when human beings abdicate personal moral responsibility through unthinking obedience, the results are never good and can sometimes be devastating. It is a plea that has historically been given a title that will and should make us uncomfortable. For, in the aftermath of World War II, it came to be known as the 'Nuremberg Defence'. When Otto Eichmann stood in the dock at Nuremberg he famously responded to the charges brought against him by asserting that he bore no guilt as he was only following orders. He did not defend himself by denying that he had been a major organiser of the Holocaust; but he did emphasise that he was not morally responsible for his actions as he was just a small cog in a vast machine.[9] He had no choice but to obey a superior's orders. Now, this might seem to be an outrageous comparison to make. How can God even be thought of as being like a despot ordering genocide? Isn't God ordering the opposite of what happened in the Holocaust – that is, commanding us to love? Surely we can have a confidence in what God commands us to do that we could never have in a homicidal dictator? But not unthinkingly . . . not if we pay attention to the commandments themselves.

The way the commandments to love are worded rules out unthinking or blind obedience – the 'just do it' approach – from the outset. The love of God that precedes the command to love each other is all-encompassing. We are to love God with all our heart, soul, strength and mind. To love God with our heart and soul speaks to a love that is emotionally intelligent and fully embodied. To love God with all our strength is to be fully committed. To love God with our mind is to love Him with our thoughts, our intellect and our reason. This is not a love that comes about because of cold, impassive, robotic compliance. To love God in this manner means that we have so knowingly adopted and internalised His way of relating to Him and to others that the resultant values lie at the very centre of our being.

This means that we cannot obey these commandments merely to be saved, because that does violence to the Gospel of Grace. We do not obey them simply because God says so, because that is not God's intention for us. A third option to consider is that we obey the love commandments to please God.

There are things I do that are intended to please my wife. I know that she finds a messy house stressful, so, if able, I tidy up, ready for when she comes home from work, so she can relax after a hard day crunching numbers. I know she occasionally likes a foot massage, as it relaxes and de-stresses her. The idea of pleasing the other party in a relationship makes a lot of sense.

Even a brief trawl through Scripture reveals that there are things that displease and please God. Among those things that God dislikes are 'haughty eyes, a lying tongue, and hands that shed innocent blood'.[10] More positively, Enoch pleased God with his demonstration of faith, and Solomon with his request for wisdom.[11] It is encouraging that God reacts to situations negatively and positively, because it means He is not observing what is going on with detached indifference. For a single human life to be lost because of the entrance of evil into the world must be more than displeasing to God. No wonder that God is said to hate certain things, so alien are they to the way He has always intended things to go.[12] To suggest, in turn, that we obey the commandments to love because it pleases God seems to have good biblical foundations.

However – while not denying that we do things that displease or please God – I suggest that this needs to be the by-product and not the goal of our relationship with Him. If we are created to please God in that way, it conjures up pictures and practices of those ancient religions that emphasised the need to please their gods to ensure survival. For example, there is a Japanese myth about a prince called Yamato Takeru, who was ordered to conquer some eastern states. As his fleet was making its way between two peninsulas, a violent storm threatened both his ships and their assignment. The solution to their predicament was provided by his wife, Ototachibana, who offered to throw herself into the sea to please and placate the sea-god who was causing the perilous weather conditions. Even as she suggested the solution, she hurled herself overboard, and according to the story the seas were becalmed.[13]

This story readily brings to mind the story of Jonah, who, just like Ototachibana, offers himself up to be thrown into the sea. However, unlike her, he has to be physically lifted and thrown overboard. The sailors' prayer before they throw him into the sea is striking, as they cry out, 'Please, O LORD, we pray, do not let us perish on account of this man's life. Do not make us guilty of innocent blood; for you, O LORD, have done as it pleased you.'[14]

I wonder what the sailors learned about the one true God, having been through this experience? Could it be that Yahweh occasionally gets displeased with one of His followers and can only be placated with their death? Given their worldview, we could not blame them for viewing this as an act of appeasement – an attempt to pacify and calm a discontented God who saw fit to display His displeasure through a storm.[15] For they also worry that they too may be sacrificed – collateral damage as a vengeful God chases down His recalcitrant prophet. They may have gone on to hear of Jonah's fantastical journey in a fish and the even more amazing turnaround in the faith of the Ninevites. However, it is suggested that from the moment Jonah went overboard, as far as they were concerned, that was it.[16]

If this were our only picture of God, He would appear to be no better than the gods of a hundred pagan myths who capriciously and arbitrarily threaten human existence unless their demands are met. The problem is, there is no meaning behind the acts that are required other than to gratify a god and bring about divine satisfaction. And this gives us an inkling as to where and how we should practise caution when it comes to the idea that we do something just to please God. It is a short step from pleasing to appeasing, from seeking merely to make God happy to attempting to dispel God's displeasure. Such a relationship is one-sided and is all about making sure I do anything and everything to please God because His anger is to be avoided at all costs.

In the same way, I might need to examine the motives behind my sometimes meagre attempts to tidy up the house. Am I just trying to get on my wife's good side and ensure that she will make me a nice dinner in the spirit of 'you scratch my back and I'll scratch yours'? This is reminiscent of the marriage saying, 'Happy wife, happy life,' which suggests that a husband can get what he wants out of his marriage if he prioritises his wife and her needs.[17] This can result in submitting to his wife's wishes and wants during every conflict and letting her hold sway when making any decision . . . but it is suggested that this 'does not lead to happiness, but to a closet full of regret, bitterness, and selfishness, which we all must open eventually'.[18]

When we love, it pleases God, for sure, but He is not a tyrant. He does not command our love of Himself and of our neighbour merely for His own pleasure. He does not use His position and power to take advantage of creatures that have no choice but to obey to avoid punishment. If He did, loving my neighbour would have more to do with *my* welfare than *their* well-being. We have arrived back at the sort of neighbourliness discussed previously: neighbourliness that is a means to an end, and not endowed with meaning itself.

So, what about a different approach to tidying the house? What if it is the result of buying into the concept of mutual submission where each pleases the other so that we join together to build towards a harmonious and deepening relationship within a desirable environment?[19] Likewise, what about a universe based on love that has the same aims? How about acknowledging that 'we love because he [God] first loved us'?[20] What if the love commands are an invitation to involve ourselves in reciprocal relationships where love and its other-centredness are the foundation of life? Hence, we don't love God just because it pleases Him, but also as a response to the love He initiates and directs towards us in the first place. And, if we note that 'God proves his love for us in that while we still were sinners Christ died for us',[21] we can appreciate that His love for me does not depend on me doing something to please Him first. Rather, the kind of love that God is looking for from us is 'our response to God's love for us, not the cause of His acceptance of us'.[22]

But, before arriving at something like a satisfactory conclusion, there is an elephant in the room to address. That is, how can love be commanded in the first place? Commanded love is like trying to draw a square circle. Love can be invited and generated through acquaintance and family ties. Love can be spontaneous, natural and instinctive. But, intuitively, someone cannot command the love of another without it becoming something other than love. Love has to come from within, rather than be ordered or decreed from without. No wonder love is considered to be elusive in nature and talked about in terms of metaphor and simile. 'Love is like a beautiful flower which I may not touch, but whose fragrance makes the garden a place of delight just the same,' advises Helen Keller. Mother Teresa suggested, 'Love is a fruit in season at all time, and within reach of every hand.' However, as Christians, we cannot leave it there. If God is love, then to move beyond figures of speech is to understand the God we worship, the God who created us.

There are a number of words translated 'love' in our English Bibles; and, despite all those sermons and talks putting them into nice neat boxes, there is a large degree of overlap in everyday use.[23] Statistically, the most important word for love in the New Testament is *agape*.[24] It is also important for our discussion, because we are invited to love (*agape*) God and love (*agape*) our neighbour. It is another of those words that is difficult to pin down. Indeed, a review of scholarly opinion comes up with sixteen different explanations, so translating *agape* solely as 'love' potentially deprives it of its richness and depth.[25]

At its core, *agape* is practical, other-centred and action-oriented. This explains the way Paul hints at its 'practical efficiency' by writing of the 'labour of love'.[26] But it is tempting to make it so practical that a robot could conceivably demonstrate *agape*. By depriving it of heart, it makes it 'a matter of decision or choice, nothing at all to do with feelings or emotions towards that individual'.[27] However, understanding that *agape* is practical and based on choice offers an elegant solution to the problem of how love can be commanded. If I do not need to express sympathy or empathy, all that is required is that I apply logic to determine whether there is a need and act on it. Hence, the injunction to love is simply a command to choose the right course of action in any given circumstance.

However, if we turn to the most famous passage on love in the Bible, we find that 'love is patient; love is kind; love is not envious or boastful or arrogant or rude. It does not insist on its own way; it is not irritable or resentful.'[28] The love that Paul so poetically presents is not just about deeds, but also about disposition. I can potentially act patiently through choice or sheer force of will, but I have to think and feel differently if I am to avoid envy or the pride that precedes boasting. In listing undesirable emotional and psychological states, Paul highlights that this is not simply about actions: for, if *agape* is to flourish, we are 'to act intentionally, in sympathetic response to others (including God), to promote overall well-being'.[29]

Nowhere is this seen more than in the life of Jesus. When He wanders providentially into a town called Nain, it is written that 'when the Lord saw her, he had compassion for her.'[30] The woman is the widow famously identified by the town in which she lives. Her life is unravelling. She has already lost her husband, and is now grieving over the loss of her only son. Her future is bleak. In a patriarchal society, a family without men can barely function economically or practically. In the face of this devastation, some translations have it that Jesus 'felt sorry for her';[31] but that does not go far enough. Even 'compassion' falls short.

When Jesus sees the woman, her plight affects His whole being. He is moved in his inward parts, from His liver to His lungs, from His kidneys to His heart[32] . . . for this is *splagchnizomai* compassion – something that does not come about by choice, but because a person is 'being moved by compassion as a strong bodily reaction'.[33] That this is involuntary is reflected in how the verb is given in the passive voice. We are moved by such compassion; we cannot move to have it. It speaks to values and principles that run deep and get triggered reflexively. It is compassion that a person cannot help feeling when seeing someone in need. To my ear, it is almost onomatopoeic in the way *splagchnizomai* sounds like the thing it describes – compassion that is a gut-wrenching reaction to human suffering. Jesus is not portrayed as giving a cold and calculated response that results in a son's resurrection. There is not a scintilla of indifference or disinterested kindness here. Rather, we see Him moved to the very core of His being and beyond. This is Jesus engaging emotionally and psychologically with the woman and her situation. In understanding people as a unity – soul, body and spirit – *splagchnizomai* compassion overcomes the entire person and is a physical, emotional and mental state.

In all three synoptic gospels, *splagchnizomai* is exclusively applied to Jesus ... except for in three parables. It is the compassion felt by a father towards his returning prodigal son in Luke 15:20, and by a master to a slave that cannot repay his debt in Matthew 18:27. It is also the word chosen to describe a Samaritan's reaction to seeing a man lying half-dead at the side of the road.[34] As it was with Jesus when He saw the widow of Nain, the Samaritan's reaction comes from the very centre of who he is as a human being. For Jesus, His compassion leads Him to touch a bier. For the Samaritan, he is compelled, 'moved with pity', and so crosses the road to tend a stranger's wounds.[35]

We too are being moved, I suggest: moved away from seeing the commands to love God and our neighbours as commands in any conventional sense. It is easy to get bogged down in the word 'commandment' – particularly if we are influenced by Jesus' conversation partner. With a nod to nominative determinism, the lawyer comes at the question like a lawyer. And we too can make this all about exemptions, clauses, conditions, terms and liability. But what if we see the commands to love God and our neighbours as being descriptive and speaking to a bigger story? What if we can detect within the love commands potential for living life to the full?

Think about living in a world where people are instinctively driven from their inward parts to reach out to those in need. Would not this more closely resemble God's ideal for us? Jesus responded with: 'Do this, and you will live,' and: 'Go and do likewise,' not just because the lawyer could then contemplate a saved life, but so he could experience a full life.[36] And, as it happens, the Bible has a phrase to describe a realm where this is more than a possibility ... for what Jesus is offering is an invitation, not an imposition. 'Jesus is not commending a new system of legalism somewhat different from the old one, but pointing to the end of all legalism,' so encouraging the lawyer that, by loving, he gets to 'live the life of the Kingdom of God'.[37] Thus, the commands to love God and our neighbours form a framework within which we can flourish and function as God created us in the first place. They have long been recognised as the key to the interpretation of the Bible.[38] But, more than that, they remind us that what the Bible is primarily about is relationships, not regulations.[39]

If we accept Jesus' invitation, is God pleased? For sure. Does this mean that you or I will then be saved? No, not in the sense that it gets us over the line, but yes, if it refers to the experience of being saved and benefiting from God overcoming evil and establishing His kingdom. Do we do it because He says so? Well, I would rather reframe the question: do we do it because this is our response to a God who is love? And the place where this is most evident? Well, that is to be found within a community of people, because 'the people who make up the church are the place where the reign of God becomes most visible.'[40]

Something more to ponder about along the way

One of the best outlooks on the Isle of Wight is to be had from the top of Culver Down. Looking to the south, it provides a stunning view of what is known as the bay area that runs from Yaverland to Luccombe. In the afternoon, the sun reflects off the water as the waves – sometimes meandering, sometimes crashing onto the beaches – create an ever-changing seascape. In the distance, the island's downs or hill formations drift in and out of sight, depending on how the clouds are feeling at the time. The view towards the north-east is previewed in the foreground by Seaview and Bembridge, the so-called posh areas that are garnished with little villages of holiday homes. In the distance is Ryde and a view of the Solent out to Portsmouth, Southampton and beyond.

I like driving or walking up to the top – not just because of the views, but also because you feel like you have risen above the world, its cares and its challenges. I can look down upon life happening below me and gain a different and refreshing perspective. However, the pleasure offered by arriving at the top was somewhat tempered by discovering that it is the favourite spot on the island for people to commit suicide. I had been oblivious to the Samaritans' notices pinned to the windswept fences that urge people to think twice and make a call before taking action from which there is no turning back. A place where I go to enjoy a fresh and different perspective turned out to be a place where others go because, from their perspective, there is no longer any point in living.

When I moved to the island, I joined a walking group to take part in and get to know others in the local community. One day, I was discussing with someone the appalling suicide rate among young people on the island. It was not a particularly pleasant conversation, but it had cropped up because Culver Down had been closed the previous day while the emergency services talked someone down off the ledge. My fellow walker mentioned to me that they had a friend who also was expressing suicidal thoughts, and this left them feeling helpless. They explained that they had no idea what to say. 'It's all right for you,' they continued; 'at least you think there is something on the other side.'

I was struck that they imagined the human story to come unstuck at the point of death. It was all so bleak. I am certain they would agree we should love our neighbour. But this was a pragmatic turn, driven by a generally kind regard for humanity. What I wanted to do (but the moment had passed) was to ask them about their bigger picture, the wider perspective, the story they believed they were living out that would bring purpose and meaning.

[1]Matthew 5:43; 19:19; 22:36-40; Mark 12:28-31
[2]Ephesians 2:8
[3]Romans 6:23; see also Romans 5:21.
[4]Luke 10:28
[5]Joseph F. Fletcher, *Situation Ethics: The New Morality* (Louisville, KY, London: Westminster John Knox Press, 1997), p. 139
[6]Exodus 20:13
[7]Matthew 5:22
[8]Peter Vardy and Paul Grosch, *The Puzzle of Ethics* (London: HarperCollins), p. 128
[9]Deborah E. Lipstadt, *The Eichmann Trial* (New York: Schocken Books, 2011)
[10]Proverbs 6:17; see also Proverbs 6:16-19; 2 Samuel 11:27; Romans 8:6-8; Deuteronomy 12:31; 14:3; Psalm 11:5.
[11]Hebrews 11:5, 6; 1 Kings 3:10; see also Numbers 24:1; 1 Samuel 12:22; Mark 1:11.
[12]For a discussion on the 'evaluative' aspect of God's love, see John C. Peckham, *The Love of God: A Canonical Model* (InterVarsity Press, 2015), p. 118f.
[13]Jan N. Bremmer, *The Strange World of Human Sacrifice* (Leuven, Belgium: Peeters Publishers, 2007), p. 232
[14]Jonah 1:14
[15]As Joyce Baldwin suggests, 'Polytheists though they are, the sailors try to appease the wrath of Jonah's God' (Joyce Baldwin, 'Jonah', pp. 543-90 in *The Minor Prophets: An Exegetical and Expository Commentary*, edited by Thomas Edward McComiskey [Baker Academic, 2009], p. 562).
[16]Baldwin, p. 564
[17]The same goes for a wife who attempts to keep her husband happy.
[18]"Happy Wife, Happy Life": And Other Misleading Advice to Young Husbands', *Desiring God*, 2018: *https://www.desiringgod.org/articles/happy-wife-happy-life* (accessed 1 July 2019)
[19]Referencing Ephesians 5:21
[20]1 John 4:19
[21]Romans 5:8
[22]Leon Morris, *Luke: An Introduction and Commentary* (Grand Rapids, MI: William B. Eerdmans Publishing, 1988), p. 182
[23]Particularly where *agape* and *phileo* are concerned (D. A. Carson, *The Gospel According to John* [Grand Rapids, MI: InterVarsity Press, 1991], pp. 466, 467).
[24]*Agape* is found 319 times in the New Testament in its various forms, whereas *phileo*, by comparison, is present 54 times and *eros* does not appear at all (Ceslaus Spicq, *Agape in the New Testament, Volume 3: Agape in the Gospel, Epistles and Apocalypse of St. John* [Eugene, OR: Wipf and Stock Publishers, 2006], p. 1).
[25]Thomas Jay Oord, *Defining Love: A Philosophical, Scientific, and Theological Engagement* (Grand Rapids, MI: Brazos Press, 2010), pp. 37, 38
[26]1 Thessalonians 1:3; Spicq, p. 171
[27]Rick Gowdy, *Agape-Love: How Important Is It Anyhow?* (Xulon Press, 2007), p. 20
[28]1 Corinthians 13:4, 5
[29]Oord, p. 47
[30]Luke 7:13
[31]For example, Luke 7:13, CEV
[32]For more on the original meaning of the word, see Johannes Louw and Eugene A. Nida, *Greek-English Lexicon of the New Testament: Based on Semantic Domains* (New York, NY: United Bible Societies, 1996), p. 293.
[33]Annette Merz, 'Ways of Teaching Compassion in the Synoptic Gospels', in: *Considering Compassion: Global Ethics, Human Dignity, and the Compassionate God*, edited by Frits de Lange and L. Juliana Claassens (Eugene, OR: Wipf and Stock Publishers, 2018), pp. 66-86 (p. 68)
[34]Luke 10:33
[35]The NRSV translates *splagchnizomai* as 'moved with pity', highlighting its dynamic nature.
[36]Luke 10:28, 37
[37]Leon Morris, *Luke: An Introduction and Commentary* (William B. Eerdmans Publishing, 1988), p. 182
[38]John J. O'Keefe, Russell R. Reno, and R. R. Reno, *Sanctified Vision: An Introduction to Early Christian Interpretation of the Bible* (Baltimore, MD: JHU Press, 2005), p. 130
[39]'A strong case can be made that the canon [the Bible as we have it] is a covenant document, depicting and regulating the relationship between God and His people' (John Peckham, *Canonical Theology* [Grand Rapids, MI: William B. Eerdmans Publishing Company, 2016], p. 21).
[40]Kevin J. Vanhoozer, *Faith Speaking Understanding: Performing the Drama of Doctrine* (Louisville, KY: Presbyterian Publishing Corporation, 2014), p. 7

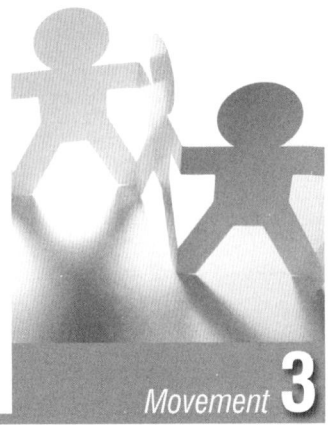

From relief to discomfort

Interpersonal intelligence, also referred to as interpersonal sensitivity, is our ability to know another person based on what they say, their body language and context.[1] We barely get time with the lawyer who features in Luke 10, so it would be pushing it to say that we can get to know him. However, this does not stop us from making some assumptions. For example, what can we make of his question, 'What must I do to inherit eternal life?' For example, why doesn't the lawyer ask, 'What must *we* do to inherit eternal life?' Would that not be more inclusive?

I have had good bosses that have used 'we' and others that were overly fond of 'I'. Eventually it would start to grate, as the latter would say things like: 'I'm going to do this,' or: 'I'm going to do that.' In the meantime, 'we' who made up the team or department would sit there and wonder what 'I' had to do with any of this, as 'we' did all the hard graft. The only work that 'I' did was to smoothly take all the credit. Because the lawyer uses 'I', we could conclude that he is concerned only about himself – but not if we take his context into account. Luke has told us that the lawyer is asking a technical question to test Jesus, and not a personal one in search of information. Furthermore, his first-century Palestinian context means the lawyer is not used to thinking about himself as being separate from the groups to which he belongs.[2] He lives in a collectivist society, and the concept that we have of being a unique, distinctive and self-governing individual is entirely alien to him. So, when he asks, 'What must I do to inherit eternal life?' the 'I' does not mean the same for him as it does for us. 'I' is instinctively understood as being indistinguishable from the 'we' who make up his group(s).

This shows how our social context heavily influences us as we read the Bible. Before the printing press was invented and the Reformation took place, there 'was no individualised "I" or "me" in relation to Scripture; it was always "we" or "us".'[3] The only way the masses accessed the Bible was by turning up to a church service and hearing it read aloud, so it was always a group activity. When Johannes Gutenberg brought movable type to Europe in the fifteenth century, he paved the way for information to be democratised – it was no longer the preserve of just a few. Even as this was one of the key drivers behind the Reformation that followed a few decades afterwards, it also changed the relationship people had with the Bible. As soon as it was translated into native languages, literacy rates increased and it was mostly read in private. The Bible may have been liberated, but it had also fallen under the influence of the so-called 'technology of individualism' – that is, the printing press.[4] The Word of God was no longer immovable, constrained and housed in church buildings – it became something that I possess and read by myself. Out of this comes the relationship we tend to have with the Bible today. 'Now, instead of asking, "What does this mean to *us?*" We are more likely to ask, "What does this mean to *me?*"[5]

We are not immune to the ebb and flow of history. Therefore, as I eavesdrop on the lawyer's conversation with Jesus, I cannot help but make it about me. I want to hear the answer to the question he raises. After all, it is one of life's great existential concerns. For Christians, it often seems to be our number-one concern – how not to die, how to live forever, to make it, be saved, inherit eternal life. That human existence is under threat was the main concern of some well-intentioned Christians in the 1960s and 1970s. Going around with seemingly permanent smiles on their faces, they intensely asked anyone and everyone, 'Are you saved?' They took the Christian concepts of joy and assurance and made them into a method of somewhat confrontational evangelism directed towards a population that mostly had no idea they needed saving in the first place. It was a noble attempt at distilling the Gospel down into a soundbite that would impact the woman and man on the street, but it resulted in a clichéd view of Christianity emerging – one in which the only concern is the saving of individuals. But we must not look down our noses at these goings-on. In reality, it is a one-dimensional picture of salvation history that many of us adopt. The Bible is often treated as if it is a manual on how to avoid those rocks at the bottom of the cliff.

Thinking about those rocks, let's go back to the man who falls off the cliff and clings to the branch before crying out to God for help. Imagine he is miraculously saved and can sit back, relieved, at the top of the precipice. If we use the story as an allegory of the experience of salvation, from what does he think he has been saved? It is suggested that the 'broad meaning of salvation in Scripture is to be saved from calamities, such as war, disease, death or other perils'.[6] But the problems are wider-ranging than that. We can imagine how Christians of every persuasion look down from the top of the cliff in relief because they have avoided the consequences of their own mortality: illness, hell, the grave, brimstone, torment, everlasting fire, judgment, punishment, the devil, a fast-deteriorating planet earth or their own bad performance. These perceived and real threats to current and eternal existence taunt us and feel as threatening as those sharp and jagged rocks waiting to greet us. It is not just about inheriting eternal life, but about what I must do to survive given all the threats I face now.

So, in response to the lawyer's questions, Jesus could have taken things in a different direction. He could have told a story that takes us on a trip from branch to cliff-top: an emotional rollercoaster of a journey from fear and trepidation to an overwhelming sense of relief at being saved. The suspense level is raised because a villain is thrown into the mix – a malevolent force that propels the man off the cliff-top to his doom. The man's drop is only temporarily halted by the branch, and his grip is undermined by uncontrollable nerves and sweat-filled palms. The odds are stacked against him. But he makes it through, because God steps in to help at last. It becomes a heart-warming tale where good triumphs over evil. It brings a tear to the eye as we watch the protagonist struggle on his way from victimhood to survivor to victor. Such a story would promise a life of hope, one where we can say everything will turn out all right in the end, 'and if it's not alright, it's not the end'.[7] At last we have a story that satisfies our desire for the happy-ever-after ending that is embedded into our psyche and seems necessary for mental well-being.

Read through to the end of the Bible and there is a happy-ever-after to look forward to. Yes, there is a malevolent force that threatens us, but he is defeated.[8] We find that God Himself will wipe away our tears; death will no longer be a threat; and 'mourning and crying and pain will be no more.'[9] It makes all the physical, psychological and emotional trauma we go through bearable to know that God is on the case . . . and we will not just get dumped back at the top of a cliff. We will be given new bodies and a newly recreated home on the new earth.[10] All the rubbish that we put up with now is balanced by the prospect of living in a city temple where God Himself will dwell with us.[11]

In the meantime, Jesus is offered as the ultimate solution in our search for respite in the here and now. He is more effective than relief sought in taking drugs, drinking alcohol or overeating. He is more real than forms of escapism such as computer games, pornography and sport. No matter what the question is, as the song goes, 'Jesus is the answer.'[12] Throw in eternal life, and the package is complete: a life with fewer problems now, and an everlasting life with no problems to come. Jesus and the religion He founded are touted around like the best insurance deal ever. More than a handbook, the Bible inclines towards being a document outlining what is and is not covered as part of a Christian's health and life insurance policy.

If relief from present and future problems is all there is to it, it is not surprising that Christians are accused of using their faith as a crutch. It is a familiar jibe. As a classic textbook of psychiatry from the 1960s puts it, religion is often seen as being for 'the hesitant, the guilt-ridden, the excessively timid, those lacking clear convictions with which to face life'.[13] Now, of course Christianity is for the vulnerable and the emotionally fraught. In answer to the question of whether the Church is full of people with mental health issues, Andrew Sims writes, 'My impression is that it contains about the same proportion of emotionally disturbed people as any other social organisation. I would like to think that it had many disturbed people. If we cannot find support and solace there, where can it be found?'[14] So, we can certainly turn to Jesus for healing: be it physical, emotional, psychological or spiritual. The problems come when we make survival and relief the core of our faith. Christianity must be more than a crutch, a first-aid box or a survival kit helping to overcome ill health, redundancy, the effects of crime, parenthood, marriage, getting old, the apocalypse and everything else we worry about.

Millennials are much maligned – often portrayed as self-entitled and lazy. But they are what the generations that came before them have made them. The lack of nuance in modernism, the liquid uncertainty of postmodernism and the failure of science to meet all their existential needs has left them with nowhere to turn. They have searched for meaning and purpose in consumerism and religion, but have found them unfulfilling. They feel as if they have been set adrift; that they are 'directionless and lost'; that, despite all the promises, they have 'become a generation of Cinderellas, told to wait for a glass slipper that no longer exists'.[15] But, even as millennials turn their backs on churches, they explain, 'We still want relationships and transcendence, to be part of something bigger than ourselves.'[16] What is perplexing is that those are among the reasons I choose to be a Christian . . . so what has gone wrong?

One answer is to be found in what Christianity came to be for millennials when they were in their teens, when it morphed into a form of moralistic therapeutic deism. It is moralistic because we are supposed to be good people and live by the rule to love our neighbour. It is therapeutic because a benevolent Creator God watches over us, ordering life, and is at the ready to solve our problems. It is deistic because God is at a distance and only gets involved when we get into difficulty.[17] This research has been criticised for showing an unwillingness to learn something new and constructive from a younger generation,[18] but it serves as a stark reminder of what happens when Christianity becomes a religion of self-fulfilment. 'Love thy neighbour' is a way to make myself feel good, and God is there to solve all my problems like a cosmic Santa in the sky. This did not come out of thin air. This was something they were taught as children and was modelled to them by their elders. It is 'no wonder consumer-oriented American teenagers accept moralistic therapeutic deism as the product churches peddle, unaware that it represents an emaciated faith, a flimsy facsimile of the grace-full life that participates in the mission of God'.[19] A one-dimensional view of Christianity that makes it all about offering relief from life's issues is as mundane as it is unrealistic. No wonder backs are being turned.

If we are willing to learn something constructive from a younger generation, we need to pursue an understanding of Christianity that is demanding, embraces the transcendent, and lives within and speaks to a bigger story. This is not about rebranding or repackaging Christianity. This is about recognising what it already is. It is about allowing the Christian story to blossom into something beyond the routine. Relief and support only go so far. What is needed is challenge.

It is undeniable that Jesus was supportive. He brought relief to a woman caught in adultery, to another who had bled for twelve years, and to a man who had not walked for thirty-eight years.[20] But, above all, Jesus was and is about challenge. When responding to the lawyer, therefore, Jesus does not unveil a drama that is focused on a man who experienced a happy-ever-after ending, but on a Samaritan whose actions were neighbourly. There is still a feel-good factor. The man who was left for dead and destined to die survives in the end. Likewise, Christianity is full of good news – but this is not where Jesus lets the lawyer focus his attention. Instead, he makes him uncomfortable and unsettled.

With whom do we most readily identify in the story? No one wants to be beaten half to death, but it is the victim of the mugging who has the more comfortable outcome. He gets to have his wounds dressed, is taken to a place of safety, does not die on a roadside but sleeps in a bed, and does not pay a penny. But identify with the Samaritan, and we have to take on the role of the neighbour. Neighbours have to go out of their way to help others – more than being inconvenienced, this means risking their lives. Neighbours have to commit to care plans by offering to pop by and pay for extra board and keep. Neighbours have to change their travel arrangements. Neighbours have less wine and oil in their possession. Neighbours have to give up what is theirs to put others first.

The victim gets rescued and metaphorically finds himself back at the top of the cliff, expressing and experiencing relief. But they are not the emotions associated with a neighbour. Jesus tells us that when the Samaritan saw the man, he 'had compassion'.[21] His is a face that shows he is 'moved with pity'.[22] The Samaritan is someone who is experiencing what it is to inherit eternal life in the present. He is not resting on his laurels. He does not have a look of satisfaction on his face because his destiny is assured. He does not pat himself on the back at having made it, but he has someone else's back. The reality of living in a world in which evil has temporarily found a home means that Christians are to take up the challenge of being present for others. It is as if Jesus is saying, 'Don't worry about inheriting eternal life and being saved – I've got that sorted. What I need you to do is to think about how you treat others now that your future is assured because of Me.' And what a challenge this is. I naturally seek to find a pathway that benefits me, yet Jesus wants me to join a community that exists for the benefit of others.

Nowhere is it more tempting to prioritise relief over discomfort than in our prayers. There is that tendency to turn them into wish lists. 'Dear Lord, please can You do this or that. . . . Please can You help in this situation or aid that person. . . . May You see fit to provide this. . . .' This is not quite a prosperity-style gospel that suggests we are to be free from illness and poverty with the right faith and attitude, but it is a move towards it. The challenges in view are all mine, but it is God who needs to take up the task of meeting them.

But 'prayers are not a means of persuasion, of modifying God's intentions or actions. What our praying can accomplish is to modify *us*, putting us at God's disposal for our own good and for the blessing of others.'[23] This change in focus can be liberating. It is extremely troubling to think that we need to convince God to do something good through prayer, as if God is holding back food from a starving child until someone gets on their knees on their behalf. Rather, prayer is a two-way process. As we receive support, we also accept the challenge to change and act.

Our prayers become not so much about what God can do for us as about what we can do for God. They permit God to use us, allowing Him to throw us out into the uncomfortable and rocky places. They give God freedom to work in our lives so He can direct us to the margins to meet people and their needs in hitherto-unimagined ways. Rather than seeking relief from the rocks below, this brings with it a different sort of danger. For the Samaritan, it meant putting his life at risk from being attacked by the same violent men that had assaulted the one he paused to help. What might it mean for us?

Something to think about along the way

Among the most awkward places in which to find yourself is in close proximity to a person who causes you, intentionally or not, to feel uncomfortable. And, like everywhere else, church communities are full of them. There is the person with halitosis who determinedly encroaches on personal space and causes you to dance around the room as you move away to escape and they insistently move towards you again. Or how about the person who prolongs meetings because they never keep up with what anyone else is saying? Or the one who irritatingly insists on asking questions already answered, or having their say over and over again? Or how about the person who asks personal questions that are intrusive or highly offensive? Or what about those individuals who always want things done their way and make a right old fuss if it doesn't happen?

That church communities are full of such people is because we probably are that uncomfortable person in our own ways. It also means that to enter into the life of a church community is to enter, inevitably, into a life of discomfort.

[1]*Interpersonal Sensitivity: Theory and Measurement*, edited by Judith A. Hall and Frank J. Bernieri (London: Lawrence Erlbaum Associates, 2001), p. xiii

[2]Bruce J. Malina, *The New Testament World: Insights from Cultural Anthropology* (Louisville, KY: Westminster John Knox Press, 2001), p. 62

[3]Eugene H. Peterson, *Working the Angles: The Shape of Pastoral Integrity* (Grand Rapids, MI: William B. Eerdmans Publishing Company, 1987), p. 92

[4]Marshall McLuhan, *The Gutenberg Galaxy* (New York, NY: Viking, 1962), p. 158

[5]E. Randolph Richards and Brandon J. O'Brien, *Misreading Scripture with Western Eyes: Removing Cultural Blinders to Better Understand the Bible* (InterVarsity Press, 2012), p. 197

[6]R. C. Sproul, *Saved from What?* (Wheaton, IL: Crossway, 2010), p. 21

[7]Attributed to John Lennon

[8]Revelation 20:10

[9]Revelation 21:4

[10]1 Corinthians 15:53; Revelation 21:1

[11]Revelation 21:3

[12]'Jesus is the Answer', words and music by Andrae and Sandra Crouch

[13]Quoted in: *Andrew Sims, Is Faith Delusion? Why Religion Is Good for Your Health* (Bloomsbury Publishing, 2009), p. 140

[14]Sims, p. 140

[15]Alicia Elliott, ' *"Directionless and Lost": What It Means to Be a Millennial*', 2020: *https://www.macleans.ca/opinion/directionless-and-lost-what-it-means-to-be-a-millennial/* (accessed 26 April 2020)

[16]Christine Emba, 'Opinion: Why Millennials Are Skipping Church and Not Going Back', *Washington Post*: *https://www.washingtonpost.com/opinions/why-millennials-are-skipping-church-and-not-going-back/2019/10/27/0d35b972-f777-11e9-8cf0-4cc99f74d127_story.html* (accessed 26 April 2020)

[17]Christian Smith and Melinda Lunquist Denton, *Soul Searching: The Religious and Spiritual Lives of American Teenagers* (Oxford, New York: Oxford University Press, 2005), pp. 162, 163

[18]Tom Beaudoin, *Witness to Dispossession: The Vocation of a Postmodern Theologian* (Maryknoll, NY: Orbis Books, 2008), pp. 79-85

[19]Kenda Creasy Dean, *Almost Christian: What the Faith of Our Teenagers Is Telling the American Church* (Oxford University Press, 2010), p. 104

[20]John 8:3-11; 5:1-15; Luke 8:43-48

[21]Luke 10:33, NKJV

[22]Luke 10:33

[23]Fritz Guy, 'Catching Up with Ellen: Five Important Ideas that Are Often Missed', *Spectrum* magazine: *https://spectrummagazine.org/views/2019/catching-ellen-five-important-ideas-are-often-missed* (accessed 18 September 2019), Guy's emphasis

From bounded to centred

He was a PK – a pastor's kid – with all the baggage and expectations that unasked-for status thrust upon him. As a rebel, he did lots of things he shouldn't have done, and imbibed lots of stuff it would have been better not to have imbibed. It wasn't that he got into bad company: often, he *was* that bad company. But here's the thing: he still attended church services intermittently. On this particular occasion he rocked up to the service late, wearing what at the time was the teen revolutionary's uniform of blue jeans and a green bomber jacket, all topped off with a face that had attitude etched all over it. For some reason, that day he was not greeted by a deacon, deaconess or usher, but one of the elders. The contrast between the two was stark. The elder – clean-cut, tall and imposing – was kitted out in a uniform of his own: a dark three-piece suit and tie, all topped off with a face that exuded attitude of a different sort.

'You're not coming in here dressed like that,' was the elder's greeting.

'Whaddaya mean?' came the response.

'You're not coming in here wearing jeans.'

The confrontation, if you could even call it that, was brief – but the fallout was much longer-lasting. The young man simply turned on the grubby heels of his Doc Martins®, wandered off into the distance, and never attempted to enter that building again.

She was about to attend a service at this particular church for the first time. It was a sad occasion, because one of her best friend's relatives had passed away. People know that there are at least a couple of times when dressing up is required, and a funeral is certainly one of them. She was not sure what to wear, but had done her best to present herself well. She walked nervously up the steps that led to imposing double doors. She, too, was greeted by one of the church's elders. Another tall and imposing figure, he too was decked out in the requisite uniform of a three-piece suit and tie and a face that expressed attitude.

'You cannot come in here dressed like that!' said the elder.

'Why?'

'You cannot come into the sanctuary wearing those clothes.'

'But I am a friend of the family and I have come to support them.'

'Not today, you haven't. You're not dressed appropriately enough.'

The conversation did not last that long, but the fallout lasted forever. She turned on her high heels and left. She did not attempt to enter that church building ever again.

One might hope that such incidents are on the decline, but both these stories are sadly true. They are not-so-subtle indicators of how people sometimes regard church buildings. They are understood to be sanctified spaces, to be protected at all costs. To step over the threshold is to enter a space where it is understood that standards need to be maintained and a certain sense of decorum needs to be upheld.

Driving this behaviour is a particular view of the church. It is seen in the way that the elders considered it to be their role – their duty, no less – to control who was qualified to view the church services, let alone take part in them. It is also suggested in how their decisions to deny entry were based on what they could *see*. In other words, they were using criteria based on appearances, on what could be evaluated with their eyes. They had no idea about what the 'offenders' were like on the inside, and seemed little interested in it. It was all about adherence to an unpublished dress code.

Similar criteria are often used by people groups, organisations and churches to identify whether a person belongs or not. For example, Scouts wear a particular uniform and promise to live up to the ideals of the Scout movement as laid out in Scout Law. Members of the local Women's Institute pay a subscription fee, must attend eleven meetings held throughout the year, and are generally female. A lawyer who wants to represent clients in court will have a law degree, will have passed the bar, will have undergone pupillage in barristers' chambers and will wear a wig and gown. Churches, similarly, have their own wide range of conditions that prospective members need to meet to be welcomed into the fold. These can include baptism, attendance at Bible classes, commitment to a set of beliefs, the signing of a covenant, and so on. Where these and similar criteria are used to distinguish between members and non-members, it results in what Paul Hiebert calls a 'bounded set'.[1]

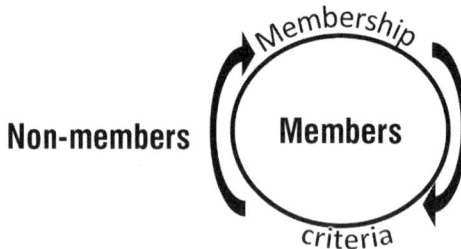

Figure 1: Bounded-set model of the church

This way of operating allows organisations and groups to function effectively. Imagine that you have set out to realise your life's ambition to form a choir. You have all sorts of plans prepared, including what genre of music you will sing and how often you will sing it. You have even come up with a name for the choir - The Semitones! How do you decide who is going to be a member of The Semitones? Generally, you are going to need people who can hold a tune. There is a certain sound you have in mind for the choir, so you will hold auditions. To make the process of learning the pieces more efficient, you want your singers to be able to read music. To ensure the pieces are performed to a good standard, you require members to turn up to a minimum number of rehearsals. There will be the cost of hiring a rehearsal room and pianist to cover, so members will agree to pay a subscription fee. Without all of these criteria in place, what audiences will hear is the wrong people singing the wrong notes with the wrong timing and in the wrong way. In this example, the boundary represents the difference between harmony and discord.

As a general rule, all human institutions and groups tend to operate as bounded sets. Setting and maintaining clear boundaries leads to stable organisations that are straightforward to manage and run. And, from a people perspective, members are clearly distinguishable and share a common identity that helps build relationships. It is for all of these good reasons that church communities are also organised as bounded sets.

Despite this, there are some limitations to consider. Firstly, there are only two types of people in this setup. A person is either a member or a non-member. Therefore, one member is the same as any other member. The Semitones might be made up of basses, tenors, altos and sopranos, but in terms of their membership they are equivalent. You are either in or out of the choir - there is no halfway house.

Secondly, it makes the process of becoming a member of a church community bureaucratic - even mechanical. Who you are as a person does not matter as long as you have achieved the benchmark. In the context of faith communities, you or I can become a member of any church or religious organisation by agreeing to the appropriate set of beliefs and by behaving, at least visibly, in the prescribed manner. This makes gaining church membership a cold and emotionless endeavour. Similarly, as important as they are, what will make members of The Semitones work together as a choir is not just their ability to read music, pass an audition or turn up to rehearsals. It is found in working to complement and build on the sounds of those around them. The best outcome will be achieved by listening to others more than yourself to achieve balance, blend, tuning and harmony. It is in feeling the ebb and flow of the music as the choir moves as a unified whole from one phrase to another, so singing with one voice.

Similarly, to be a member of a church community takes more than fulfilling a list of externally verified membership requirements. It is about becoming and being a Christian. It is what goes on inside a person that is most important. It is about having attitudes and dispositions characterised by repentance, forgiveness, selflessness and surrender. Jesus characterises this as the new-birth experience.[2]

To be a Christian is more about the unseen than the seen. It is about the Spirit and relationships. It is about an alternative way of being that Jesus characterised as denying oneself, taking up one's cross and following Him.[3] There are extrinsic or external criteria, but they are driven and motivated by an inner transformation that is most often referred to as 'conversion'. Above all, Christianity at its core is a connection with God the Father, Son and Holy Spirit that then informs us and brings us a fresh understanding as to how to relate to others. Belonging to a church community is about more than just assent and action: it is a Spirit-filled enterprise based on relationships.

Here's the issue: we can try to set up boundaries that represent what separates a member from a non-member, but Christianity is about what is happening on the inside: and, if knowing who's in and out is about relationships, then we need access to a person's heart, mind and soul . . . and only God has that.[4]

Bearing this in mind, what does a model based on relationships look like? Hiebert offers up an answer even as he recognises that 'we cannot see into the heart of people.'[5] This second model focuses not on the boundaries, but on the centre, and so is called a 'centre set'. Membership depends upon the connection a person has with the centre. Members of the group are those who are moving relationally towards the centre, and non-members are those who are going in the opposite direction. What is at the centre of a church community? Taking into account the three-fold nature of Christianity, it has to be God the Father, the Son and the Holy Spirit.[6] The concept can be visually represented as follows, noting that each arrow represents an individual's journey of faith:

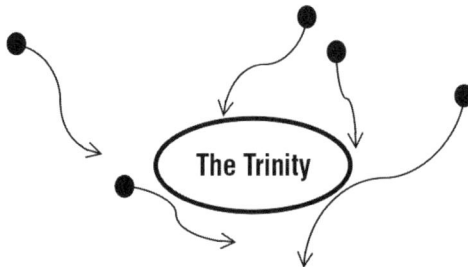

Figure 2: Centre-set model of the church

The positive thing about a centre-set view of the church is that it readily encompasses the diversity of Christian life. It does not matter how far away a person is from the centre: as long as they are moving in the right direction, they are recognised as being part of the group. This reflects the reality of church communities, because not everyone is in the same place in their relationship with God or with other members; and so the individuals who make up the community can never be thought of as being uniform in the way that is suggested by a bounded set. Another advantage is that there is a sense of journeying involved, as it is a dynamic concept that recognises movement.[7] The idea that a person is moving from A to B coheres with the use of 'walking' as one of the Bible's 'most vivid metaphors for how godly people should live'.[8] As it is a model that can only be fully comprehended by God, our limited human perspective means we are only catching glimpses of reality. This imposes on us a need to be humble when making assessments and evaluations about others.

Despite the attractiveness of a centre-set model, the bounded-set concept of church cannot be thrown out. To a certain extent, both models are extremes, yet remain able to describe different aspects of how we relate to others when in groups. The bounded-set view of the church describes its corporate structure and the institution, while the centre-set view brings into play the idea of the church as a covenant community of believers. In reality, a centre-set church will still have boundaries, not least of which is the boundary line of conversion. We know it exists, but we also know that only God understands where it might be in relation to an individual's life. Likewise, a bounded-set church will still have a centre to which members relate. The most important thing to address is where we focus our attention. Is it on the centre or on the boundaries?

Some of the issues that come with focusing on boundaries are seen in the passage in Luke 10. The lawyer's question, 'Who is my neighbour?' shows that he wants to distinguish between those who qualify to be his neighbour and those who do not, constituting a bounded set as follows:

Not Neighbour **Neighbour**

Figure 3: Neighbours as a bounded set

Jesus undermines and transforms his thinking in two ways: firstly, by choosing a Samaritan as the parable's hero – a man from a different people group with whom it is culturally inappropriate to interact – someone who, by tradition and custom, is to be despised. This boundary-breaking move confronts the lawyer with the idea that *anyone* in need is worthy of his attention, inside or outside the boundaries of his closely defined community.

Secondly, Jesus asks the lawyer to consider being a neighbour. This moves the lawyer's focus away from the boundary to a centre that is about people and his relationship with them. In Jesus' model, to move away from others by excluding them is the very opposite of neighbourly. Neighbours move towards people and grow in relationship with them.

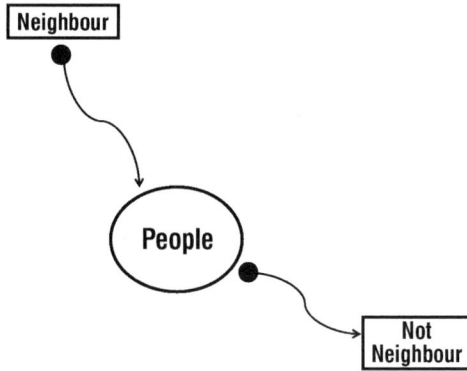

Figure 4: Jesus' view

This highlights a problem with boundaries. Yes, they help administratively, but they can also develop into walls of exclusion and inclusion . . . and it's not only first-century Jewish lawyers who do this. We too can construct inappropriate boundaries based on everything from ethnicity and culture to custom and tradition. We might even see justification for them in the Bible.

For example, in Galatians, Paul writes of those who are 'born of the flesh' and compares them with those who are 'born of the Spirit' – and, just in case we are not sure how to distinguish the two, he gives us a list of characteristics:

Table 2

Works of the flesh[9]	Fruit of the Spirit[10]
Fornication, licentiousness, impurity, idolatry, sorcery, enmities, strife, jealousy, anger, quarrels, dissensions, factions, envy, drunkenness, carousing	Love, joy, peace, patience, kindness, generosity, faithfulness, gentleness, self-control

Even though we might practise works of the flesh, and the fruit of the Spirit can be no more than aspirational at times, it is easy for a bounded-set mentality to be imposed, arriving at something like this:

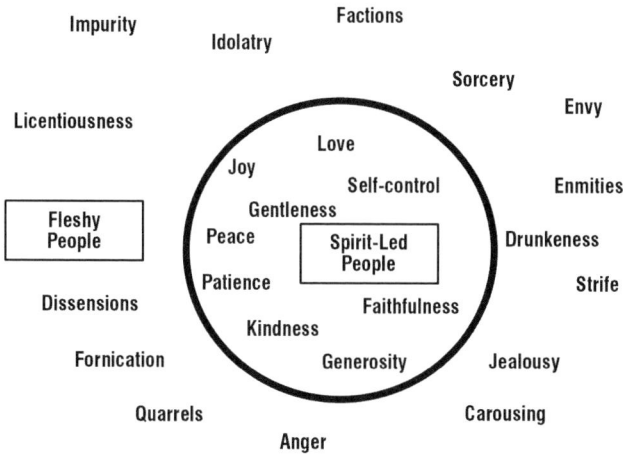

Figure 5: Works of the flesh vs. fruit of the Spirit

Paul similarly distinguishes two groups in opposition in Romans 12, where he writes, 'Do not be conformed to this world, but be transformed by the renewing of your minds, so that you may discern what is the will of God – what is good and acceptable and perfect.'[11] Again, a bounded-set mentality sees these verses as setting up in/out criteria that look like this:

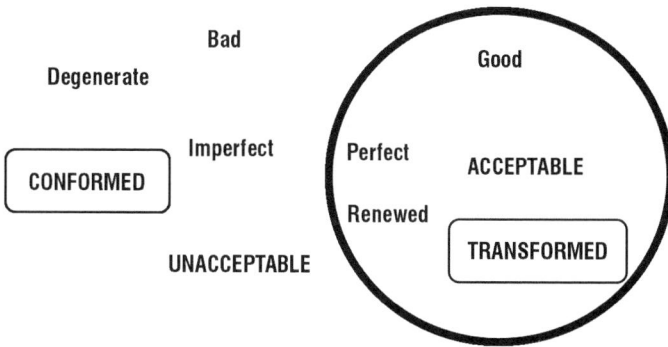

Figure 6: Conformed vs. transformed

Not only does this generate boundaries and emphasise difference, but it also seems to suggest that we who have accepted Jesus as Lord of our lives are not just different from those who have not done so, but are better than 'they' are. And isn't that the case? After all, Paul exclaims, 'If anyone is in Christ, there is a new creation,'[12] and they are 'changed into his [the Lord's] glorious image'.[13] Thus there are benefits in the here and now, because I follow Jesus. And do not the pages of Scripture and a relationship with God bring a different perspective on the world and its problems? Don't we gain a sense of peace, despite how tumultuous our lives get, because of a grounding in Christ? And what about the enhanced life that comes from communing and fellowshipping with like-minded souls who are on the same journey?

The Gospel is transformative, and encountering Christ through the pages of the Bible changes us. It is full of advice and instructions encouraging its readers to change or modify their behaviour. Jesus, referring to the second-greatest commandment, exhorted His disciples to 'love one another'.[14] John takes this directive and applies it to its utmost in that 'we ought to lay down our lives for one another.'[15] Very practically, James encourages the recipients of his letter to 'let everyone be quick to listen, slow to speak, slow to anger'.[16] Peter tells his correspondents to live their earthly lives 'no longer by human desires but by the will of God'.[17] If these instructions did not result in change, then the Bible would be nothing more than a book of wise and aspirational sayings. The transformation I undergo as an individual, and as a member of a church community, because of my faith in Jesus, lies at the heart of the Gospel. It would be ridiculous if that relationship and state of being were to make me worse, or even if it had a neutral effect. So, doesn't this mean that we who are 'in Christ' are inevitably better than those who are not? The answer to this question depends upon which frame of reference is being used.

One legitimate frame of reference is ourselves. Because I have access to my own heart, I can compare the 'old' me to the 'new' me. We each have a story that tells us where we have come from and where we are now. More than that: in allowing my story to be shaped by the biblical narrative, my future conceivably includes, by God's grace, a post-resurrection existence characterised by imperishability, glory, and strength.[18] But this is no reason to feel superior. Contemplation of what God has in store for me shows that, no matter where I think I have arrived at on my Christian journey, there is always further to go. The ultimate 'benchmark' is Christ, the second Adam, in whom humanity has reached its fullest and most complete expression.[19] To compare myself in my fallen, broken and weak state with Christ is always to fall short. 'The closer you come to Jesus, the more faulty you will appear in your own eyes; for your vision will be clearer, and your imperfections will be seen in broad and distinct contrast to His perfect nature.'[20] Neither frame of reference ever allows us to think we have 'made it', and so both of them demand humility at the same time as they speak to our potential through the Spirit. Innately, for both comparisons, any conclusions are unquantifiable, because they are relational in nature.

Alternatively, problems start to emerge if I take other people as my frame of reference. As tempting and as easy as it is to measure myself against others, it would be a project doomed to failure. I cannot compare the transformed and transforming version of me with someone else and conclude that I am somehow better than they are. If I think I am better than them, I start to use my characteristics and humanness as some sort of benchmark to which others need to aspire. It misses the point that intrinsic or internal factors, such as a faith relationship, are only visible to God. In Romans 12, Paul installs guardrails to protect his charges from such a destructive impulse. Having promoted the notion that we should be leading transformed lives, he writes, 'I say to everyone among you not to think of yourself more highly than you ought to think.'[21] Then, ensuring that the correct frame of reference is employed, he goes on to write, 'Think with sober judgement, each according to the measure of faith that God has assigned.'[22] In other words, think about the faith God has given you, and not about the faith God has given someone else!

Something to consider along the way

Politician Norman Tebbit is known for stirring up several controversies over the years, but none is more famous than the time he devised a loyalty test that came to bear his name. The Tebbit Test *involved asking which team people support when England plays their country of birth at cricket. Mainly directed at people originally from Asia and the Caribbean, it was proposed that not supporting England showed they were insufficiently integrated into the UK - they were not properly 'one of us'.*

One day, at one of the churches we attended as a family, a white person decided to stand at the door of the church building and 'discourage' black people from entering. It was like apartheid had come to the Home Counties. The irony was that this person was there visiting some of his relatives - he was not even a member. But he had decided that something needed to be done about the number of people who were viewed as taking over the church and who were not 'one of us'.

On another occasion, I had a conversation with a woman who had been part of a church for quite some time. Eventually, her attendance started to dwindle, and then it just stopped. Upon visiting her, I found out that she felt isolated and alone because she was the only white person in a black-majority congregation. 'I've no one I can really talk to,' she said, 'because there is no one like me.'

For a church community that operates focusing on boundaries, there are only two sorts of people - those who are on the inside, and everyone else. The people on the inside are, by definition, indistinguishable from each other, as they have all fulfilled the same 'membership' criteria. In such a church, it is not the members' job to be like those to whom they are reaching out. Rather, the burden of responsibility is placed firmly upon the shoulders of the outsider to become like the members.

[1]Paul G. Hiebert, 'The Category "Christian" in the Mission Task', *International Review of Mission*, vol. 72, issue 287 (1983), pp. 421-27; Paul G. Hiebert, *Transforming Worldviews: An Anthropological Understanding of How People Change* (Baker Academic, 2008), p. 38f.
[2]John 3:1-21
[3]Mark 8:34
[4]1 Samuel 16:7
[5]Paul G. Hiebert, 'Conversion, Culture and Cognitive Categories', *Gospel in Context*, 1.4 (1978), pp. 24-29

[6]Hiebert puts Jesus at the centre, but a more balanced theology involves seeing Christians as engaging and relating to all the members of the Godhead – see Tihomir Lazić for more on this approach (Paul G. Hiebert, *Transforming Worldviews*, p. 281; Tihomir Lazić, *Towards an Adventist Version of Communio Ecclesiology: Remnant in Koinonia* [Cham, Switzerland: Springer Publishing Company, 2019], p. 186).

[7]Paul G. Hiebert, 'Conversion, Culture and Cognitive Categories', *Gospel in Context*

[8]*Dictionary of Biblical Imagery*, edited by Leland Ryken, James C. Wilhoit, and Tremper Longman III (InterVarsity Press, 2010), p. 923

[9]Galatians 5:19-21

[10]Galatians 5:22, 23

[11]Romans 12:2

[12]2 Corinthians 5:17

[13]2 Corinthians 3:18, NLT

[14]John 13:34

[15]1 John 3:16

[16]James 1:19

[17]1 Peter 4:2

[18]1 Corinthians 15:42-44

[19]Romans 5:12-21; 1 Corinthians 15:21, 45

[20]White, Ellen Gould, *Steps to Christ* (Pacific Press Publishing Association, 1892), p. 64

[21]Romans 12:3

[22]Romans 12:3

The story of Anywhere Church: from best practice to tradition, and from doctrine to people

W hen Anywhere Church started, there were tough but rewarding times to begin with. The small community of ten people pulled together in the face of adversity. What made them stand out was, astonishingly, that all the members were left-handed. At first, this was a bit of a quirky coincidence that made them smile, but soon they started to find they had a sense of togetherness and identity because of their shared left-handedness. When they met and greeted each other, it was not with the right-handed shake of hands that a right-side-dominated society demanded of them, but with heartfelt left-handed shakes. They started to vote with their left hands, high five with their left hands . . . never had they experienced such freedom to be who they really were.

Initially, they seemed to attract only left-handed people, and the bond between them just grew stronger. At the Anywhere Church, there was a lack of restrictions found nowhere else in town. Even the guitarists played left-handed instruments instead of being forced by a biased right-handed society into using right-handed equipment. When they eventually moved into their own building, the doors were designed for the benefit of left-handed people. In the stationery cupboard could be found only left-handed scissors and pencil sharpeners. The kitchen was stocked with all sorts of left-handed equipment ranging from can openers to peelers.

From time to time, some right-handed people began to turn up. They were heartily welcomed, of course, but remained in the minority. The two hands lived happily together – the left-handedness of the majority dominated how things were done, while the right-handers who came were quite content just to fit in. As every instrument and utensil was designed for the left-handed, they were satisfied to do no more than the most menial of tasks.

Months turned into years, and eventually became decades. Anywhere Church had continued to welcome the right-handed, but was still a church where the vast majority were left-handed – and it was this group that continued to flourish and dictate how things should be done. But, one day, a group of right-handers moved into the area and started to attend Anywhere Church. There were thirty of them. As they settled, it seemed they took what was a left-hand-dominated church in their stride. Then things started to go wrong. Right-handed children were learning to play musical instruments, and one young lad had the temerity to turn up to the service asking to help out with the music. Wouldn't you know it – he was playing a right-handed guitar. In the nicest possible way, the local left-handed elder suggested that, before the young person played, they ought to take it to the church board.

At the next board meeting, the subject of the influx of right-handers was at the top of the agenda. It turned out that right-handed guitars were not the only problem disturbing the relative calm and tranquillity normally to be found in the Anywhere Church. At first, there were just whispers. These became suggestions. Soon they turned into reports. Appallingly, some of the people were coming to church and shaking hands, and they were not doing it with the correct (left) hand! Some members were beside themselves to think that people had brought right-handed grips into the church building. Others thought that this was an anti-left-handed conspiracy designed to split the church apart and bring in dubious right-handed theology. One person suggested that promoting this new form of handshake was all down to a local secret society who they had heard was trying to infiltrate Anywhere Church. The elder was tasked with going back to the young lad's parents and politely declining the offer to help out with the music for worship in the future. The deacons were charged with keeping an eye out for and then eradicating right-handed shakes with a firm but fair dose of policing. Now, right-handed people were tolerated rather than welcomed, and later they stopped attending at all.

No one can blame left-handed people for being left-handed. It is like trying to blame basketball players for being tall. Yet this church community allowed one aspect of who they were to turn into a boundary that many others could not breach. It was not there to begin with, but was constructed slowly over time, brick by brick, thought by thought, act by act, all building on what came before until it seemed as if it had been there all along. It is illustrative to see how socially complex church communities can be as they form boundaries within boundaries.

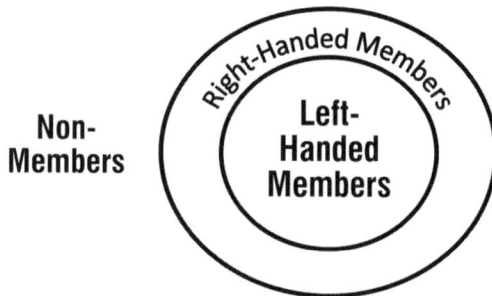

Figure 7: The Anywhere Church

But this all seems far-fetched, doesn't it? This would never happen in our church communities. Unlike the left-handers of Anywhere Church, we are flexible and don't insist on a certain order or type of service. We don't stick to language, Bible versions or structures that once met needs but are now out of date. We have not taken context-based practices that had very sound reasons for being adopted, and made them as sacrosanct as the laws of the Medes and Persians. Except we have, but are probably not aware of how, or that this has even happened, because the process is subtle yet powerful.

A broad rule of thumb for how these circumstances develop goes something like this (see Figure 8). A particular situation leads to a particular task being done in a particular way. After some time, that practice becomes a tradition. As it becomes concretised, the tradition gets turned into a rule, and eventually the rule gets spiritualised and becomes doctrinal in nature. The *situation* in Anywhere Church was that they were all left-handed. They started to *practise* left-handed shakes because it naturally suited the people who were all left-handed. They also did things like using left-handed implements, because it was less awkward for them. After a while, these *practices* became part of their *tradition* or norm. Given enough time for the tradition to bed in, it developed into an unwritten *rule* that was subsequently seen as being *doctrinal* in nature. Finally, through a process of interpretation, theological implications came to light, such that right-handed shakes were deemed unethical and unspiritual.

SITUATION	WE ARE ALL LEFT-HANDED
PRACTICE	WE USE LEFT-HANDED THINGS
TRADITION	WE ALWAYS USE LEFT-HANDED THINGS
RULE	WE MUST USE LEFT-HANDED THINGS
'DOCTRINE'	GOD REQUIRES US TO USE LEFT-HANDED THINGS

Figure 8: From situation to 'doctrine'

We are all faced with situations that lead to certain practical outcomes, and that is fine. That is living. If left-handed people want to use left-handed implements, then that is both practical and understandable. It becomes an issue when practices turn into traditions because, very often, people start to get marginalised. In the above scenario, once the group of thirty right-handed people arrived, there was no inclination to adapt to a changing situation. By now, the tradition and rules that had arisen out of a particular left-handed context were seen as more important than people, regardless of whether the individuals coming into the church were right-handed or not. And therein lies the problem.

As we move down the scale from situation to 'doctrine', we move further and further away from the people context that generated the practice in the first place (see Figure 9). By Jesus' day, the people context in which the Sabbath was created had faded from view, so Jesus was moved to remind the Pharisees (and us) that 'the sabbath was made for humankind, and not humankind for the sabbath.'[1] The Sabbath would be meaningless were it not for the people for whom it was created – people living in a relationship with their Creator. Of course, this does not mean there are no doctrines and absolutes – but if we were to make the beliefs themselves the most important thing, we would not only lose sight of the people context, but also force God into the background. Doctrines are important expressions of belief, but they are only relevant because they reflect a reality that is founded on a relationship with a Triune God and with each other. This is why everything important can be summed up by the commands to love God and love our neighbour. It is the reason Paul writes, 'For the whole law is summed up in a single commandment, "You shall love your neighbour as yourself." '[2] And, as Jesus is demonstrating to the lawyer in Luke 10, this does not lessen our obligations, but rather broadens them. It is far easier to maintain a rule than it is to maintain a person-centric life.

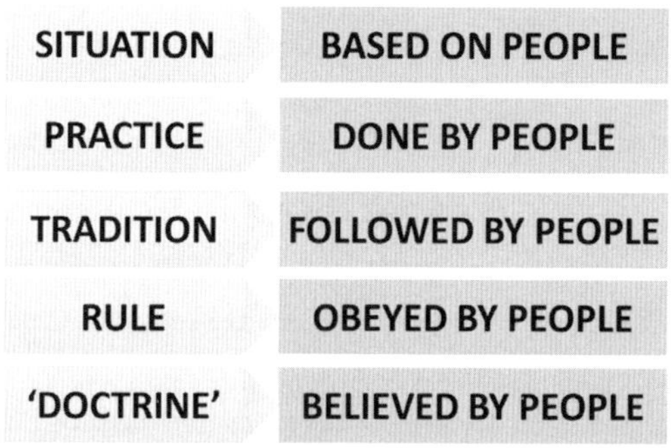

SITUATION	BASED ON PEOPLE
PRACTICE	DONE BY PEOPLE
TRADITION	FOLLOWED BY PEOPLE
RULE	OBEYED BY PEOPLE
'DOCTRINE'	BELIEVED BY PEOPLE

Figure 9: Situations, doctrines and people

Therefore, we need to continually review practices to ensure that they fit the current context. Otherwise, we will lose sight of *why* we do what we do. For example, in the situations in which I pastor, it is common practice in a communion service to cover the bread and wine with an ornate white cloth. This is solemnly removed by deaconesses before the breaking of the bread, and replaced afterwards with an equal sense of occasion. My wife finds this practice amusing and frustrating in equal measure, because now it makes no sense. We have allowed the context in which this practice arose to get lost in the mists of time, so we have no idea why this started or why we still do it. Was it once done to protect the bread and wine in pursuit of good food hygiene or keep them out of sight until they were needed? Was it a way of giving females something to do in what is a highlight of a church's calendar but can be a male-dominated affair? There is no ready explanation. Certainly, there is nothing in the Bible that speaks to this.[3] This may sound trivial, but, because the practice-to-doctrine model is working overtime, it is regarded by some as a theological issue. The thinking goes that if we need a special cloth to cover the bread and wine, it must be because the emblems are sacred. This makes them become more than the symbols proclaiming Jesus' death that we know them to be.

Similarly, the Bible has nothing to say about church services predominantly being held in buildings, in the mornings, with the congregation sat in rows. Scripture does not tell us there must be a sermon or that we must use a certain translation of the Bible. We need to be constantly vigilant to ensure we have the right focus. To let our guard down is to let our practices become embedded, fossilised, spiritualised and depersonalised. I was going to write that there is no right way to 'do church' – but such a statement is trite and can be taken out of context. The right way to **be** church is to turn our gaze from boundary issues to the core. It is found in respecting God's ideal that we love Him and our neighbours. It is about being recognised as Jesus' disciples because we love each other.[4] It is through understanding how important people are to God, and so adopting the best people-focused practices possible. The key, I think, is in the questions we ask. For example:

It's not,
'What music is right?'
But,
'What music will best help those we are reaching encounter God in worship?'

It's not,
'What is the dress code?'
But,
'What do we need to wear to reach out to others?'

It's not,
'What is the right diet for a Christian?'
But,
'In what ways is my diet hindering or helping my relationships?'

We readily turn things like music, dress and diet into boundary issues, even as God would like us to focus on the core. These questions might make some feel uncomfortable, because they are open-ended and appear to veer towards situational ethics – which is why someone once asked, if the situation demanded it, whether I would turn up to a service naked. However, not only would that be distracting and disturbing, but it would also miss the point. To reach out to people is to walk alongside them as they enter into a living, breathing, life-enhancing relationship with God in three Persons and with others. It is this that can both frame and ground our discussions on such topics. For example, it is not about playing attractive music, but worshipful music. If the lyrics do not help people encounter God, then they are not fulfilling their purpose. If the style of music is inviting but distracts worshippers from meeting with the Truth (that is, Jesus), then it is falling short. This can be the case with an ancient hymn that is mumbled and stumbled over, as much as it can be for a more contemporary or upbeat song.

Thus, in the spirit of reflection, we could ask, 'Why are we doing this?' and 'What are we trying to achieve?' These are useful questions, but they are not as valuable as asking, **'How would God like us to treat people in this situation?'**[5] I hesitate to beat down on the priest and the Levite, but I wonder what would have happened if they too had asked themselves that question. Would it have changed the outcome? Would they have been able to see how they had allowed themselves to be boxed in by tradition, rules and 'doctrine'? When confronted by a wounded, half-dead man on the side of the road desperately in need of help, would they respond, or continue to believe that God required them to move on?

[1] Mark 2:27
[2] Galatians 5:14
[3] See Luke 22:14-23 and 1 Corinthians 11:17-34, for example.
[4] John 13:35
[5] Andy Stanley has a useful list of questions that help this process of reflection. See Andy Stanley, *Deep and Wide: Creating Churches Unchurched People Love to Attend* (Grand Rapids, MI: Zondervan, 2016), pp. 287-89.

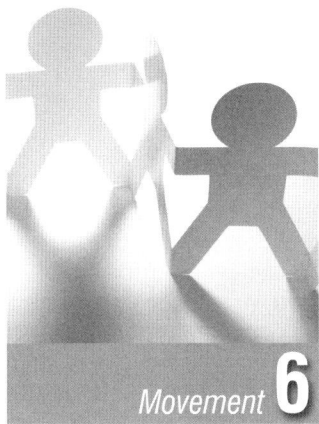

From person to personhood

It should not need stating that we need to treat people as people. Of course we should treat people as people! How else would we treat them? However, it does not take too much knowledge of world history – contemporary and ancient – to acknowledge that this concept very much needs stating again and again. The worst human-on-human atrocities throughout the ages have been brought about by some person(s) treating individuals or groups as if they no longer fully belonged to the human race. Near the top of the list is any time someone is enslaved. It is sad and shocking that, even though we are well into the twenty-first century, slavery is not yet something that has been consigned to history. At the time of writing, the anti-slavery charity *The Walk Free Foundation* are reporting that there are 40.3 million slaves found on six of the seven continents.[1] To the list of atrocities can be added relatively recent and higher-profile occurrences, such as the acts of torture carried out at Abu Ghraib, the oppression that different people groups experienced through the institution of systems generated by Jim Crow and apartheid, or the genocidal acts arising out of conflicts in places ranging from Rwanda to Bosnia. If we were there on the Jerusalem-Jericho road, we could see a man who is treated not as a person, but as a source of clothes and money and therefore ripe for a mugging. If we were to hang around, we could watch as a priest and a Levite pass by the victim of the assault, seeing him not as a human being, but as a carcass to be avoided.

It is easy to look at these awful events that pepper human history with a sense of detachment. Yes, they happened, but surely *I* could never be part of them. This is especially the case if the events that scarred the twentieth century are taken into consideration. Surely anyone with a sense of morality, civility and decency would not have taken part in the killing of millions of Jews in World War 2, for example? It seems straightforward to conclude that a scrap of humanity and some common sense would certainly have prevented this. And yet we have to come to grips with the fact that, during that awful episode in human history, people were treated as far less than people on an industrial scale.

More formally, not treating people as people is known as 'depersonalisation'. This is just the first step on a downward spiral that eventually results in dehumanisation. To depersonalise someone involves depriving them of their individuality, and is often achieved through labelling. So the people standing in front of us are no longer Abraham and Sarah, with individual histories and attributes, but 'Jews'. The process is nudged along through the addition of the definite article as individuals are further denied their identity by being grouped with others. Now, Abraham and Sarah are not simply Jews, but 'the Jews'. The next step sees the person or group denied human characteristics. Rather than living, breathing, autonomous and free-thinking human beings, Abraham and Sarah belong to a group that is deemed to lack generosity and a sense of humour. As dehumanisation sets in, Abraham and Sarah cease to be seen as members of the human race, and are viewed as objects, animals or pests, and consequently are treated as such. Finally, the dehumanised entities are no longer viewed as benign, but represent a threat to safety, security or well-being. It is this type of process that led to the Holocaust. Where the 'Nazis were most successful was in the depersonalisation of the Jew. . . . Depersonalisation increased the already existent widespread indifference of German popular opinion and formed a vital stage between the archaic violence of the pogrom and the rationalised "assembly-line" annihilation of the death camps.'[2] The indifference is shocking, and yet it was that indifference that led to unthinkable, dehumanising behaviour.

While on holiday a few years back, my wife and I decided to visit the Mauthausen Concentration Camp Memorial in Austria. As we walked around, it was difficult not to feel the weight of history. It was tough not to shudder as we came across specially constructed 'showers' capable of exterminating one hundred and twenty people at a time. As we walked through the sleeping quarters where single beds had housed multiple inmates, it was challenging to appreciate just how badly human beings were treated in what appeared to be such a mundane setting. We read how the camp and its satellite sites were in the main designed to kill people through forced hard labour. We – who, by the grace of God, would find it intolerable to take a single person's life – struggled to come to terms with the sheer scale of the operation. Despite Mauthausen being thought of as a 'softer' concentration camp, it is estimated that 90,000 out of the 190,000 people imprisoned in the main camp died because of the treatment they received.[3] We had to constantly remind ourselves that those numbers represented people, individuals with personal stories, families, hopes and dreams. We kept asking ourselves how the officials running the camp could look into prisoners' eyes and behave so badly towards them. What we were struggling with the most was that the camp's staff were not seeing a person – a daughter, son, mother or father – but a dehumanised object to be treated like an animal, abused or even eliminated.

But move away from camps to battlefields and the problem lingers. As the Allied and Axis powers faced each other in World War 2, both sides needed to treat their enemy as less than human. Look down the sight of a gun and see someone with a biography and personality, and we will see someone we are unlikely to pull the trigger on – even for a righteous cause. It is why sailors living under the threat of twenty-first-century maritime piracy and kidnapping are told, 'Humanise yourself. It's a lot harder to kill someone when you view them as a person – it's easier to shoot an object.'[4] It takes a high degree of sociopathy, even in the heat of the battle, to kill your enemy, unless they are no longer thought of as a fellow member of the human race. It is a totally different ball game if your enemy is regarded as an invading army of cockroaches that threatens your country's well-being. Similar narratives were carried through into the popular press and culture on both sides in World War 2. For example, it is suggested that the most popular float in a parade in New York in 1942 depicted a bomb falling on yellow rats. It was clear to all that those peculiarly coloured rodents represented dehumanised Japanese people who 'deserved' extermination.[5]

But are these extreme cases to bring up, given our context? What has this to do with us who live in the twenty-first century? Even more so, what has it to do with Christians who are part of a church community? Perhaps we need to take note when it is suggested that dehumanisation is 'profoundly intertwined with the human experience'.[6] As a result, it has been going on for far longer and is more widespread than we think.

It is sobering to understand the reason dehumanisation is so widespread: it's because anyone caught up in the right circumstances and systems is capable of it. In the notorious Stanford Prison Experiment, psychologist Philip Zimbardo recruited students from Stanford University to take part in a trial to investigate the psychology of power.[7] A mock prison was set up in the basement of Stanford's psychology department and populated by students who were arbitrarily assigned to play the role of guard or prisoner. The experiment was designed so the guards held the balance of power. They were told not to use physical intimidation, but were encouraged to challenge the prisoners psychologically. The inmates were known only by a number, dressed in ill-fitting prison clothing, housed in 6x9-foot cells and made to attend headcounts day and night.

All of the participants were chosen for their mental stability and came from healthy, middle-class families . . . but it is remarkable and disturbing how quickly they took to their roles. After just a few days, the guards were psychologically abusing and intimidating the prisoners and were humiliating them by forcing them to perform lewd acts. Many of the prisoners were unable to cope mentally with the conditions, succumbing to depression and anxiety. Consequently, the experiment lasted only six of its planned twenty-one days. Zimbardo agrees that this rapid descent into unacceptable behaviour is 'hard to imagine'.[8] What makes it particularly difficult to comprehend was that there was no difference between the two groups. 'They all began the experience as seemingly good people. Those who were guards knew that but for the random flip of a coin they could have been wearing the prisoner smocks and been controlled by those they were now abusing.'[9] It was concluded that it was not because of a person's personal qualities that abuse happened, but because of 'powerful situational and systemic forces'.[10]

The participants were put into a situation where they behaved in a way the system 'expected'. I could not imagine myself ever abusing another human being as the students who took on the role of the guards did. But that is the point. Before twelve students had volunteered for the experiment and were assigned to be prison wardens, they probably could not have imagined that either.

Not only is this a warning to be mindful of how systems and the power that lies within them can influence us, but it is also a demonstration of the impact that belonging to a group has. Researchers have demonstrated that as soon as we become part of a group, our behaviour changes. Our identity is immediately tied into the group, so that we define those in the group as 'us', and those outside as 'them'.[11] And, no matter who we are, we are members of many groups – each of which allows us to distinguish ourselves from others. For example, I am currently part of groups that can be defined as white, British, English, European, Protestant, able-bodied, vegetarian, Arsenal-supporting, non-Marmite-eating and so many more.

When we meet someone for the first time, part of the process of getting to know them is searching out which groups we have in common. This allows for shared identities and stories to be used to build rapport. Finding that you are from the same town, or the same country when meeting abroad, or have the same interest in basket-weaving, immediately helps break the ice. Dropping group language into the conversation strengthens the bond further. This is because much of a group's personality comes from the language that is used: 'Our lingo is our identity.' For example, Anglican vicars employ a quintessentially English sense of humour when referring to a 'fish and chips service'. This came about because *Abide With Me* and *Loving Shepherd of Thy Sheep* are so often sung at funerals that they are seen together as frequently as fish and chips.[12] Such terms act as an in-group language, so are only understood by those in the know. If someone were to use terms like 'hard block', 'centre trio', 'bootleg' or 'zebra', I would be completely baffled by this American football jargon. This lack of knowledge on my part would promptly identify me as an outsider, and in certain situations it would mean I am excluded.

It is not just about a shared language, but also having a common history. I loved playing cricket when I was a lad. I must have spent hundreds of hours out on the school field, batting, bowling and fielding, never quite being able to play enough to be content. There came a time when I was moved to another school, and so I was looking forward to joining in with at least one of their cricket teams. But, very early on, it was clear that my ambitions were to be severely curtailed. I had not been drilled in the art of playing cricket in the same way as those who had attended the school from day one. I also had not built up the necessary connections over time with teammates or coaches. Maybe it was also that I was not good enough. I found there was little chance of getting near the second or third teams, let alone the highly esteemed first team that played on a fantastic pitch and used equipment I could only dream about. There was more in-group language to learn as I was directed towards playing OAS cricket. 'What's OAS cricket?' I asked. 'That, my friend,' came the reply, 'is "odds and sods" cricket.' Not being good enough for the 'proper' sides meant being labelled as an 'odd or a sod' in that educational establishment.

Thinking about my school experience all these years later, only now do I realise that something unexpected happened. Instead of looking enviously at the other teams, I came to be proud to be part of the odds and sods. I revelled in the camaraderie built on the good times we had together. I came to enjoy the down-to-earth games we had, because we were nice, friendly and reasonable. By contrast, the members of the other teams, especially the first team, were seen as over-competitive, stuck-up and big-headed. I had ended up pitting one group against another; and, as soon as that happens, a very subtle yet pervasive form of dehumanisation called *infrahumanisation* takes place.[13]

Infrahumanisation occurs when a person considers those outside their group as below, or less than, human. We do this by subconsciously depriving them of human-defining characteristics. My school cricketing experience led to the first team being seen as lacking compassion, contentment and satisfaction. This reflects how infrahumanisation leads us to doubt the ability of non-group members to respond with the full range of human emotions.[14] More explicitly, this is the 'tendency to internally attribute sophisticated, uniquely human, secondary and higher emotions more to in-group members than out-group members'.[15] Lower, or primary, emotions are the instinctive, unthinking emotions that come on strongly, are easily identified, and can be experienced by animals as well as people. Secondary emotions come in response to primary emotions, and are more complex and difficult to pin down. For instance, the primary emotion of fear can lead to the secondary emotions of helplessness or feeling weak; joy can be followed by happiness or delight.

Infrahumanisation is not so easily identified because it does not necessarily lead to obvious acts of aggression towards outsiders. It is not even that group members dislike non-group members. Rather, it is that membership of a group increases the likelihood of feelings of indifference or apathy because non-group members are deemed to have reduced mental capacities; and if I am feeling indifferent or apathetic towards another person or group, I will not be inclined to want to connect or establish a relationship with them. Why would anyone want to associate with someone they consider to be not quite as human as they are? This means I will distance myself from them and feel even greater attraction towards the other members of my group – increasing the bonds between us.[16]

Forgive me for using another sporting example, but an obvious and extreme case of where this occurs is between rival football fans.[17] As previously mentioned, I support Arsenal, and the few times I have been to watch my team play, at some stage during the match, regardless of whom the opponents are, the crowd chant, 'Stand up if you hate Tottenham!' It reflects and maintains the traditional rivalry that exists between Arsenal and their

North London neighbours, whose stadia are only five miles apart. Now, I do not particularly want Tottenham's fans to be happy because their team is successful, and that is probably not a healthy, or indeed Christian, attitude. However, I do not hate them. I know a few people who support Tottenham Hotspur, and there is no animosity on my part towards them at all. So, when feeling brave, I have refused to stand when the call rings around the ground to rise up in collective hatred – potentially risking the ire of fellow supporters. But it goes deeper than what at first has the feel of a pantomime act. I sometimes listen to Arsenal podcasts to provide a bit of light entertainment. On one in particular, whenever the topic of Tottenham and their supporters comes up, the hosts immediately question our rivals' mental capacity and cognitive abilities. Contributors refer to them as being Neanderthal, uncivilised and barbaric. Now, it is not as if all Arsenal fans belong to Mensa and are capable of producing a Shakespearean-style sonnet, of course. Putting any irony to one side, the key point is that the Arsenal in-group sees the Tottenham out-group as being less than human, and so infrahumanisation takes place. For the sake of balance, Tottenham fans also infrahumanise Arsenal fans, because this works both ways.

There was the same dynamic in play between the Jews and the Samaritans – one that makes Jesus' choice of a Samaritan as the hero of His parable such a provocative one. That there was animosity between the two groups is well known. That infrahumanisation was a result is seen in the suggestion that the 'Jews regarded Samaritans as half-breeds, the offspring of resettlement policies of the cruel Assyrians.'[18] Evidence of distancing between the groups is plainly expressed when the narrator comments in John 4:9 that the 'Jews do not share things in common with Samaritans.' The New King James Version emphasises the gap still further by interpreting the same verse as saying, 'For Jews have no dealings with Samaritans.'

The implications of this can readily be transferred to a church context. Being a member of a faith community has all sorts of positive psychological and health benefits, and this has been verified in several studies.[19] Taking into account the research on groups, we can now add to these benefits the increased connectivity that comes from being part of an in-group. But, at the same time, we also have to think about the effect of psychologically dividing those inside and outside the church community into 'us' and 'them' because of the tendency for this to lead to infrahumanisation. 'They' do not know what 'we' know. 'They' live debauched and reckless lives outside the saving and transformative influence of the Holy Spirit. 'They' are not saved, but rather are lost. Because 'they' have not accepted the Gospel, 'they' are more likely to get involved in criminal activities because of their lower moral standards. While missing out on the wonders of a heart and life made new, 'they' will be less adept in forming meaningful and rich relationships. The problem is clear: 'they' end up being understood as not quite as human as those of us who are inside the church and are members of the religious in-group – the way 'they' are distanced is almost palpable.

1st Stage ➡ **2nd Stage** ➡ **3rd Stage**

My Group   **Us**   **Human**

Not My Group   **"Them"**   **<Human**

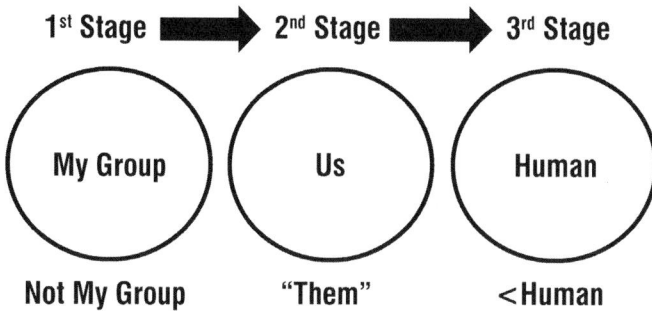

Figure 10: From 'not my group' to 'not quite as human'

As with the two sets of football fans, infrahumanisation goes both ways. Christians are regarded as being hypocrites, intolerant, judgmental, deluded, out of touch and archaic. Such statements are made without actually knowing the people being spoken about – any individual's identity is bound up and inseparable from the group identity. There is, therefore, a sociological phenomenon at work here, because wherever 'the ratio of what is known to what needs to be known approaches zero, we tend to invent "knowledge" and assume we understand more than we actually do'.[20] A pretty harmless example of this is the assumption that I like to drink tea because I am English. I have often encountered looks of surprise on people's faces when making pastoral visits when I tell them I only very occasionally partake of hot drinks, and do not actually like the taste of tea or coffee. 'You're not very English, are you?' I have often been told. I resist the temptation to respond by telling them, 'But I am very me.'

Herein lies the solution. To combat the tendency to infrahumanise others, we need to avoid the steps that lead to it happening, or at least consciously reverse them. The primary task involves extracting individuals from the groups to which we assign them, or with which they identify themselves. Just because someone has darker or lighter skin pigmentation does not mean they are the same as those who look similar. Just because I identify as 'English' does not mean I drink tea, wear a bowler hat to bed and apologise too much. As a person is extracted from their groups, this allows stereotypes and labels that such groupings encourage to fade away. 'Us' and 'them' are no longer adequate terms to use; rather, 'Jill', 'Jane', 'Joan' or 'John' becomes an appropriate term as a living, breathing individual with a unique set of gifts, talents, hopes, desires and characteristics starts to emerge. Eventually, a one-to-one relationship is established where knowing is a dynamic process not driven by assumption, but by interaction and the sharing of stories. This surely is part of what it means to 'love your neighbour', because to know is to love.

The apostle Paul does just this as he counterintuitively both removes labels and at the same time groups everyone together in a notable passage in his letter to the Galatians. He writes, 'for in Christ Jesus you are all children of God through faith. As many of you as were baptized into Christ have clothed yourselves with Christ. There is no longer Jew or Greek, there is no longer slave or free, there is no longer male and female; for all of you are one in Christ Jesus.'[21] Here, the labels that were potentially used to depersonalise every living human being in Paul's day are taken off the table, for everyone was and is either a Jew or a non-Jew, male or female, slave or free.[22] This new, label-free status comes about for those who have a relationship with Christ because they have been and are baptised into Christ, have put on Christ, and so belong to Christ. Is Paul merely establishing a new and exclusive group with a new label – a group that differs from those who have not encountered and responded to Jesus? Of course not: he is giving us a glimpse of the type of community that God intended for all of the nations, tribes and people in the first place and is working towards right now. He is telling us that this does not come naturally, as our instinct is to split off into different groups. So, to experience this new status, we need to be recreated in Christ.

Clearly, we who are part of church communities also need to fight the tendency to infrahumanise those we see as not being part of us. When it comes to the outgroup, there is a ready vocabulary available to apply – one that comes tied to stereotypes and that includes 'the world', 'worldly', 'unchurched', 'pagan', 'new-agers', 'secular' and so on. In not recognising the effects of using such terms, we fail to see the way they encourage feelings of superiority – feelings that lead to the physical and relational distancing that was in evidence in Jesus' day between the Jews and the Samaritans.

If we allow ourselves to be caught up in infrahumanising others, the effects on mission are potentially devastating as real human interaction is discouraged. But, in reversing the process of infrahumanisation, we can establish authentic relationships. And – because this works both ways – in doing so, we allow others to humanise Christians and challenge the assumptions made about those of us who choose to follow Jesus.

But, having arrived at a more positive position, one of the potential complications to be faced is that there are times in the Bible when labels are applied, and a 'them and us' attitude appears to be adopted or even encouraged. Some of the clearest examples of this are found in John's letters where, for example, he writes, '*They* are from the world; therefore what *they* say is from the world, and the world listens to *them*. *We* are from God.'[23] It is challenging to try and unravel what John means by the term 'the world', because he uses it to refer to different things in different places. The world is to be loved and saved, while, at the same time, it is to be avoided and is in opposition to God.[24] Indeed, it is suggested there is such a 'constant shift of meaning, or rather connotation, [it] makes it impossible to give any single definition'.[25]

What does John mean in practice? Does this give Christian communities leeway to set themselves up in opposition to others? Not if we take into account the fact that, in John's writings, 'although the "world" does constitute a sphere that is indelibly and constitutionally opposed to God, it is not by the will of God or by some act of exclusion or omission on God's part.'[26] In fact, God does not erect boundaries, but rather sends His Son as 'the atoning sacrifice for our sins, and not for ours only but also for the sins of the *whole world*'.[27] That means everyone. Rather than giving permission to erect boundaries, exclude and infrahumanise others, we are to identify with all of humanity, who all need saving. Hence, 'Evangelism is just one beggar showing another beggar where he found bread.'[28] We are all beggars in need of the Bread of Life. Christian or non-Christian, we are all beggars just the same.

Here we see a key step to take in treating people as people. Where infrahumanising encourages us to distance ourselves from others, to humanise is to identify with 'them' and reduce the gap. The way Jesus closed the distance between Himself and humanity profoundly illustrates how far God is willing to go. Jesus became human. He identified as human, dwelt among us, lived with all our foibles and quirks, and placed Himself in the centre of the rough and tumble of life. How far am I willing to go to identify with the people to whom I am being neighbourly?

This movement started with the apparently obvious statement that we need to treat people as people. We have found that this is easier to write than to do. It is with little effort that I might start to think that people from the areas of town in which I live are more civilised than those living in the rougher parts of town, or even a rival village just down the road. Those moments of humour that happen when Americans tell jokes about Canadians, the British about the Irish, and the Irish about people from Limerick, are underpinned by an innate understanding that the humour is revealing a lack in those who are the subject of the jokes. How about the temptation to consider vegetarians like myself as consuming a balanced and healthy diet, but see vegans as taking it too far, and meat-eaters as being lost souls who unnecessarily kill innocent animals? It comes naturally to regard students who attended the same educational institutions as me as being more rounded and intelligent than those who went to other places or no places at all. In the US, it has been found that Princeton is thought of as being academically rigorous, but too exclusive and hierarchical. MIT has brilliant students, but it is socially unpleasant. The University of Pennsylvania is altogether too career-minded. There are similar dynamics in play in the sometimes hostile rivalry between Britain's two greatest universities, Oxford and Cambridge: a rivalry that goes back to the thirteenth century.[29]

Maybe one of the reasons Jesus tells us not to judge people is that we cannot judge others without somehow making them less human and encouraging us to feel in some way superior.[30] It is comforting for us, then, that God the Father and the Son are our judges, because their judgments enhance rather than diminish our humanness.[31] This is where the centre-set model of church can be a powerful tool. In fact, I suggest that what is needed is centre-set *thinking*. This is where the only difference between me and any other person is that we are on a different journey with respect to the Trinitarian centre. There are no boundaries to help distinguish, exclude and promote labelling, just individuals who are being influenced by the Holy Spirit in different ways at different times.

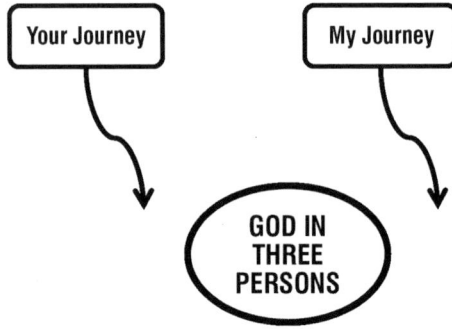

Figure 11: Different journeys

Imagine a community of people that we call church who, rather than depersonalise and dehumanise, enhance and help establish each other's personhood and humanity. Imagine a church community where the priority is to get to know each other so that each individual is valued as a person in their own right. Imagine a community where the use of labels is minimised, and the power of relationships is maximised. Imagine a place where 'the world' is being encouraged to partake in the plan of redemption, just as we who are Christian have already done so.

Something more to think about along the way:

'I was travelling abroad and felt as if I was treated like baggage at the airport. When I checked in, employees asked my companions questions about me and did not speak to me.' Stopped from getting to the aircraft in her own wheelchair, the story continues, 'The man pushing me spoke to my companions, but not to me, other than to tell me no when I put my hands on the wheels. I felt powerless, as if I were just an object that needed to be moved from one place to another.'[32]

'Any time someone reduces a human being to a single characteristic, especially a negative one, they are dehumanising.'[33] Those with visible disabilities can have their external identities condensed and squashed until they become their disability and not a person with a disability. Disability can be seen as a negative characteristic that in turn leads to ableism – the privileging of the able-bodied over the disabled – such that it is thought, 'It is better for a child to walk than roll, speak than sign, read print than read Braille.'[34]

Dehumanisation of people with disabilities happens when they are *thought not to have feelings and emotions; not to feel pain, cold or hunger; not to be able to make worthwhile contributions to society; or to be incapable of making decisions for themselves.*[35]

[1]Antarctica is the only continent without slaves: *www.walkfree.org.*

[2]'The Persecution of the Jews and German Popular Opinion in the Third Reich', in: *The Nazi Holocaust, Part 5: Public Opinion and Relations to the Jews in Nazi Europe,* edited by Michael R. Marrus and Ian Kershaw (Wesport, London: Walter de Gruyter, 1989), pp. 86-114 (p. 112); see also Julia Boyd, *Travellers in the Third Reich: The Rise of Fascism Through the Eyes of Everyday People* (London: Elliott & Thompson, Limited, 2018).

[3]'The Mauthausen Concentration Camp 1938-1945 – History – KZ-Gedenkstätte Mauthausen': *https://www.mauthausen-memorial.org/en/History/The-Mauthausen-Concentration-Camp-19381945* (accessed 9 October 2018)

[4]Tarrol Peterson: *https://www.dockwalk.com/news/taken-hostage-how-to-survive*

[5]Steven Bender, *Mea Culpa: Lessons on Law and Regret from U.S. History* (New York: NYU Press, 2015), p. 162

[6]David Livingstone Smith, *Less Than Human: Why We Demean, Enslave, and Exterminate Others* (New York: St Martin's Press, 2011), pp. 1, 167

[7]Philip Zimbardo, *The Lucifer Effect: How Good People Turn Evil* (London: Random House, 2011)

[8]Zimbardo, p. 172

[9]Zimbardo, p. 172

[10]Zimbardo, p. 381

[11]Adam Waytz and Nicholas Epley, 'Social Connection Enables Dehumanisation', *Journal of Experimental Social Psychology*, 48 (2011), pp. 70-76

[12]Susie Dent, *Dent's Modern Tribes: The Secret Languages of Britain* (London: John Murray, 2016), p. 8

[13]The prefix 'infra' means 'below'. Thus, the word 'infrasonic' refers to sounds that have frequencies below what humans can hear, and the word 'infranatural' means the opposite of 'supernatural'.

[14]J. P. Leyens et al., 'The Emotional Side of Prejudice: The Attribution of Secondary Emotions to Ingroups and Outgroups', *Personality and Social Psychology Review*, 4.2 (2000), pp. 186-97

[15]Graham M. Vaughan and Michael A. Hogg, *Social Psychology* (French Frost, NSW: Pearson Higher Education AU, 2013), p. 349

[16]Or, as originally put, 'Social connection may therefore benefit intragroup relations, but impair intergroup relations' (Waytz and Epley, *Social Connection Enables Dehumanization,* p. 75).

[17]For more information, see Desmond Morris, *The Soccer Tribe* (New York, NY: Rizzoli International Publications, 2016).

[18]Gerald L. Borchert, *John 1-11* (Nashville, TN: B&H Publishing Group, 1996), p. 199

[19]See, for example, M. A. Bruce et al., 'Church Attendance, Allostatic Load and Mortality in Middle-Aged Adults', *PLOS ONE*, 12.5 (2017): *https://doi.org/10.1371/journal.pone.0177618*; S. Li, T. J. VanderWeele, and T. H. Chan, 'Association of Religious Service Attendance With Mortality Among Women', *JAMA Intern Med*, 176.6 (2016), 777-85: *https://doi:doi:10.1001/jamainternmed.2016.1615.*

[20]James M. Henslin, *Down-to-Earth Sociology, 14th Edition: Introductory Readings* (New York, NY: Simon and Schuster, 1981), p. 331

[21]Galatians 3:26-28

[22]Paul uses the label 'Greek' here to denote all non-Jews, and not just those who are ethnically Greek. See *Theological Dictionary of the New Testament*, edited by Gerhard Kittel, Geoffrey W. Bromiley, and Gerhard Friedrich (Grand Rapids, MI: William B. Eerdmans Publishing Company, 1964), p. 513.

[23]1 John 4:5, 6

[24]Positive allusions might be found in John 1:9, 29; 3:16, 17; 4:42; 6:33, 51; 8:12; 12:47); negative ones are in John 12:25, 31; 14:30; 15:18; 16:11, 33.

[25]John Ashton, *Understanding the Fourth Gospel* (Oxford; New York: Oxford University Press, 2007), p. 396

[26]Judith Lieu, *I, II & III John: A Commentary* (Westminster John Knox Press, 2008), p. 66

[27]1 John 2:2

[28]Attributed to D. T. Niles

[29]*https://www.cam.ac.uk/about-the-university/history/early-records*

[30]For example, see Matthew 7:1-5 and Ephesians 4:29.

[31]The role of God the Father as judge is a familiar one. However, it often gets overlooked that Christ also acts as judge. See 2 Corinthians 5:10; John 5:22, 27.

[32]Michelle R. Nario-Redmond, *Ableism: The Causes and Consequences of Disability Prejudice* (Hoboken, NJ: John Wiley & Sons, 2019), p. 57

[33]Sherry Hamby, 'What Is Dehumanisation, Anyway?' *Psychology Today*: *https://www.psychologytoday.com/blog/the-web-violence/201806/what-is-dehumanization-anyway* (accessed 12 October 2018)

[34]Nario-Redmond, *Ableism*, p. 5

[35]Tom Nelson, 'Dehumanisation, Discrimination, and Segregation', *Disability Justice*: *https://disabilityjustice.org/justice-denied/dehumanization-discrimination-and-segregation/* (accessed 3 May 2020)

From worshipper to 'worshopper'

'Can you remember where you were when . . . ?' It is that classic conversation starter that offers up a variety of evocative 'whens': be it when JFK was assassinated or men first landed on the moon, mega musicians performed for Live Aid or the scenes of 9/11 left viewers dumbfounded around the globe. Tragic or uplifting, these moments are memorable because they are shared experiences on a psychological level due to their propensity to affect emotions, thinking, values and attitudes . . . *and* because they impact more than those who are directly involved.

For my grandparents' generation, their list of global life-changing events is inevitably dominated by the two world wars. For millennials to whom I have posed the question, it is terrorist atrocities ranging from 9/11 to the Charlie Hebdo massacre that come most easily to mind. For my own generation, the list includes the gulf wars and the Falklands conflict. Naturally, which situations elicit such a reaction change over time, as memory ebbs, flows and falters as things move forwards from one era to the next. Despite historians' best efforts to immerse us in the meaning and emotion of events, they eventually become somewhat one-dimensional as the subjective aspects fade.

An evocative and unique occasion that still lingers in our collective consciousness occurred on 15 April 1912 when the RMS *Titanic* sank off the coast of Newfoundland. Although romanticised on page and screen since, at the time it hit home because it tragically highlighted several unsafe assumptions in the way ships were starting to be built and operated. Famously, it has ensured that never again should seagoing vessels be allowed to journey without enough lifeboats for *all* crew and passengers. But it is the psychological after-effects at the time that strike a chord; for it served as a stark reminder that, despite the recent growth of and reliance on technology, human beings lived in a world where they were forced to face their own vulnerability.[1]

On a more positive note, the events surrounding the sinking of the *Titanic* added to the legend of British chivalry. It offered up a picture of heroic men as they desperately and valiantly braved the elements to ensure that women and children should come first (WCF). This principle – that women and children should come first – was ingrained into British thinking and was one of the principles that formed part of my education growing up, both formally in the classroom and informally in social settings. It was drummed into us as boys that, to be a proper man, we had to understand how to become a gentleman. At the time, it did not seem to take much to attain to the required level of refined masculinity. We simply had to learn to usher females through open doors and give up seats for the 'fairer' sex. Of course, nowadays, such attitudes are regarded as outdated and chauvinistic. But, in times gone past, it was suggested that a sign of a civilised society and nation is found in its menfolk's willingness to treat females and children well – especially in dire situations.

At no time was this found to be more significantly applied than on that fateful day in April. The numbers and identity of the survivors of the *Titanic* disaster shout out that WCF was heroically applied. Only 19% of the male passengers were saved, but 75% of the women and 54% of the children survived the ordeal. The captain, Edward Smith, as expected and required, went down with his ship: thus conjuring up the evocative picture of a smartly dressed skipper resolutely and stoutly saluting in a final act of defiance as the icy waters fatally rise to engulf him.

But take a more generalised view and the picture is not so rosy. In the period from 1852 to 2002, research shows that women (26.7%) and children (15.3%) had on average the lowest survival rates when compared with male passengers (37.4%) and crew (61%). While many of the captains dutifully went down with their ships, getting towards half (43%) refused to do so. And as for British chivalry? A self-portrait would once have resulted in a nostalgic image of men with immaculate uniforms and stoicism bravely taking the fight to the elements on listing decks. Mostly, this turned out to be a work of fiction. The heroism on display in the sinking of the *Titanic* was no more than an outlier. The concept of women and children first was, alas, nothing but an ideal. The conclusion of the researchers is a rather sorry one for humanity – for, in one damning sentence, they conclude that 'human behaviour in life-and-death situations is best captured by the expression, "Every man for himself." [12]

When the Levite and priest do not stop to help the victim in the parable, is there an element of 'every man for himself' going on here too? Yes, there were the religious and cultural practices that too easily persuaded them to cross the road to the other side. But, as the casualty lay there half-dead and half-naked, he would have presented a graphic reminder of human vulnerability. Rather than the awesome and overwhelming power of nature, it was the forces of evil residing in the hearts of men that threatened. From this point of view, to pass by was as much an act of self-preservation as anything else; for an 'every man for himself' approach means looking after number one when exposed to threats and danger – just as the Levite and the priest were on the Jerusalem-Jericho road that day.

Such an attitude is not confined to nineteenth- and twentieth-century British sailors, or perhaps priests and Levites in parables. Every so often, you hear someone quoting Philippians 2:12 as evidence that, at its root,

Christianity is similarly an 'every man for himself' religion, as Paul commands, 'Work out your *own* salvation with fear and trembling.' It is a phrase that is stark enough to cause a reader to experience a flash of human vulnerability . . . not because technology has let us down, but because the verse appears to stand a person alone, isolated and exposed, just like the victim in the parable. Here there appears to be biblical support for Christianity being all about the individual. When it comes to whether you will walk the streets of gold in the bejewelled New Jerusalem of Revelation 21 – well, that, my friend, is all down to you, and you alone. Only your decision to accept and believe in the death and resurrection of Jesus counts where *you* are concerned. No one can choose for you.

Perhaps Paul just needs his beloved charges in Philippi to aspire to a more mature concept of faith. Could it be similar to that moment growing up when parents no longer bail you out, instead telling you it is 'time to take responsibility for your own actions'? Suddenly, you have metaphorically been cast out to sea in a boat for which you alone are going to have to pay; you alone are going to have to make all the navigating decisions; you alone do all the rowing (should you even own oars); you alone find food, water and shelter from the elements. It's scary, but apparently it is 'all just part of growing up'.

So, when Paul instructs us to 'work out [our] own salvation', it could be assumed to be part of the same narrative. At some stage, we are going to have to take responsibility for our own actions and our own destiny. God is there with us all the time, giving, empowering, persuading and encouraging, but there is a part to play in the process that is ours alone. I am reminded of the time my pastor looked me intently in the eye and asked, with what seemed a rather forced neutrality, 'Do you want to be baptised?' Try as he might, he could barely cover how eager he was for me to say, 'Yes.' Yet, ethically, he could not and must not force the issue. 'It's up to you,' came the qualifying phrase to ensure that this was the case.

And this all seems to make some sense, right? If 'by grace you have been saved through faith', and even if 'this is not your own doing; it is the gift of God', grace and faith are not things someone else can receive or have for us.[3] Many a parent who agonises over the salvation of their children has dreamt of the tantalising possibility that their belief will be enough for errant Jane or Jimmy to 'make it'. But, alas, it does not work like that.[4] Jesus' brother James tells us that faith without works is dead.[5] And, no matter how many acts of service such as feeding the destitute or clothing the naked I perform to enrich my faith, it will not help yours. The bottom line is, we cannot substitute in someone else to believe, have faith or serve for us. We all have to take responsibility for our own actions.

Taken to its extreme, or even its logical conclusion, there are benefits to be had from looking at it this way. Attend a church service and glance at the person sat next to me, and I can breathe that little bit easier knowing that I only have to consider my own salvation and not theirs. And, anyway, worrying about my own stuff is frankly enough of a burden. Taking responsibility for someone else's spiritual health and eternal destiny is too much to contemplate. Interpreting the verse in this way brings with it a sense of relief. Ultimately, when that longed-for moment finally arrives and Jesus returns in the clouds of glory, if they do not make it then it's their decisions and attitudes that have swung it either way – their fault, not mine, in other words. This does not mean I do not look fondly on my companions – care for them, love them, witness to them, desperately want them to make it – but it's every man, woman and child for him or herself at the end of the day.

However, once that sense of relief and release has ebbed away, the consequences of such a view might start to kick in. Look once more at that person sat next to me. I may have no responsibility for their salvation, but they also have nothing to do with mine. In fact, everyone should be looking at each other, shrugging their shoulders in forced indifference. Members may meet up once or twice a week, but if you cannot believe for me, have faith for me, or perform works of service that bring that faith alive for me, then I guess I am on my own. I need to ensure I look after myself through carrying out my obligations and duties. Looking after number one has rocketed to the top of the list. If I have to work out my own salvation, I need to ensure that I am in the best place to do that. My evaluation of the service at the closing hymn would be driven by how it had helped me achieve my personal aims. What if the Bible studies are dull and repetitive, or the music is dreary and lifeless, or the sermons are long, unstructured and uninspiring? If there's any sense that anything fails to live up to the goal of providing for me and my salvation, then I must find a place that does. If the church down the road has a young and vibrant speaker, a semi-professional worship band or a Bible study run by biblical scholars, that's where I'm headed. Loyalty to any given church depends on what it offers me and my salvation.

Over the years, churches have either raged against such a destructive philosophy or, in the spirit of a *fait accompli,* have embraced what, at its root, is a form of consumerism. It is suggested that nowhere was this seen more than in seeker-sensitive churches that have been criticised for catering to the lowest common denominator to be attractive.[6] A more charitable evaluation is that they were responding to the context in which they found themselves – one where potential church attendees behave innately like consumers. So the wisdom of business gurus was used to reach out to the unchurched, de-churched, non-churched or any other church 'consumer' category we care to name. Such consumers were unlikely to find forty-five-minute expository sermons that challenged and pricked consciences palatable, so shorter, story-based talks were delivered. They were paired with flashy, multi-media presentations and music that would not disgrace Glastonbury. Christianity's unique selling points were found in a gospel framed as meeting 'felt needs', so providing for those missing links in one's life. Ultimately, the consumer was king, the local community was the marketplace, and advertising and marketing techniques were the methods of choice. Attendees were attracted, engaged and entertained, but in the worst cases rarely contributed – because consumers, inevitably, naturally just consume, after all.

Ah, it is easy to criticise other churches and their methodology, because then we do not have to look at ourselves. Shouldn't every church community be warm, inviting and accommodating when it comes to guests and visitors? Where possible, should not all church communities provide moments when the deep things of God are communicated on multiple levels, including for the unchurched? Through thoughtfully selected music and carefully crafted messages, doesn't every church need to speak to people in their own context? Without a doubt, programmes should be run that address felt needs and holistically deal with everything from mental health to homelessness.

But what every church community also has in common is that they are all in a fight – a fight to resist encouraging people to be consumers. All churches are in a battle to resist being a community where people turn up to be served, entertained and have their needs met rather than participate. Every church struggles against the inclination we all have to act as individuals, rather than as participants with a role to play in the community. Each church is striving to be a place where worshippers rather than 'worshoppers' are found.[7]

'Worshoppers' act like the ultimate consumers with little brand loyalty, jumping from church to church, browsing for the one that best fits their personal requirements. Taken to its extreme, it ends up being a parody of church where everyone takes, because it is their duty to work out their own salvation. Ultimately, it can lead to people searching for solutions outside their faith community once the church's resources are exhausted.

To interpret Philippians 2:12 in such an individualistic manner does violence to the context that Paul sets it in. Not only does it fail to take into account the values that he proposes, but it also runs counter to the ultimate where-were-you-when moment that he sets before the Philippians and before us who read his letter to this day. We shall return to all of this shortly . . . but first we have to go to the beginning of the passage in which this verse is found to help set the scene.

Something to think about along the way

Some colleagues and I were eating at The World Buffet[8] *– a restaurant where, for a reasonable price, one could sample with abandon around two hundred dishes from approximately fifteen different countries. It was a fascinating opportunity to people watch. It was difficult not to question the culinary choices that led to plates being piled high with noodles, chips and lasagne, garnished with a couple of samosas and breaded mushrooms.*

The complexity and scale of the operation was astounding – truly a marvel of mass catering. But, unsurprisingly, this meant the food was not necessarily of the best quality. There was no limit on how much you could eat, and this too is not always a good thing. No matter if I had a word with myself beforehand to ensure a degree of self-control and self-discipline: the nature of the enterprise meant I always seemed to consume too much. And, in the aftermath, it was not as if I ever particularly enjoyed what I had eaten.

One day, someone commented, 'Wouldn't it be great if church were like this – catering to and for everyone's needs, adapting what is on offer to reach the maximum amount of people?' On the surface, this seemed like an interesting, if unattainable, ideal. It conjured up the picture of a church where there was an unlimited supply of a variety of spiritual dishes to suit everyone's tastes. But it occurred to me there was something not quite right about this idea. And it was not just because I used to leave the restaurant feeling full but dissatisfied.

Then it came to me. Think about the 'normal' process that is undertaken when eating out at a restaurant. It starts with deciding what sort of food you are in the mood for: Indian, Chinese, British, Mexican and so on. Once at the establishment of choice, the menu is presented and scanned, and selections are made. Starter and main course are chosen to begin with, and maybe a dessert to come later. The selection process is vital because there is a certain amount of risk involved. Once you have placed your order, quality issues excepting, that is it: the die is cast. Throughout this process, there is discernment, commitment and uncertainty. But at The World Buffet *these elements are either missing or limited. If I choose to go Indian and then find that I am not in a mood for a curry, I can discard my plate and go and get some pizza. If I fancy inventing my own fusion experience, I can readily combine chips with sushi. If that proves to be disastrous, that's fine: I can move on to the next idea. The bottom line is that it all doesn't matter. My choices have few consequences beyond an overly full stomach. With this in mind, what if there were an equivalent place of worship called the* World Buffet Church? *Would it be the same?*

---

[1] The *Titanic* became 'a potent symbol of technological hubris and human vulnerability' (Jeffrey Sconce, *Haunted Media: Electronic Presence from Telegraphy to Television* [Durham & London: Duke University Press, 2000], p. 73).

[2] Michael Elinder and Oscar Erixon, 'Gender, Social Norms, and Survival in Maritime Disasters', *Proceedings of the National Academy of Sciences of the United States of America*, 109.33 (2012), 13220-24

[3] Ephesians 2:8

[4] There is what is called 'household salvation', where one member of the family's belief leads to all being baptised, as in Acts 10 and 16. However, without denying the strong influence relatives can bring to bear on each other, it still comes down to individual acceptance (Ezekiel 14:12-20). For a more detailed exploration of this subject, see David Matson, *Household Conversion Narratives in Acts: Pattern and Interpretation* (Sheffield: Sheffield Academic Press, 1996).

[5] James 2:14-17

[6] John Drane, *The McDonaldization of the Church: Consumer Culture and the Church's Future* (Macon, GA: Smyth & Helwys Publishing, Incorporated, 2012)

[7] Term borrowed from Martyn Percy, *Engaging with Contemporary Culture: Christianity, Theology and the Concrete Church* (London; New York: Routledge, 2016), p. 53.

[8] Name has been changed.

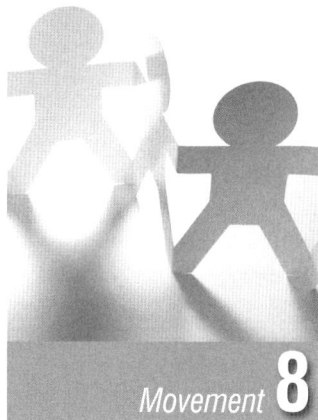

From worthiness to citizenship

The coronation of Queen Elizabeth II was a momentous occasion. The pomp and ceremony, extravagant robes, crowns and coronets just added to scenes immortalised by artists, poets and painters. A cast of thousands was joined by a TV audience comprising seventy-five percent of the UK.[1] Although Elizabeth was technically already monarch with the passing of her father, the coronation broadcast the concept that here was someone special, someone set apart from the man or woman in the street. Just four miles separate the Queen's and my own birthplace, but the distance between us socially, economically and politically is vast. She was born at the home of the Earl of Strathmore in upmarket Mayfair. I arrived in a hospital built originally for the poor of the parish in a North London suburb. She is my Queen, and I am her citizen. The difference in status could not be greater – whether I am a royalist who acknowledges that or not.

In order of importance, it is suggested that Jewish society could be neatly packaged into priests, Levites and Israelites.[2] The priest's importance is seen in an ordination service that lasted not one day, like the coronation, but seven. It comprised six steps involving washing, clothing, anointing, and baking. The most important element was the sacrificing and eating of the 'ram of ordination', because this led to Aaron and his family being recognised as Israel's spiritual leaders.[3] So, even though the whole nation was called to be holy,[4] the priests were holy on another level. They were set apart to offer effective service and 'were the servants and guardians of the covenant relationship' God had established with His people.[5] Levites, too, were singled out for service – in their case through an eight-step process that included purification, the shaving of the body, washing clothes, presentation at the Tent of Meeting, the laying on of hands, and a series of offerings and sacrifices.[6] Both from the same tribe, although with slightly different roles, the priests and the Levites had therefore undergone a process that broadcast they were special in a way not open to those who merely stood and watched them carry out their duties.[7]

Consequently, they are no ordinary men who rush past and ignore the victim on the side of the road. Yes, ordination and consecration conferred status, but they also called for certain behaviours. The holiness laws that dominated their lives were not meant to be just about a lack of ritual

73

impurity, but designated them as 'a force for good in society'.[8] Yet, when the priest and the Levite come across a man in desperate need of help on the Jerusalem-Jericho road, their actions fall short of what is required. For sure, Jesus' audience is stunned that the hero of the story turns out to be a Samaritan, but are they already in a state of shock that the two who serve in the temple turn out to be the villains? The men who were engaged in administering the sacrificial system fare badly when compared to a 'Samaritan who pours out the true offering acceptable to God'.[9]

In Paul's letter to the Philippians, we also have heroes and villains. The latter we shall return to . . . and the heroes? They too have expectations laid upon them, for they are described as those who are called to 'live . . . in a manner worthy of the gospel of Christ'.[10] The need to live a worthy life is one of Paul's favourite themes.[11] But what does he mean by this?

On a spectrum of worthiness, at one end is the divine worthiness found in the Father's creating and sustaining and the Son's sacrifice and victory upon the cross.[12] Now, it is clearly ridiculous to claim to be worthy in the way They are. In terms of status, They are unique. It is not that the Father and Son have been set apart by any ceremony, as They have always been worthy of worship because of who They are. But at the opposite extreme is a type of worthiness that is something else altogether.

When I worked in the food industry, I would often get to taste-test food. This sounds great. A foodophile looking in from the outside might think sampling food and getting paid to eat for a living is a dream come true. But munching on the thirtieth version of the same product was as far from fine dining as you could get. On the healthy foods side of the industry, the worst products to eat were those that were better for you than they tasted. More often than not, they were coloured brown – an unpalatably dark brown highlighted with flecks of grey. They were stodgy, grainy and dense. They consistently seemed to have the ability to rapaciously remove moisture from your mouth and throat. They were saleable only to that portion of the market with a puritanical streak running through their veins. Rather than for pleasure, they were especially suitable for those who want to eat healthily and *experience* the food's healthiness as they endure, endlessly chew, and eventually, hopefully, swallow. There was something about their make-up and structure that meant such products were unanimously and solemnly pronounced 'worthy'.

So, whenever I read Paul's instruction to the Philippians to live 'in a manner worthy of the gospel of Christ', I think of those experiences, and certainly not the unattainable divine worthiness on display in the heavenly throne room. A worthy Christian, in this sense, sounds as winsome as a worthy food product – unattractive and hard to be around. As Billy Sunday, tongue firmly in his cheek, suggests, for some Christians, 'If they smile it looks like it hurts them, and you're always glad when they stop smiling. If Paul and Silas had had such long faces as some church members have on them, when they went into the Philippian jail, the jailer would never have been saved.'[13]

To unpack this, we need to note a couple of things Paul is not doing. Firstly, 'worthy' is not being used to denote a cheerless and pietistic manner. Indeed, Paul feels able to celebrate the Philippians' 'joy in faith' and wants them to 'complete' his joy.[14] And, in thinking of Paul's own disposition when in Philippi itself, he was wonderfully positive, despite suffering time in jail.[15] Secondly, Paul is not suggesting that to be worthy of the Gospel of Christ is to attain to a certain level of inner holiness or righteousness. 'Worthy' is being used as an adverb and not as an adjective here. It is not describing the way the Philippians are to be in and of themselves, but the manner in which they are to behave. It is, therefore, an 'outside' challenge to do with worthy actions, not an 'inside' challenge that sees value in a certain level of personal goodness, purity or sinlessness.

What, then, is worthy behaviour – behaviour worthy of the Gospel of Christ? There are those who believe this involves good time-keeping (turning up to services on time). Some stock responses might include 'prayer', 'reading your Bible', and 'being good to others'. The list might be expanded to include fasting, serving, tithing, practising good stewardship, eating and drinking right, dressing appropriately, using spiritual gifts, embodying the fruit of the Spirit, being a disciple and more. However, even though many of these things are commendable and related to what Paul has in mind, they are not the specific behaviours for which he is looking. Rather than leaving us to speculate, he elaborates as follows: '. . . whether I come and see you or am absent and hear about you, I will know that you are standing firm in one spirit, striving side by side with one mind for the faith of the gospel, and are in no way intimidated by your opponents.'[16]

Much of what is thought of as 'worthy' Christian behaviour has me focusing on myself. But, surprise, surprise, Paul is more concerned with how the Philippians behave collectively . . . for the standing and striving of which Paul writes cannot be accomplished by furrowing a lone path. And Paul is consistent with this understanding of worthiness. Paul asks the Romans, as a group, to welcome Phoebe in a worthy manner.[17] In the letter to the Ephesians, Paul encourages that community to 'lead a life worthy of [their] calling' by 'bearing with one another in love, making every effort to maintain the unity of the Spirit in the bond of peace'.[18] Hence, worthiness is found in how people interact and work with fellow believers. Instead of *'I need to . . .'* Paul is looking for a *'we need to . . .'* approach, as in: '**We need to** *stand firm in one spirit.* **We need to** *strive side by side with one mind for the faith of the Gospel. And so,* **we are** *in no way intimidated by* **our** *opponents.'*

In the Philippians' case, such behaviour is not just life-affirming: it is life-saving. Togetherness counts. Go it alone, and they will be lost. Musk oxen know this instinctively. Despite their name, musk oxen are the largest goats in the world. Although only one and a half metres tall, they weigh in at a hefty quarter of a tonne. Their main defensive strength is found in the ten-centimetre-wide horns that sit atop their eight-centimetre-thick skulls. Their first instinct upon sensing danger is to run to higher ground before turning to stand shoulder to shoulder to form a defensive circle around the calves and females. Only a foolhardy wolf or bear would dare try to breach such a formidable barricade.[19]

Likewise, in Philippians 1:27, 28, it is the church of 'Onward, Christian Soldiers' that comes into view. Paul is using military language to describe the strategy needed to face off against wily opponents. The Philippians are to stand firm, a posture reminiscent of a phalanx of soldiers 'locking shields, standing their ground together, not breaking ranks in the face of external opposition, attack, persecution or pressure'.[20] They are to be seen 'striving together side by side' – 'striving', as in 'to engage in competition or conflict', provoking images of teams of athletes in a tournament, or, again, of a close formation of soldiers in battle.[21] Unlike the stance of the musk oxen, this is not just a defensive move. These Christians standing as a group side by side are not to act as a barrier to keep others from the Gospel, but are together 'for the faith of the gospel'. Positively, 'The team effort supplied by the church would present the Gospel to the world' despite, or in the face of, opposition.[22]

So much for the heroes in the story; but what of the villains? Figuring out who the Philippians' opponents are is one of the great scholarly debates.[23] However, the key thing is that their influence will falter if the Philippians stand together and 'are in no way intimidated by' them.[24] One outcome, however, is unanticipated: for, in taking this approach, it provides 'evidence of their destruction, but of your salvation'.[25] This is not the clearest thing Paul has written, and a more literal translation highlights how ambiguous it is: 'This is to them a sign of destruction, but of your salvation.'[26] It follows that the salvation being spoken of is the Philippians' . . . but it is not so clear whose destruction it is.

It could be the church's destruction, or apparent demise, in the face of overwhelming persecution. Even though they are suffering and consequently seem on the brink of being destroyed, it is paradoxically at the same time a sign of their salvation and victory. This is much in the same way as Jesus' death and victory on the cross appeared to be a defeat to His adversaries.[27] The more obvious option is that it is their opponents' destruction. But what does it look like, and when does it happen – now, or in the future, at the conclusion of time as we know it?[28]

A reality for Christians is that we live in the tension between the 'already' and the 'not yet' – between the partial and complete fulfilment of God's purposes.[29] For example, the Philippians are already experiencing unity in Christ, but are not yet living out the unity in all its richness, which is yet to come. Even so, their experience now anticipates the unity to come. Therefore, the Philippians are an 'in-between people' living out lives of cosmic and future significance in the present.[30]

This same mix of present reality and future promise is seen when comparing Philippians 1:27, 28 with Philippians 2:12, 13 (see Table 3). Each pair of verses addresses similar concerns, allowing them to have a 'conversation' that leads to each illuminating the other.

Table 3

Only, live your life in a manner worthy of the gospel of Christ, so that, **whether I come and see you or am absent and hear about you**, I will know that you are standing firm in one spirit, striving side by side with one mind for the faith of the gospel, and are in no way intimidated by your opponents. For them this is evidence of their destruction, but **of your salvation**. *And this is God's doing*. **Philippians 1:27, 28**	Therefore, my beloved, just as you have always obeyed me, **not only in my presence, but much more now in my absence,** work out **your own salvation** with fear and trembling; *for it is God who is at work in you,* enabling you both to will and to work for his good pleasure. **Philippians 2:12, 13**

There are three things to look at here. Firstly, as highlighted in bold, their worthy behaviour is not to depend on Paul. It should not be that while the cat is away, the mice will play. Rather, it is God's presence through the Spirit that is key. Secondly, Paul makes sure we understand that our salvation is because of what God does, and not because of what we do (see italicised text). Finally, if we allow the context of the later passage to be informed and enlightened by the first, it suggests that working out our own salvation is not about individuals setting off on solitary spiritual journeys in the hope of being saved. Rather, it is about saved people working in and behaving as a community. It is about standing shoulder to shoulder with other Christians, unified with one purpose and 'one spirit'.[31] This *'we need to . . .'* approach is a future orientation that has present-day significance. In other words, we can already start to adopt and benefit from the attitudes of those who will gather in the New Jerusalem of Revelation 21.

There is yet more to consider here, because Paul draws the Philippians into something bigger, deeper and life-orientating. Paul's customary term for everyday Christian living is the Greek word for 'to walk'.[32] For example, later on in the letter Paul encourages the Philippians to 'join in imitating me, and observe those who *live* [walk] according to the example you have in us' (Philippians 3:17).[33] However, here in Philippians 1:27, he uses the Greek word for 'citizenship'.[34] Hence, the New Living Translation renders verse 27 as: 'You must live as *citizens* of heaven.'[35] Paul is thought to be doing two things here. Firstly, he butters up his audience, because the residents of Philippi were very proud when they were made a Roman colony by Caesar Augustus.[36] As Paul too was a Roman citizen, he would no doubt have appreciated how the accompanying privileges and prestige enhanced a person's self-esteem.[37] Gaining Roman citizenship set one up as a cut above the rest. Paul's use of 'citizen' and its associated high status meant that he was already starting to push the Philippians' buttons.

The second thing he was doing was redefining citizenship in the context of a Christian community. The citizenship that Paul wants the Philippians to live out has nothing to do with responsibly subjecting themselves to the governing authorities, even though he supports this approach elsewhere.[38] Neither is he looking for people who salute their nation's flag and know every word to all the verses of their national anthem. He has something else in mind – something bigger in scope and of eternal significance. This is in view when, later in the letter, Paul describes how *'our citizenship* is in heaven, and it is from there that we are expecting a Saviour, the Lord Jesus Christ.'[39] The opponents make another appearance here too, and are described as those who are 'enemies of the cross of Christ'.[40] Their impending ruin, first revealed in Philippians 1:28, also gets another mention as Paul declares, 'Their end is destruction; their god is the belly; and their glory is in their shame; their minds are set on earthly things.'[41] By contrast, the citizens of heaven will be transformed and be 'conformed to the body of his [Christ's] glory' at the Second Coming.[42]

To see this as confirmation that everything for a Christian is about a future reality is to miss the impact of what Paul is affirming. He wants the Philippians to catch hold of this Christ-centred vision that speaks to a glory-filled future because of what it can do for them as they face their opponents in the present. Be a citizen of this future reality today, he is telling them. Live life as a citizen of the Kingdom of Heaven right now in this city named after the father of Alexander the Great. Be a part of an alternative community whose membership is more life-defining than it is even to be a Roman citizen.

When Paul put quill to papyrus to write to the Philippians, it was around the time that Nero ruled the roost.[43] Therefore, the Praetorian Guard mentioned in Philippians 1:13 and 'those of the emperor's household' who send greetings in 4:22 are all likely in the employ of one of the most notorious Roman leaders in history. Nero was reigning just forty years after Augustus had established the emperor as 'a conqueror, a legislator, a builder and a priest'.[44] The power was absolute, even though Augustus was wise enough to wield this power subtly.[45] When Queen Elizabeth II ascended to the throne in 1952, the British Empire was in the middle of being dismantled, having reached its peak under her grandfather George V. Her mix of religious and military titles – for example, 'Defender of the Faith' and 'Commander-in-Chief of the British Armed Forces' – are but echoes of the power wielded by her predecessors. Hers is a constitutional monarchy, and certainly cannot be compared to the position of authority in which Nero revelled. But, despite the requirement to be non-political and having no executive role, she is more than a person. She 'acts as a focus for national identity, unity and pride [and] gives a sense of stability and continuity'.[46] She is the figurehead of an institution, the head of state and the primary public representative of the countries over which she reigns. She is a reminder that for me to be a British citizen is to be part of something bigger than myself – something with a history, a present and a future.

And, here in this letter, Paul is saying to the Philippians that all of this goes for you too. You might be struggling against persecution and opponents, but this is worthwhile because you belong to a movement founded and grounded on King Jesus. When caught up in the minutiae of life and the daily grind, it helps to know that it all has significance because we are part of a bigger story. We can be encouraged that there is value and worth in what we do, because we belong to a kingdom over which Christ reigns. Rather than being lost and hopeless, and powerlessly caught in the ebb and flow of history, we are a part of something that matters.

This sounds great: but, generally, this is not something that sits well with people in a Western context. Let me illustrate this by further exploring my own identity. Not only am I British, but I am also English. This identity rarely rears its head, and does so mostly when England competes with other nations on the sports field. What being English means is difficult to pin down, and has often been assumed more than articulated.[47] It is an identity that is tied up in colonialism and fighting world wars. But, as time moves on, these aspects of history that once acted as anchors seem more and more irrelevant. As Jeremy Paxman wrote of the English in 1999, 'The new generation are refining their own identity, an identity based not on the past, but on their needs. . . . the most vital sense of national identity is the individual awareness of the country of the mind.'[48] This shift in emphasis from a big story to a personal one is one of the major movements that began to take root in the latter half of the twentieth century. The big stories with their solutions that once seemed so compelling had proved to be pipe dreams at best, or works of fiction and ways to manipulate power at worst. The expectation that science could lead to a 'better world for all human beings' or that Marxism could deliver a 'utopia of international socialism' had long been undermined.[49] Now, the understanding is that there are no legitimate secular metanarratives or explanations of the world that can be universally applied. We are left with personal stories in which to ground our identity and being. My story is as good as your story or any other story.

So, in the context in which we are living, what Paul is proposing is not just countercultural, but hyper-countercultural. The Philippians, with their strong sense of community identity, had to be persuaded to join another community with another identity. By contrast, we have to be persuaded to take part in and have our identity associated with a community at all.[50] They had no concept of separating everyday living from their religion. Now, public expressions of faith in the workplace are frowned upon.[51] Then, the home was the place where church was most visible.[52] To peek behind the curtains presently is to see mostly a privatised version of Christianity – one that makes it seem as if church is barely, if at all, necessary.[53]

We may wring our hands as we watch Christianity's public face become about reducing numbers and increasing insignificance, but are we partly responsible? Is this because we have not communicated how big and significant the Christian story is? Do we make it too much about individual salvation and what it will take to get over the line? Have we allowed it to shrink and shrivel, to 'collapse' the Bible's huge narrative into 'my story' and miss out on the significance of 'our story?'[54] Have we made it so much about the future that in the present it is diminished and limited? 'When we all get to heaven, what a day of rejoicing that will be,' is understandably sung with feeling. Given all the suffering that goes on 'down here', no wonder there is a desire to 'sing and shout the victory' because we have seen Jesus.[55] Yet all the time we are turning present-day Christianity into a waiting-room experience. Taking the idea to its extreme, churches simply become places where individual saints gather to grit their teeth as they make their way through life's difficult circumstances until Jesus comes in the clouds of glory.

However, does a bigger story matter if no one is going to buy into it given the current antipathy towards them? In taking the Bible seriously, Christians have no choice but to live within its big story and embrace its metanarrative.[56] But it is more than something with which we are stuck. Big stories matter because they bring hope, and we need hope to survive. They matter to modern generations even as they paradoxically reject them. They matter because they look around to see a world lacking in spirituality, community and promise. Therefore, millennials understand that there is no choice but to embrace a big story – because without one there is no hope.[57] In the end, an individual's story is important, but is not enough: 'Authentic happiness requires a meta-narrative, a full story which offers long-term hope, not a midi one focused on the immediate.'[58]

This means that part of the challenge is to tell the right story using the right language – 'we' language. The other part is to live it out – to be in-between people awaiting the return of Christ who are proactive, not passive: standing firm, side by side, shoulder to shoulder, living out the benefits of the future in the present. This is a people exhibiting behaviour that can be called worthy because it is collective behaviour based on unity, spirit and purpose – a people who are citizens of the kingdom over which King Jesus already reigns.

Something to think about along the way

The United Nations Children's Fund suggests the following ways to defeat racism:

- *Listen to and amplify black voices.*
- *Call out bigotry and hate speech.*
- *Teach kindness, fairness and human rights.*
- *Stand up for people being harassed – intervene if it is safe to do so.*
- *Support human rights organisations.[59]*

Thinking about this list in the context of Paul's urging the Philippians to stand shoulder to shoulder, striving together side by side, is racism a worthy opponent against which Christians should contend?[60] If so, how do we make a stand in the spirit of what Paul intended?

To stand with people who look, think and act like me is easy. Social media offers a quick and clean platform for making statements and sharing anti-racism posts that make me think I have done 'my bit'. Making a donation to Amnesty International can be done at the click of a keyboard. While not denying the benefits of these actions, they do not sound too much like they involve striving. To strive is 'to labour alongside of, to toil with'.[61] To strive takes effort, sweat and tears. It means standing shoulder to shoulder with people who do not look, think or act like me. To strive is to risk calling out casual racism among close friends and family. To strive means taking time out to listen to others' stories. To strive is to practise kindness, fairness and human rights when others cannot or will not. To strive with others may be a moment of strength, but it is probably not a moment of comfort.

Even as I might struggle with this, and even as there are those who think, 'This is not my fight,' I am moved by Isaiah 58:6 where the prophet writes, 'Is not this the fast that I [the Lord] choose: to loose the bonds of injustice, to undo the thongs of the yoke, to let the oppressed go free, and to break every yoke?'

[1]There were 8,251 guests, and 30,000 members of the armed forces and police taking part in the procession (Rose Slavin, '50 Facts about the Queen's Coronation', *The Royal Family*, 2017): *https://www.royal.uk/50-facts-about-queens-coronation-0* (accessed 10 May 2020).

[2]Although there were other groups, such as the Essenes, Pharisees, Sadducees and Zealots, 'priest, Levite and Israelite' were the 'main divisions of respectable society' according to the Mishnah – see Bernard Brandon Scott, *Hear Then the Parable: A Commentary on the Parables of Jesus* (Minneapolis, MA: Fortress Press, 1989), p. 198.

[3]Exodus 29:1-37

[4]Leviticus 19:2

[5]Walter A. Elwell and Barry J. Beitzel, 'Priests and Levites', *Baker Encyclopedia of the Bible* (Grand Rapids, MI: Baker Book House, 1988), p. 1755; Hannah K. Harrington, *The Purity and Sanctuary of the Body in Second Temple Judaism* (Göttingen: Vandenhoeck & Ruprecht, 2019), p. 21

[6]Numbers 8:5-13 - note that God explicitly commanded that they be set apart (see Numbers 8:14).

[7]Although there was much overlap in practice, the Levites were to 'assist their brothers [the priests] in the tent of meeting in carrying out their duties, but [were to] perform no service' (Numbers 8:26). For more on their different roles, see R. Dennis Cole, *Numbers: The New American Commentary* (Nashville, TN: Broadman & Holman Publishers, 2000), pp. 147-48.

[8]Harrington, *The Purity*, p. 22

[9]Syliva C. Keesmat, 'Strange Neighbours and Risky Care', in: *The Challenge of Jesus' Parables*, edited by Richard N. Longenecker (William B. Eerdmans Publishing, 2000), p. 281

[10]Philippians 1:27

[11]Romans 16:2; Ephesians 4:1; Colossians 1:10

[12]Revelation 4:11; 5:12

[13]William Ellis, *Billy Sunday: The Man and His Message* (Moody Publishers, 2013)

[14]Philippians 1:25; Philippians 2:2

[15]Acts 16

[16]Philippians 1:27, 28

[17]The New Revised Standard Version uses 'fitting' rather than 'worthy' in Romans 16:2. However, it is the same word in the Greek.

[18]Ephesians 4:1-3

[19]'Species Spotlight: Musk Ox', Alaska Wildlife Alliance: *https://www.akwildlife.org/news/specie-spotlight-musk-ox* (accessed 11 May 2020)

[20]Ben Witherington, *Paul's Letter to the Philippians: A Socio-Rhetorical Commentary* (Grand Rapids, MI/Cambridge, UK: William B. Eerdmans Publishing, 2011), p. 102

[21]For differing views, see Kittel and Friedrich, *Dictionary*, p. 167; Richard R. Melick, *Philippians, Colossians, Philemon: The New American Commentary* (Nashville, TN: Broadman & Holman Publishers, 1991), pp. 89, 90; Witherington, *Paul's Letter to the Philippians*, p. 102.

[22]Melick, *Philippians*, p. 90

[23]The suggestions as to whom the opponents might be include a group with a perfectionist tendency or faulty eschatology, or Gentile agitators, or teachers with questionable morals. For an overview, see Martin,

Philippians, pp. 43, 44; Moisés Silva, *Philippians* (Grand Rapids, MI: Baker Academic, 2005), pp. 9, 10.
[24]Philippians 1:28a
[25]Philippians 1:28b
[26]G. Walter Hansen, *The Letter to the Philippians* (Grand Rapids, MI/Cambridge, UK: William B. Eerdmans Publishing, 2009), p. 99
[27]Stephen E. Fowl, *Philippians* (Grand Rapids, MI: William B. Eerdmans Publishing, 2005), p. 67f.
[28]For the Jews, the 'Day of the Lord' was the locus of such events. See, for example, Isaiah 24:21, 22; Zephaniah 1:14-18; and Jeremiah 46:10.
[29]The most quoted example is the way that the kingdom is simultaneously both here (Matthew 12:28; Luke 11:20) and still to come (Luke 19:11, 12).
[30]I have taken a phrase first coined by Bosch and reassigned it. His original intent was that it referred to church communities who are part of and yet different from the wider community. See David Jacobus Bosch, *The Church As the Alternative Community* (Potchefstroom, South Africa: Instituut vir Reformatoriese Studie, 1982), p. 28.
[31]Philippians 1:27
[32]Περιπατέω or *peripateo*
[33]The New King James Version's more literal translation is, 'Join in following my example, and note those who so *walk*.'
[34]Πολιτεύομαι or *politeuomai*
[35]See also the International Standard Version for another example.
[36]Fee, Gordon D., *Philippians*, vol. 11 (Downers Grove, IL: InterVarsity Press, 1999), p. 77
[37]The benefits for Paul are seen during his adventures in Acts 16:37-39; 22:25-29; 25:7-12. For further explanation of rights and privileges, see Gerald F. Hawthorne, Ralph P. Martin, and Daniel G. Reid, *Dictionary of Paul and His Letters: A Compendium of Contemporary Biblical Scholarship* (Downers Grove, IL: InterVarsity Press, 1993), pp. 139-41.
[38]See for example Romans 13:1-4.
[39]Philippians 3:20
[40]Philippians 3:18
[41]Philippians 3:19
[42]Philippians 3:21
[43]Tradition has it that Philippians was written from Rome in AD 60 to 62. Nero reigned from AD 54 to 68. See Melick, *Philippians*, p. 40.
[44]Barry Strauss, *Ten Caesars: Roman Emperors from Augustus to Constantine* (New York: Simon and Schuster, 2020), pp. 44, 45
[45]Thus he 'hid it behind existing offices, misleading titles, invocations of the republic, charismatic authority, and a degree of deference to the Senate' (Strauss, *Roman Emperors*, p. 45).
[46]Kirsty Oram, 'The Role of the Monarchy', *The Royal Family*, 2016: *https://www.royal.uk/role-monarchy* (accessed 17 May 2020)
[47]Studies into English identity did not really start until the late 1990s. Partly, this is because Englishness has been seen as being the same as Britishness. See Professor Krishan Kumar, *The Idea of Englishness: English Culture, National Identity and Social Thought* (Farnham, Surrey: Ashgate Publishing, Ltd., 2015), pp. 1, 203, 204.
[48]Jeremy Paxman, *The English: A Portrait of a People* (London: Penguin Books, 1999)
[49]Stanley James Grenz, *A Primer on Postmodernism* (Grand Rapids, MI: William B. Eerdmans Publishing, 1996), p. 44
[50]For further discussion on this, see Philip F. Esler, *The First Christians in Their Social Worlds: Social-Scientific Approaches to New Testament Interpretation* (London; New York: Routledge, 2002), p. 29f.
[51]For example, those in the medical profession in the UK are prohibited from expressing their faith to their patients.
[52]Acts 2:2; Romans 16:5; 1 Corinthians 16:19; Colossians 4:15; Philemon 2
[53]See for example Kelly Bean, *How to Be a Christian Without Going to Church: The Unofficial Guide to Alternative Forms of Christian Community* (Grand Rapids, MI: Baker Books, 2014).
[54]N. T. Wright, *Paul and the Faithfulness of God: Two-Book Set* (Minneapolis, MN: Fortress Press, 2013), p. 165
[55]Lyrics taken from 'When We All Get to Heaven', words by Eliza E. Hewitt, music by Emily D. Wilson.
[56]Unless we 'reduce our beliefs about the creative and redemptive activity of God to a set of metaphors about something else, something purely immanent or existential'. See Nicholas M. Healy, *Church, World and the Christian Life: Practical-Prophetic Ecclesiology* (Cambridge, UK: Cambridge University Press, 2000), p. 145.
[57]'Metanarratives can't be trusted, but without a metanarrative, there is no hope.' See Tom DeBruin, 'That's So Meta: The Post-Postmodern Church', *Adventist Today*, 23.3 (2015), 8-13 (p. 11).
[58]Sylvia Collins-Mayo and others, *Making Sense of Generation Y: The World View of 15-to-25-Year-Olds* (London: Church House Publishing, 2011), p. 170
[59]'5 Ways to Stand Up Against Racism and Injustice', UNICEF USA: *https://www.unicefusa.org/stories/5-ways-stand-against-racism-and-injustice/37355* (accessed 15 June 2020)
[60]Philippians 1:27, 28
[61]Louw and Nida, *Greek-English Lexicon*, p. 514

Kayleigh was scrolling through Facebook one day when she saw that one of her friends had shared a post about twenty-nine-year-old Louise, who was in desperate need of a new kidney. She had never met or spoken to Louise, but, from the information given, she recognised that she had the same blood type and so might be able to donate one of her kidneys. That Kayleigh was willing to do this for a complete stranger had Louise baffled. 'She just kept asking me: "Why? You don't even know me." And, honestly, I don't know why. If someone you loved needed a kidney and someone else could help them then you'd want them to, wouldn't you? From the moment I saw that post I wanted to do it.' As a consequence, Kayleigh was instrumental in saving Louise's life.[1]

What is it within some of us that compels us to respond positively to another's need, even if we do not know them? What does it take to undergo major surgery on another's behalf or to hang around in dangerous and bandit-filled countryside to the north-west of Jerusalem and give aid to a stranger? What was the difference between the Samaritan who helped and those who shuffled past with their heads down?

Look deep within a person, and we will find that what influences our actions the most are our core values. They are there even if we are not aware of them and cannot begin to put a name to them. They act as filters that help us prioritise our actions and determine whether, in broad terms, we think independence or community, privacy or openness, rules or relationships matter most.[2] So, even as the Samaritan spots the man on the side of the road, his values system is working overtime impacting his assessment of the situation and the courses of action he sees open to him. The same is as true for groups as it is for individuals. Where there is a shared group identity, there will also be shared values arising out of that identity.[3] And, because this includes church communities, it explains why Paul is concerned about the values the Philippians embody.

Now he transitions from writing about the church of *Onward Christian Soldiers*, who stand shoulder to shoulder, to the church of good Samaritans. The foundation remains the same – the unity mentioned in Philippians 1:27 – but now he comes at it from a different angle, composing and combining four phrases that can productively be organised into two pairs:

'Be of the same mind,'
'having the same love,'
'being in full accord'
'and of one mind.'[4]

The outer 'pair' appeals for the same thinking, while the inner 'pair' speaks to a community whose internal life is unified and grounded in *agape* love. Oh, and when Paul asks for the group to be of the same mind, that is the 'same mind . . . that was in Christ'.[5] This is a tantalising possibility. Any meeting that I have to chair as a pastor would last minutes and never hours. There would be no discussion. One person's suggestion would resonate with everyone else, and so all decisions would be harmonious and all votes unanimous. There would be no heated debates or 'intense' moments in our fellowship – it sounds wonderful. But we live in the real world, where unity thrives in diversity, not a robotic one which is based on everything and everyone being the same. Paul's conception is based on patterns, not prescriptions – he is not pushing for bland uniformity here, because there is a richer experience for which to aim. It is based not on individual thoughts, but on the community's collective dispositions or inner attitudes.[6] They are to sing from the same song sheet, many diverse voices seamlessly blending to produce a symphonic masterpiece whose melody has been premiered in the life of Christ. The things that make music live are the key, tempo and time signature, the elements that dictate how the notes flow from page to ear. The values Paul now lays out for them perform the same function. They are values to be found at the very core of a Christian community that thinks with the same mind as Jesus. Paul expresses them both negatively and positively as follows:

'Do nothing from selfish ambition or conceit, but in humility regard others as better than yourselves.'

'Let each of you look not to your own interests, but to the interests of others.'[7]

At first glance, they might be regarded as rather extreme, even as a recipe for disaster. What about self-esteem and self-worth? What about the balance between looking after yourself as well as others? Is Paul really suggesting that my needs are to be subsumed and absorbed into the collective? Am I to become a mere instrument of others and their demands? Won't I end up bogged down in a quagmire of self-doubt that results in an all-consuming inferiority complex?

Particularly where the second set of values is concerned, there is a suspicion that some scribes may have seen fit to soften the force of Paul's instruction. We can see this in those versions that have something along the lines of: 'Let each of you look *not only* to his own interests, *but also* to the interests of others.'[8] That sounds more reasonable and manageable for sure. It is a bit like the safety instructions that are given just before take-off on an aeroplane when we are told to put our safety masks on first, before helping others. The difference arises because of one Greek word missing in a number of manuscripts, and just that one word goes some way towards easing the burden Paul is placing on the Philippian community.[9]

When considering which translation to favour, it seems the thrust of Paul's argument remains the same, in that our focus and efforts should at least include, if not necessarily fully prioritise, others' concerns. But a softer reading fails to do justice to the example of Christ that Paul sets before us in verses 6 to 11. Christ is at the centre of this endeavour, and that is where Paul instinctively places Him. Any notion that we are to set off on our own path working out our individual salvation is overwhelmed and washed away like a sandcastle at high tide by what comes next. He does this by presenting an amazing and profound where-were-you-when moment. This event is one that is more widespread in its effect than any other we care to mention, and it goes deeper beneath the surface than the iceberg that sank the *Titanic*. He brings to the table a moment and a Person in history that affected and affects much more than those in the immediate vicinity, and does so on multiple levels: at the very least psychologically, spiritually and cognitively. It is a moment that speaks to the vulnerability of a human being, but, in this case, it is a vulnerability that comes with facing off against a rising tide of evil. But, paradoxically, we discover that vulnerability and apparent weakness are how God overcomes all that is bad in our world.

This moment is presented to us in the form of what some call a hymn and others a poem.[10] One of the most theologically significant passages in the whole of Scripture, it comprises just seventy-six words in the original language. It charts the descent and rise of Christ, and at the same time offers a glimpse of some of the deeper things of God and His ways. It comes not just at the centre of this section, but is the centrepiece of Paul's letter to the Philippians as a whole.[11]

As we follow the Son's descent into slavery, we unexpectedly, in fallen, human terms, find ourselves looking up at an example of humility and self-giving that is simply breath-taking. 'Let the same mind be in you that was in Christ Jesus,' is Paul's introduction and command: one that purposefully provides both a setting and objective for why the hymn is being utilised.[12] This might well trip easily off the tongue because we are so used to thinking of Jesus as our example. *'Be like Jesus, this my song, in the home and in the throng; be like Jesus, all day long! I would be like Jesus,'* we sing, almost with abandon.[13] Biblical support for any given position makes us comfortable as Christians, and here it does feel as though we are on safe ground because of the many verses throughout the New Testament that hold Jesus up as the pattern for Christian behaviour.[14] The WWJD movement founded in the 1990s took this idea forwards and at the same time to an extreme. It worked on the premise that at any given moment we should ask, *What Would Jesus Do?* Famously, there were, and indeed still are, wrist bands to act as a constant reminder to ask this searching question. However, the movement floundered because the practicalities of this were difficult to follow through on. If we find ourselves aboard a boat, should we refuse the offer of a life-vest because, if called upon, we could simply walk our way to safety across the oceans just as Jesus did on Lake Gennesaret? At those times when we are caught short on the catering front, would blessing a few loaves and fishes and distributing them in baskets be the way forward? Would it be appropriate to wield a whip and show anger in the face of injustice and disrespect for God's purposes, as Jesus did in the temple? What about those situations that Jesus did not encounter? Which would Jesus choose: an Android or a Mac; the conservative, liberal or socialist candidate? Would He advocate for a market-based or a planned economy?

Of course, it is good to set ourselves goals, and they by necessity need to be both attainable and stretching. Goals that make no demands of us lead to apathy and boredom. Mediocre goals infamously result in mediocre results, so experts suggest that to achieve outstanding results we should set ourselves courageous goals.[15] But the goal to have the same mind as in Christ that Paul sets before his group over there in Macedonia is most definitely not a mediocre one. To suggest that this is the objective for Christians feels like it is way beyond courageous . . . especially if we take a look at what comes next:

'Let the same mind be in you that was in Christ Jesus, who, though he was in the form of God, did not regard equality with God as something to be exploited, but emptied himself, taking the form of a slave, being born in human likeness. And being found in human form, he humbled himself and became obedient to the point of death – even death on a cross. Therefore God also highly exalted him and gave him the name that is above every name, so that at the name of Jesus every knee should bend, in heaven and on earth and under the earth, and every tongue should confess that Jesus Christ is Lord, to the glory of God the Father.'[16]

Paul lays out before us the story of God as told through the life of Christ. He sets before us Someone who did not take advantage by grasping at or holding on to the benefits of Divinity (verse 6). Our example, Paul writes, is the Person who left the glories and comfort of Heaven, giving up more than we can possibly imagine. He did this not to become the expected king or emperor, but a slave, forever changed by becoming human (verse 7). We should be left in no doubt that it will take an eternity to begin to understand what led the Son to walk among us as a first-century Palestinian Jew. The sacrifices made, even before the events of Good Friday, are astonishing. But a life characterised by humility and obedience is what leads to the ultimate sacrifice at Calvary (verse 8). It is no wonder that everyone will confess that He is Lord (verse 11).

Therefore, the subject of this magnificent hymn is not someone who holds back. Christ gives everything in and for the interests of others, to the point of death on the cross. This is what makes this passage so daunting, and why on balance the stronger reading of verse 3, found in the New Revised Standard Version and elsewhere, better makes Paul's point. There is no sense of comfort. There is no reasonableness. It is 'all in'. It is about regarding others as better than ourselves and putting others' interests first, just like Jesus.

But isn't this ridiculous? It's a bit like nervously attending a first singing lesson and finding you are stood next to Andrea Bocelli or Beyoncé, or whoever your most admired singer is, and the first instruction is: 'Sing like her,' or: 'Perform like him.' Imagine standing there as Bocelli's metallic tones, underpinned by exemplary breath control and the ability to use every bone and fibre of his being to reinforce the resonant quality of his voice, fill the space in an awesome display of vocal power. Or think about listening to Beyoncé from a few short feet away as she effortlessly performs vocal acrobatics, blending trills, runs and melisma, smoothly transitioning from one vocal register to another. For most, it would just be embarrassing to attempt to follow them with our comparatively feeble squeaks and warbles. These comparisons are daunting enough, but they do not do justice to the example Paul is putting before us here: for Christ gave up more than we can even contemplate giving up. His sacrifice was and is beyond measure. In an attempt at understanding Paul's intention, it is suggested he is using hyperbole to get his charges to aim for Mars in the hope that they land on the moon;[17] but even that analogy does not bring us close. Rather, Paul seems to be asking humanity to reach for the stars, when by contrast we can barely get off the ground. But maybe that is the point after all – if Christ can do that much, then the little being asked of us pales by comparison.

Think about those times when we might struggle to give up our favourite seat for someone who turns up late for a service. Or how about vacating the church car park to make sure that visitors always have somewhere to put their vehicles? What about giving up music that suits our taste, our prescribed way of 'doing church', having our say, asserting our rights and pushing our personal agendas, all with the express purpose of meeting others' needs? Yes, there are familiar ways we can apply this concept – clothing the naked, feeding the hungry and sheltering the homeless[18] – but, in the complex world in which we live, it is often the intangible losses that mean the most. Think about forgoing the approval of a peer group by standing up against racism, misogyny or oppression.[19] Think about Jesus telling us to lay down our lives for our friends, and then contemplate what it would be like to lay down our reputation, status, position, prestige and dignity.[20] Consider a man who breaks through racial and religious divides by crossing the road to help someone who has been beaten half to death, and then remember that *this* is an example of neighbourliness. Then again, think about anything we do or do not do, and consider how ludicrously insignificant it is in comparison to Christ and the sacrifice He made on our behalf.

To bring some perspective at this juncture I will mention three things. Firstly, none of this means that what we do does not matter. The 'smallest' gesture can prove crucial in advancing the kingdom. Secondly, Paul is not attempting to get a response by laying on the guilt – because, finally, Paul does not write: 'Do what Jesus did,' but: 'Let the *same mind* be in you that was in Christ Jesus.'[21] In other words, this is all about *thinking* in the same way that Jesus did. This is about patterns of behaviour, and not specifics.[22] Paul is not being prescriptive, but opening up possibilities. This is still a daunting prospect to consider, of course, but it provides space to breathe and move things forwards. Even though we cannot possibly do precisely the same things that Jesus did in the same way that He did them, we can adopt and follow His pattern because our thinking, acting and feelings are influenced and governed by the same values. These values, taken together, are the absolute opposite of an 'every-man-for-himself' way of thinking – rather, it is an 'everyone-for-everyone-else-and-no-one-for-only-themself' philosophy.

We might be moved to ask, *'But what about me? Don't my needs matter?'* The answer to these questions lies in the beautiful symmetry that exists when these values are applied to and by more than one person. A community where everyone puts others' needs first and looks after others' interests rather than their own is a community where no one's needs are neglected. In such a church community, I do not need to look after my interests, because there is a whole group of people bearing my concerns in mind. If I regard everyone else as better than me, they all, in turn, will regard me as better than them. In other words, I trust you to have my best interests at heart, just as your best interests are important to me. This is not superficial. This is a place where everyone's self-giving and other-awareness results in deep community, and where the organic ebb and flow of humble service means that all are genuinely supported as and when needed. It is a community where there is complete freedom to concentrate on others because there is no danger of being hung out to dry as far as your own needs are concerned.

It feels right to pause a while and contemplate this elegant and grace-filled conception of church community founded and grounded on Christ. But then the cold, hard reality of church life on a sinful planet kicks in and reminds us that we are often a long way from achieving this ideal. The sort of community being described thrives on full participation and calls for high levels of trust – and churchgoers know we can fall short on both counts. Frequently, we do not trust the people in our church community and can even have more confidence in those on the 'outside'. There are many reasons why this is the case, but arguably one of the biggest issues is that 'trust is choosing to risk making something you value vulnerable to another person's actions.'[23] In taking up the challenge of fully adopting these values I am required to risk my reputation, my well-being, in fact my all, on the understanding that at all times you will have only good intentions for me. Referencing the team-building activity that is often used to promote the idea of trust, this is much more than relying on someone to catch us if we fall backwards. This is more akin to relying on someone to ensure our safety if we metaphorically fall off a cliff.

It is both fascinating and telling how the business world has taken up the challenge of generating trust in organisations because of the way it benefits companies and their employees.[24] High-trust companies have been shown to not only produce better numbers, but also have higher levels of productivity and superior product or service quality.[25] In citing this example, this is not a case of bringing business practices into a church setting (something that has not always been to the Church's advantage). Rather, it is an example of how biblical values work even in an environment that tends to define success almost entirely financially. It is exciting to think of the potential for high-trust church communities – that higher levels of 'productivity' and 'service' can be achieved through the adoption of values that innately demand trust.

And as to the issue of participation? The announcement goes out that volunteers are needed to tidy up the grounds that surround the church building. You look around expecting to see the usual reticence from most and begrudging acceptance from those who always step forward. Instead, you are startled to see one hundred hands shoot up. Disbelief is soon replaced by pride at belonging to such an active and willing group. The day dawns dull and overcast. It's the only day of the week you're going to get a lie-in. The bed feels just that bit more comfortable than usual, and the duvet is reluctant to release you out into the world. An inner monologue ensues. Weren't there ninety-nine other people who volunteered? Won't their enthusiasm and skills make up for my absence? Would I do much good if I turned up anyway? Guilt is easily assuaged with those immortal words: *'They won't miss me.'* A sigh of relief is expelled, and you snuggle down for a few more precious moments of R&R . . . except there is more than one bed still occupied when the work is due to commence.

This is what is known as diffusion of responsibility – where we fail to help others because we believe someone else will do it.[26] No wonder this leads to the application of the 80:20 principle that in a church setting means 80% of the talking in a Bible study class is done by 20% of the attendees; 80% of the offering is given by 20% of the members; 80% of the food at shared lunches is provided by 20% of the diners; 80% of the moans are heard from 20% of the members; 80% of church activities are carried out or managed by 20% of the available workforce.[27]

When it comes to assigning roles within a church community, there are always positions that are viewed as hot potatoes to be avoided. Sometimes when people do step forward they hang around just long enough to feel disenfranchised, worn through and burnt out. Eventually, a natural reaction is to assert one's right not be taken advantage of, and that holistic, interconnected community generated by other-centred values seems unachievable.[28] Does this mean we should give up or not bother trying?

I don't want to lay on the guilt, but this is where the challenge of what Paul is saying in this passage in Philippians gets uncomfortable. Paul's flow of thought means that entertaining any concept of diffused responsibility, or refusing to trust or take risks, needs to be placed to one side. Why? Because we once again have to allow ourselves to be confronted by the example that he offers up for us to consider – that beyond-comprehension example of Jesus. That 'where-were-you-when' moment when Christ came and gave what others could not, was humble to the point of death, and did not take advantage of His divinity. By definition, He could not step back in a pique of diffused responsibility or refuse to take the risk . . . for if He had, where would we be? In a word – lost.

> ## Something to think about along the way
>
> *The unexpected note from a loved one or friend can make your day . . . even your week. Sue came out to her car and found that her 8-year-old son had left her a note wishing her a nice day and telling her that he loved her. He'd even arranged a light breakfast of an apple and a yoghurt. Sue felt as if her heart would burst.*
>
> *Janey was busy organising and running programmes for the youth in her church. She would spend hours planning, phoning people and setting up things so the young people could experience fresh new ways of understanding the Gospel, no matter what their learning style, prior knowledge or level of enthusiasm. As she went into the church hall to finish tidying up after one particularly inspiring session, she noticed that someone had left a note on a pile of books. Was it to thank her for all her hard work? Was to it to acknowledge how she was connecting with the youth and helping them to connect to God? No. It read, 'Dear Janey, please do not place books on top of the Holy Bible.' Janey also felt as if her heart would burst.*[29]

[1] Marie-Claire Chappet, *How It Feels to Save a Life*, BBC Three, 2019: *https://www.bbc.co.uk/bbcthree/article/477ad856-eb03-437d-85ce-0948be720077* (accessed 10 February 2020)

[2] M. Neil Browne and Stuart M. Keeley, *Asking the Right Questions: A Guide to Critical Thinking* (Prentice Hall, 2010), p. 160f.

[3] Susan E. Cross and Jonathan S. Gore, 'Cultural Models of the Self', in: *Handbook of Self and Identity*, edited by Mark R. Leary and June Price Tangney (New York, NY: Guilford Press, 2012), pp. 587-616 (p. 590); see also Llewellyn Edwards, *Values-Led Lives: The Way Jesus Wants Us to Think and Act* (Grantham, UK: Stanborough Press Limited, 2017).

[4] Philippians 2:2b – this structure is proposed by, among others, Witherington, *Paul's Letter to the Philippians*, p. 118.

[5] Philippians 2:5

[6] The original word in the Greek for 'mind' is *phronein* and refers to inner dispositions, not just thinking. See Kittel and Friedrich, *Dictionary*, p. 221.

[7] Philippians 2:3, 4

[8] English Standard Version – similar translations of this verse are seen in the King James Version, New Living Translation, International Standard Version and others.

[9] In essence, there is a contentious *kai* missing in some manuscripts that can be translated as 'also'. For a more in-depth discussion on this issue, see Bockmuehl, pp. 113, 114.

[10] The originator of the understanding that this is a hymn is famously Lohmeyer in: Ernst Lohmeyer, *Kyrios Jesus: Eine Untersuchung zu Phil. 2, 5-11* (Sitzungsberichte der Heidelberger Akademie der Wissenschaften, Philosophisch-historische Klasse, Jahrgang 1927/28; see also Hansen, *The Letter to the Philippians*, pp. 122, 123.

[11] As mentioned previously, the section runs from Philippians 1:27 to 2:16 or 18.

[12] Philippians 2:5

[13] James Rowe, 1911

[14] See, for instance, 1 Corinthians 11:1; Ephesians 5:1, 2; 1 Peter 2:20-22; 1 John 2:6.

[15] See for example Kenneth McIlroy, *The Pragmatic Leader: A Guide to Mastering Key Management Concepts* (New York; Lincoln; Shanghai: iUniverse, 2003), p. 144; Robert C. Crosby, *The Teaming Church: Ministry in the Age of Collaboration* (Nashville, TN: Abingdon Press, 2012), p. 49.

[16] Philippians 2:5-11

[17] Ben Witherington, *The Letters to Philemon, the Colossians, and the Ephesians: A Socio-Rhetorical Commentary on the Captivity Epistles* (Grand Rapids, MI: William B. Eerdmans Publishing, 2007), p. 131

[18] This is, after all, a biblical mandate – see Isaiah 58:7; Matthew 25:31-46; James 2:14-18; 1 John 3:17, 18.

[19] Again, this is biblical – see Deuteronomy 10:18; Isaiah 1:17; 10:1-4; 58:6; Jeremiah 22:3-5.

[20] 'No one has greater love than this, to lay down one's life for one's friends' (John 15:13).

[21] Philippians 2:5

[22] Although, still with a focus on behaviour, a more dynamic and helpful translation to consider is: 'Let this be your pattern of thinking, acting and feeling, which was also displayed in Jesus' (Fowl, p. 88).

[23]Another major factor is that church communities can develop shame cultures that make trust almost impossible – see movements 13 to 16. Here I'm quoting from Charles Feltman, *The Thin Book of Trust: An Essential Primer for Building Trust at Work* (Bend, OR: Thin Book Publishing, 2011), p. 7.
[24]See for example Stephen R. Covey and Rebecca R. Merrill, *The SPEED of Trust: The One Thing that Changes Everything* (New York, NY: Simon and Schuster, 2008); Robert C. Solomon and Fernando Flores, *Building Trust: In Business, Politics, Relationships, and Life* (Oxford: Oxford University Press, 2003).
[25]John Hall, 'Why a Focus on Employee Trust Is Essential', *Forbes*, 14 March 2021: *forbes.com/sites/johnhall/2021/03/14/why-a-focus-on-employee-trust-is-essential/* (accessed 14/6/2022)
[26]Saul Kassin, Steven Fein, and Hazel Rose Markus, *Social Psychology* (Belmont, CA: Cengage Learning, 2010), p. 409
[27]Also known as the Pareto Principle, where roughly 80% of effects are due to 20% of possible causes. See Richard Koch, *Living the 80/20 Way, New Edition: Work Less, Worry Less, Succeed More, Enjoy More* (London: Nicholas Brealey Publishing, 2011).
[28]There are ways around this, including promoting people to ministries based on their gifts, as advocated by the Natural Church Development movement, for example: *www.ncd-international.org* or *www.ncd-uk.org*.
[29]The stories are true, but the names have been changed.

From worrying about me to being a star!
Movement **10**

Wine is mentioned just a few times in Luke's gospel.[1] It makes an appearance when a Samaritan pours it on wounds, hoping that its disinfectant properties will combat the diseases and germs that are already working away unseen as a man lies injured beside the road. The tender and compassionate way the Samaritan ministers to the victim with wine contrasts greatly with a scene depicted thirteen chapters later. Now, Jesus is hanging on the cross and desperately needs to quench His thirst. Soldiers respond by bringing him cheap sour wine blended with taunts: 'If you are the King of the Jews, save yourself!' they say mockingly.[2] Even though this bargain-basement wine was thought to have health benefits, the difference in motivation is stark.[3] One application of wine is intended to bring healing, while the other is to generate added humiliation. And when Christians sit down at the communion table to remember Christ, it can similarly bring healing or something else altogether.

The Lord's Supper is on Paul's mind in 1 Corinthians, as is, once again, worthy behaviour. 'Whoever, therefore, eats the bread or drinks the cup of the Lord in an unworthy manner will be answerable for the body and blood of the Lord. Examine yourselves, and only then eat of the bread and drink of the cup.'[4] These verses provide a ready-made excuse to some and terrify others – especially after they have 'examined' themselves. Excuses can come thick, fast and varied when the opportunity to partake of foot-washing, bread and wine is given. And that 'unworthy manner' comment doesn't help, as it can be taken to suggest that it is open only to those who are, or at least feel, holy or clean in some sense. And who wouldn't want to avoid the possibility of the condemnation Paul refers to in verse 34?

However, as was the case with the Philippians, the unworthiness Paul is speaking against has to do with how the community as a whole are behaving, rather than a lack of individual righteousness or cleanliness. 'I hear that there are divisions among you,' Paul writes.[5] And, showing a degree of pastoral caution, he believes this charge to 'some extent'.[6] As we've seen, unity is important for Paul. But we also know that if a bunch of people get together and call themselves a church, disagreements follow. And this is no mere squabble: it is a schism that could potentially split the church in two.[7] So we wait with bated breath to find out what is causing this terrible state of affairs, and we read, 'For when the time comes to eat, each of you goes ahead with your own supper, and one goes hungry and another becomes drunk.'[8] Paul is aghast at their 'contempt for the church of God' and how they 'humiliate those who have nothing'.[9] So we find that there is impatience, gluttony and disrespect. Some of the group seem to be more interested in eating and drinking than in the reason they are gathering as a church community in the first place. This is about more than overindulgence, as some have not just fallen ill: they have died.[10]

Paul's solutions to these problems are wonderfully practical and almost mundane. This issue does not require a committee meeting, a big debate or disciplinary measures. There are no instructions to undertake all-night fasting sessions and prayer vigils followed by self-flagellation that some might suggest should precede attendance at a Lord's Supper. It is not pietistic attempts to attain to the required level of sanctity that are needed – rather, it is that each person is to consider how they treat other people within their community. 'So . . . when you come together to eat, wait for one another. If you are hungry, eat at home' first.[11] Paul basically tells the Corinthians to stop the bad behaviour that has disturbingly resulted in some losing their lives and the lowliest in the group going without food altogether. Their bad behaviour is so easily remedied that it would almost be humorous were it not for the grim consequences.

In Corinth, this is not an internal matter that can be kept behind closed doors. The behaviour in view on this most spiritually significant of occasions is no different to that seen at any other social event you might wander into.[12] They are doing no better than what is seen among the so-called heathens, running counter to the concept of functioning as communities that stand out because they embrace Spirit-empowered and life-enhancing values in a manner not seen in general. Rather, there is the same emphasis on one's position in society that promotes difference. The rich and those of high status are served first with the best food, and the slaves and poorer classes get the scraps and leftovers towards the end. The messages being thrown around are clear: '*I have, and you do not.*' '*I am held in high regard, and you are not.*' This all threatens the unity and harmony Paul is encouraging and sees as exemplifying the body of Christ.

That such concerns are on Paul's mind is seen in the enigmatic phrase, 'For as often as you eat this bread and drink the cup, you *proclaim* the Lord's death until he comes.'[13] What does Paul mean by saying that these actions are a proclamation? 'To proclaim' conjures up a picture of a town crier standing on a street corner, ringing their bell and delivering their message in a loud voice that cannot be ignored. People sat indoors eating bread and drinking wine do not seem to fit the bill.

The same word is used in Acts 13:5, where the word of God is proclaimed 'in the synagogues of the Jews', and in Romans 1:8, where the Roman Christians' 'faith is proclaimed throughout the world'. This strongly suggests that 'to proclaim' has a public dimension, 'so that all may see what is displayed'.[14] Therefore, as meaningful as the Lord's Supper is for the worshipping community, it is also a demonstration to those who look in from the outside – because, in 'eating this bread and drinking the cup, the whole assembled congregation stand in the witness box and pulpit to proclaim their "part" '.[15] Such occasions carried great weight and responsibility, because 'meals, perhaps more than any other social event in antiquity, encoded the values of a society, or, if it was a sectarian meal, of the sect itself.'[16] Simply put, how the Corinthian church community behave towards one another speaks volumes about their values, their relationships, and the Gospel of Christ they claim to live by: but what is being displayed to outsiders is a profoundly significant Christian meal marred by overindulgence, discrimination and difference.

What does the way we conduct ourselves when taking part in the Lord's Supper say about our communities in a contemporary context? Nowadays, there is little possibility of getting inebriated or eating ourselves to death, because the usual practice is to have what might be called a 'miniature fast food meal'. The bread and the wine have become symbolic in name and quantity; and, even though we might practise 'open communion', the doors are closed, and any proclamation appears to be limited.

However, there are messages we send to ourselves and then on to others: for example, the one that speaks to the issue of equality. No matter who you are, no matter your bank balance, ethnicity or status in society – all of that fades into the background when seated at the communion table. Church communities are not hierarchical entities that function via a chain of command based on a ranking system. Rather, they are founded on the death and resurrection of Jesus Christ. It is this and more that is proclaimed each time the meal is celebrated.

In the shadow of the *Windrush* controversy that is still swirling around the UK as I write, I was recently talking to someone whose parents were passengers on that historic voyage in 1948. The HMT *Empire Windrush* has come to be associated with a whole generation that has subsequently been mistreated by being wrongly detained and deported, despite being British citizens and long-term UK residents. This highlights the fact that, although looking fondly and with loyalty upon the 'mother country', there is a sense in which people from the Caribbean have found themselves occupying an in-between space where they are neither accepted as truly British, nor, in the case of the person to whom I was talking, truly Jamaican. She told me, 'As a black woman, I have never been fully accepted into society.' Such a liminal, or in-between, existence is challenged at the Lord's Supper where equality, identity and inclusion hold sway. In eating and drinking together, we are acknowledging that we are part of each other. We are proclaiming that all belong.

In one of the areas in which I was pastoring, I invited a civic dignitary to an event we were running. This particular church community comprised people from more than twenty ethnicities, hailing from five of the seven continents. He, however, was used to attending a local church that was almost entirely made up of one ethnicity. He told me that to sit and worship with such a diverse group came as a pleasant surprise to him. I realised, thinking back on our conversation, that, until then, I had taken the ethnic makeup of the congregation somewhat for granted and had failed to appreciate the message we were proclaiming: that, despite racial tensions flaring up around the city at the time, here was a group of people who, because of Jesus, were able to worship and fellowship together – a group that sat peaceably together around the same table.

Similarly, there is a proclamation in the air when Paul encourages the Philippians to 'work out [their] own salvation with fear and trembling'.[17] This particular verse has sparked a degree of controversy over the years, and appears in books looking at the 'hard' sayings of the Bible.[18] To a Protestant, there is a perilous-looking mix of 'your own', 'work' and 'salvation' that could lead to a form of legalism. Partly, the issue has to do with what Paul means by 'salvation'. We are back to the 'small versus big' story we looked at in Movement 8. There is a popular, but limited, view of salvation that sees it as being all about making it through the pearly gates into a heavenly realm populated by harpists. This view of salvation focuses on escaping this rotten planet and all its problems with the goal of swanning around in celestial safety on clouds of glory. It makes salvation all about individuals, their conversion and their story. But, as we have seen, Philippians 2:12 is set in a passage that is far from being so individualistic.

Logically, if salvation were 'just' about liberating individuals then things could have been brought to a conclusion after the resurrection, as Jesus' atoning death and resurrection are all that is needed for you and me to 'make it'.[19] But God has a grander plan on His mind, one that involves reconciling to Himself through Christ 'all things, whether on earth or in heaven, by making peace through the blood of his cross'.[20] More than just about individuals, therefore, God's plan of salvation involves bringing a lasting and peaceful solution to the problem of sin as experienced by the whole universe. Because of this, we get to look forward to the time when evil has been eradicated, relationships are made whole again, and God's reputation has been restored. And, rather than a disparate group of individuals occupying the city temple, the final and future picture of the people of God in the Bible is of a community who are dwelling with God and the Lamb.

With this broader outcome in mind, the sign of the Philippians' salvation that is on view as they stand together starts to make more sense:[21] for, by striving together in unity and in the one Spirit, God's plan to reconcile relationships – both vertical *and* horizontal – is being played out for all to see. Thus, their harmonious existence hints at what is to come when God's plan comes to fruition.

And as to those values that come in Philippians 2:2-4? They provide a context through which to understand the work that is being done in verse 12; because we are simply unable to put others' interests first, to think of others as better than ourselves in a loving and self-giving way, and to have the same mind as Christ's mind unless we are 'in Christ'. In more simple terms, an 'other-person-centred' life is beyond us unless we have been born again. So, by the time we get to verse 12, Paul has already been describing the post-conversion experience of salvation to be had in the present. And, coming towards the end of a passage that emphasises unity, the context is, therefore, church community.[22] It is not about who is or is not going to make it, but a group of believers whose Spirit-empowered life of togetherness is evidence of their collective salvation – one that hints at the rich community to come.[23] More than an ideal, Paul wants the Philippians 'to work out for themselves what this business of being saved will mean in practice'.[24]

In 1 Corinthians 11:26 the collective way of being at the Lord's Supper is itself a proclamation – in that case, of Jesus' death and resurrection. In Philippians 1:27 their togetherness proclaims their salvation. And there is more: for Paul tells the Philippians, 'Do all things without murmuring and arguing, so that you may be blameless and innocent, children of God without blemish in the midst of a crooked and perverse generation, in which you shine like stars in the world.'[25] By standing together, putting others first, having the same mind that is in Christ and working out the results of their salvation together, they can live in a way that is in stark contrast to what is seen in society in general. And so different are they that their witness will have a star-like quality. Because of who they are in Jesus, they will stand out.

This is both exciting and challenging. It is exciting because Paul has revealed the potency church communities have, in their collective behaviour, to act as beacons of hope by demonstrating and promoting human flourishing. As Kevin Vanhoozer suggests, 'The aim of Christian theology is not merely to add to our stockpile of theoretical knowledge, but to cultivate disciples who can *display* the mind of Christ in every situation.'[26] In some ways echoing Philippians 2:15, he goes further by proposing that our purpose is the 'living out of the Christian faith in the theatre of the world'.[27] And it is challenging, because the question that immediately comes to mind is: 'How does this work in practice?' How does this happen in churches that are mostly being church behind closed doors?

Something to consider along the way

Every time I drive past this particular church building, I cannot help but look. It occupies a prominent position on a main road leading out of the second-biggest town on the island. It's as if it has been designed to draw the eyes, and the occupants want you to do more than take a glance. Pretty much the whole of the front of the church is glass – a massive complex of windows through which any passer-by can see the main worship space with its chairs, lectern and musical instruments. There is nothing hidden away from public view – what you see is what you get. Drive or walk past on a Sunday morning, and you can observe people praying together, singing and worshipping. Here is a group of Christians who are literally putting on a show each time they meet. I cannot recall seeing a church building designed

> *in quite the same way before. When I asked someone what the thinking behind the design was, they said it was simply 'because we want people to see us'. Not for them, then, some cheesy poster with a catchy phrase or two written in Christianese - a phrase that only those of us in the know are ever going to understand.*

[1] Apart from the instances referred to in this chapter, wine is mentioned in the context of John the Baptiser's Nazirite vow in Luke 1:15; 7:33 and also features in a parable in Luke 5:37.

[2] Luke 23:37

[3] That's whether taken internally or applied externally. See Bryan D. Spinks, *Do This in Remembrance of Me: The Eucharist from the Early Church to the Present Day* (London: SCM Press, 2014), p. 439.

[4] 1 Corinthians 11:27, 28

[5] 1 Corinthians 11:18

[6] 1 Corinthians 11:18, as noted by Johnson, Alan F., *1 Corinthians, The IVP New Testament Commentary Series* (Westmont, IL: IVP Academic, 2004), VII, p. 204

[7] Indeed, the Greek word he uses is *schismata*, from which the English word 'schism' comes.

[8] 1 Corinthians 11:21

[9] 1 Corinthians 11:22

[10] 1 Corinthians 11:30

[11] 1 Corinthians 11:33, 34

[12] As Witherington says, 'Neither of these problems . . . was at all uncommon at Greco-Roman meals, especially at the drinking portion of the event.' See Ben Witherington, *Making a Meal of It: Rethinking the Theology of the Lord's Supper* (Waco, TX: Baylor University Press, 2007), p. 49.

[13] 1 Corinthians 11:26

[14] Anthony C. Thiselton, *The First Epistle to the Corinthians: A Commentary on the Greek Text* (William B. Eerdmans Publishing, 2000), p. 209

[15] Thiselton, *The First Epistle to the Corinthians*, p. 887

[16] Witherington, *Making a Meal of It*, p. 13

[17] Philippians 2:12

[18] Manfred Brauch, *Hard Sayings of Paul* (Downers Grove, IL: InterVarsity Press, 1989), pp. 218-222; Walter C. Kaiser Jr and others, *Hard Sayings of the Bible* (Downers Grove, IL: InterVarsity Press, 2010), p. 645f.

[19] This truncated and diminished version of events is being challenged in a number of quarters - see, for example, Anthony C. Thiselton, *Life After Death: A New Approach to the Last Things* (Grand Rapids, MI: William B. Eerdmans Publishing, 2011); Tom Wright, *Surprised by Hope: Original, Provocative and Practical* (London: SPCK, 2012).

[20] Colossians 1:20; see also Ephesians 1:10.

[21] Particularly as we have seen in Philippians 1:27; 2:1, 2.

[22] Philippians 1:27

[23] For more on this, see Paul Hartog, ' "Work Out Your Salvation": Conduct "Worthy of the Gospel" in a Communal Context', *Themelios*, 33.2 (2008), 19-33 (pp. 22-23).

[24] Tom Wright, *Paul for Everyone: The Prison Letters - Ephesians, Philippians, Colossians and Philemon (New Testament for Everyone)* (London, 2002)

[25] Philippians 2:14, 15

[26] Vanhoozer, p. 21

[27] Vanhoozer, p. 24

From purity to disgust

I once had a neighbour who used to clean his car every weekend . . . and I mean *every* weekend. Its chrome always gleamed, its carpets were spotless, and never was a smear seen on windows buffed to perfection. What was at first amusing became baffling, as he would wash the car even when the previous weekend's sparkle still caught the eye and any blemishes were imperceptible. It might be concluded that here was someone who prioritised and took pride in how his car looked.

We all have priorities we live by and that help direct our behaviour. And, like values, we might not have them written down or be conscious of them, but they are there all the same. For example, someone who thinks it is important to care for the environment will be more likely to recycle their waste and stop using plastic bottles; a person who prioritises time over tidiness will skip making their bed to save those few extra seconds; and so on. But, even if we believe actions speak louder than words, we cannot reasonably draw conclusions about someone based on their behaviour. For instance, when I got to know my neighbour a bit better, it turned out he was not cleaning his car as a matter of pride or because of a devotion to vehicular hygiene. He described how stressful his job had become recently, and how the one moment in the week when he could forget all his troubles was when he cleaned his car. The behaviour in view had more to do with stress management than cleanliness.

Such a cautionary tale suggests that we might make the same mistake when drawing conclusions about the priest's and the Levite's priorities. But, in their case, Jesus compels us to evaluate them by asking the question, 'Who was a neighbour to the man?' And, in comparison with the Samaritan, the pair of passers-by do not come off well. Appearances might suggest that an injured person lying by the side of the road was not as much of a priority for them as the religious system they were assiduously upholding, for example.

There is a good reason to examine the story in this way, and it is not to make us feel good as we get to condemn two men and laud another. Jesus uses parables to bring about change: be it to the lawyer, the crowd, the disciples, or those of us who interact with the story two thousand years later. Allowing parables to challenge us realises their potential to be windows into the Kingdom of God. More than that, they serve as mirrors encouraging us to look at ourselves.[1] Parables encountered in this way are confrontational and transformational. They niggle away at our presuppositions and prejudices, confronting the way we think and behave.

So, even as we assess the priest and the Levite, we also might ask ourselves the following questions to gauge where our own priorities lie. For example, is society as a whole more important than the individuals who make up that society? And do the needs of the individual outweigh the needs of the collective? How we answer these questions depends greatly on where we have been raised. People in the UK, Germany and North America, for example, prioritise the individual and their freedom, independence and rights; whereas societies such as those found in Japan, China, India and first-century Palestine tend or tended to prioritise one's duty to the family, community and society. Consequently, everyone is understood to be interdependent – what affects you affects me.

These biases towards either the community or the individual influence the decisions we make. For example, if I have grown up where the community matters most, I am likely to seek agreement from both my family and the family of the person I intend to marry before proceeding with marriage. However, if I come from an individualistic culture, I will probably choose my partner with little, if any, consultation with even my own family. And, of course, there are other priorities to consider. Do I choose to marry because of romance, love or commitment? Or how about stability, economics and status? Or is there a sense of duty driven by moral or religious concerns?

According to Richard Shweder, these are the sorts of things we consider, knowingly or unknowingly, when making any decision. He groups them into three ethics or categories: namely, autonomy, community and divinity.[2] Autonomy and community are relatively straightforward and relate to the question of the importance of the individual and the community, as discussed above. The divine ethic is more nuanced, and is based on what a person finds disrespectful and degrading. It is about human dignity and a person's concept of the divine. Despite its name, the divinity ethic is not about whether someone is religious, and does not depend on belief in God or god(s):[3] hence Shweder's calling it 'divinity', not 'Divinity'. However, because this can be distracting and misleading, from this point on it will be referred to as the 'sanctity ethic' for reasons that will become clearer.

The sanctity ethic is best understood by way of an example. Before becoming a pastor, I had the opportunity to take one of my employer's customers to see England play football at Wembley Stadium. We were merrily chatting away during the build-up to the match when an intense look suddenly came over my companion's face. Without warning, he stood up, holding his right hand across his chest. At first baffled, I eventually realised that I had been so caught up in the conversation that I had failed to notice that the band was playing the national anthem; and, by continuing to talk, I had not just shown a lack of awareness, but also disrespect. I had been disturbing the way things should be, based on country, monarch and national pride. He was not impressed. And, despite the nature of the words being sung,[4] this had nothing to do with God. His reaction was driven by his sanctity ethic.

This model is especially useful for understanding behaviour in church communities. Many of our heated moments that disrupt our fellowship come about because individuals differ on which category or ethic is the most important. Attend a church committee or board meeting and the different priorities people have are there for all to see. An all-too-familiar debate is over what chairs to have in a church building, for example. Those prioritising the divinity ethic might well push for pews, because that is the natural order of things for a church, and because pews promote reverence by being different from everyday seating. Those who are focused on individuals will push for the seating options that provide the greatest comfort for the largest number of people. If the church functioning as a community is of primary importance, then others will raise concerns about how the chairs affect the layout of the room and how this, in turn, affects social interaction. These examples demonstrate how the three ethics form two groups (see Figure 12). Community and autonomy are people-focused. The sanctity ethic, which features so strongly in church communities, is about something else altogether.

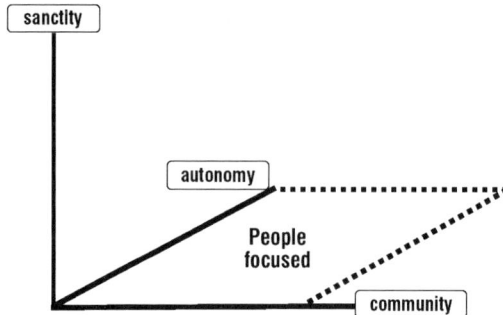

Figure 12: The three ethics or categories in relationship

The sanctity ethic is driven by two major concepts: an up-down hierarchy and a purity metaphor. The up-down concept is present because we generally think the higher up you are, the better you are. When a person gains a promotion at work, for example, they might be told they are climbing the ladder. Move to a better neighbourhood or buy a boat, and you may be told you are going up in the world. If a person experiences several personal crises, such as debt, marriage breakdown or acute health issues, it is often suggested they are on a downward spiral. This idea comes naturally to us and is, therefore, more familiar than it might seem at first. It is also found in the Bible. In Psalm 8, for example, we find:

> 'Yet you have made them [human beings]
> a little lower than the angels,

> *and crowned them with glory and honour.*
> *You have given them dominion over the works of your hands;*
> *you have put all things under their feet,*
> *all sheep and oxen,*
> *and also the beasts of the field,*
> *the birds of the air, and the fish of the sea,*
> *whatever passes along the paths of the seas.*[5]

The psalmist suggests a natural order of things that sees God at the top, followed by angels, humankind, and finally the other animals. To move up the scale is to move nearer to God and away from the less desirable behaviours and attributes associated with the beasts of the field.[6] This means that human beings are deemed to be 'nearer' to God than chickens, for example. This is not only intuitive, but endowed with theological significance.

UP

↑ **DIVINE**

 HUMAN

↓ **BEASTS**

DOWN

Figure 13: Up-down metaphor

Moving up or down the scale is both possible and culturally informed. To brawl in the street might be considered animal-like behaviour and so move one down the scale. In a Christian setting, it may be that praying or fasting is considered to move a person upwards towards God. Or, even though Jesus never wore a tie, to accompany one with a suit when attending church is perceived to move a person upwards and away from the earthly/beastly end of the scale.[7] In the days when men tended to own only two sets of clothes, the 'lower' outfits were the ones they wore day in and day out as they earnt their keep. However, on one day a week, men donned their 'Sunday best'. These garments were cleaner and in better condition than the normal workday clothes, and so suitable for special occasions like weddings and funerals. To wear a tie and one's best suit was to move away from the earthly struggle to survive, and upwards towards a higher plane of existence.[8]

This can be a very physical thing. Church buildings are designed and used to promote the feeling of upward movement towards a divine Other. To enter a church building is to move into a space that is qualitatively holier than the everyday, earthlier spaces outside. Religious buildings are where the barriers between heaven and earth seem thinly veiled. Such structures, particularly cathedrals, are environments where clothing, music, furniture and behaviour are different and set apart. Religious architects purposefully incorporate a design that draws the eyes upward and heavenward, away from the chaos and dirt of everyday living. This all makes entering a church building a religious experience, even though the New Testament does not support the idea that any construction on earth is holier than any other.

The other aspect of the sanctity ethic is the matter of purity. As a person moves up the scale they are regarded as becoming cleaner and less polluted.[9]

To move upwards is to attain to a status associated with God Himself by becoming ever more holy, righteous and sanctified. At the other end of the scale, we find the opposite: the unholy, the unrighteous, the unsanctified and the impure.

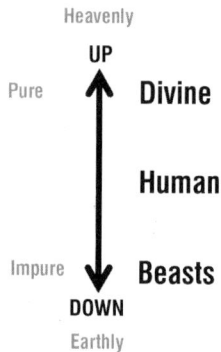

Figure 14: The up-down scale

For instance, if someone were to defecate on the pavement in a town centre, it would provoke a range of responses from surprise to horror. Such an act would go against the natural order of things which says that evacuating one's bowels must be done in private, in specially designated places called toilets. To do otherwise is chaotic and beast-like – more akin to how dogs behave. It would also be a matter of purity, because it would be seen as contaminating the environment.

This brings us to another characteristic of the sanctity ethic. Imagine you are given an empty cup and are asked to spit into it. After waiting five minutes you are instructed to drink the contents of the cup. What do you do? To date, when conducting this exercise, not one person has agreed to take so much as a sip, reflecting rather more rigorous research reported elsewhere.[10] As Beck points out, this makes no sense at all, because we swallow our saliva all of the time. So what is the problem? One answer is found in acknowledging the difference between saliva in the mouth and the cup, and the boundary that exists between them. Spit into a cup, and your saliva goes from inside to outside and is no longer thought of as being part of your body or its systems. Once in the cup, it is out of place and is thought of as being disorderly and chaotic. Any sense of ownership is much diminished, as it has come to be considered as waste that is contaminated and impure – maybe even toxic, polluting or defiling. Our natural response is one closely associated with the sanctity ethic . . . disgust.

Why does any of this matter? The autonomy and community ethics, in different ways, prioritise people. However, once the sanctity ethic starts to dominate our decision making, the focus on people can be reduced or even lost. In a church setting, which is and should be all about people, the sanctity ethic turns our attention elsewhere – towards artefacts, traditions and rules. Remember the stories of the two elders who acted as gatekeepers to their church? The lack of a tie on the young man's part and the revealing clothing in the young woman's case were both violations of the elders' sanctity ethic, because they were showing a lack of respect towards the space they were about to enter. Add in the purity aspect, and it means they were threatening to contaminate the 'holy' space merely through their presence. Hence, the elders reacted with disgust. Never mind how the two young people felt – they were of secondary importance in the elders' minds, because their decision-making processes were being governed by the sanctity ethic, and not concerns to do with autonomy and community.

It is important to note that the sort of contamination being referred to here is irreversible. For example, I recently found that a spider had chosen to take up residence in my glass of water. Few people would simply remove the spider and carry on drinking. The sense of how things should be ordered has again been disturbed. The spider, having broken the boundary between food and non-food, is in the wrong place. And, once contaminated, there is no way to restore the water to its former purity – at least, not by simply removing the spider. Because contamination only flows from the impure to the pure, there is no sense in which the water 'cleanses' the spider. The now impure water is unwanted and 'disgusting'.[11]

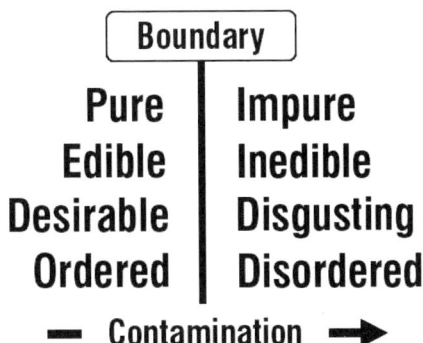

Boundary	
Pure	Impure
Edible	Inedible
Desirable	Disgusting
Ordered	Disordered

— Contamination ➡

Figure 15: The boundary effect

Disturbingly, this is not just about insects: it can also be about people. It is shocking to think that we might consider another person to be a contaminant, but this is not without historical precedent. The Athenians in the fourth and fifth centuries BC excluded those who were thought to threaten the order and stability of society.[12] There were the Dalits or 'untouchables' of India, who were 'widely deemed to be ritually and physically defiling to the rest of the Hindu nation' and even to this day experience discrimination, albeit in more subtle forms.[13] Closer to home, it is suggested that the caste system upon which this is based was mimicked by the British class system, which reached its peak in Victorian times and led to certain members of society similarly being excluded or ostracised.[14] Do we now know better? Well, it might not be so overt or organised, but it exists all the same.[15]

The island I call home notably does not have any travellers living on it. 'Traveller' is the politically correct term for those who were once called Romany or gypsy, or, more pejoratively, 'pikey'. They are frequently treated as outcasts and made unwelcome because of their perceived high levels of anti-social behaviour, tax avoidance and environmental pollution. If they set down roots in a town or village, usually on a piece of land they do not own, uproar follows as crime rates go up and house prices plummet . . . but not here on the island, where, according to some, their absence makes the island a safer and cleaner place to live, a place free from the contaminating presence of undesirables.

Excluding someone through physical distancing or by shutting down communication is 'most commonly a response to deviant or inappropriate behaviour, or, in some instances, to one or more physical characteristics of the individual that sets him or her apart from the rest (for example, physical handicap, colour, carrier of disease, and so on)'.[16] A moment's thought might see us add migrants, those with mental health issues, refugees and addicts to that list. The effect on the individual is powerful because it 'carries with it the message that something about that individual is bad or unwanted' and leads to 'an internalised belief in one's undesirable nature and shortcomings'.[17] In other words, once excluded, we can *feel* like we are out of place and contaminating in some way.

We like to think that church communities are different: but, even as we have similar issues to society at large, we add to the problem by struggling with those who fail to conform, or believe and behave differently, or are of alternative sexual orientations or look different because of tattoos, and so on. It is not just priests and Levites who get to walk past people.

Something to think about along the way

Mike[18] *walked into the church building that day without a care in the world, and with no inkling of what was about to hit him. As soon as one of the senior men of the church saw that Mike was present, he marched over and told Mike they needed to have a word with him. They trooped round the back into one of the side rooms, and suddenly Mike found he was outnumbered three to one. There were no pleasantries exchanged, no small talk to ease people into the conversation, just a barely disguised statement of condemnation: 'Mike, it has come to our attention that there may be issues over your choice of . . .' (the speaker hesitated to take time to search for the right word) '. . . your choice of partner.'*

Now Mike had much more than a care in the world, and could only guess at what was about to hit him. He'd been to a restaurant with his latest beau. He suspected that, despite attempts at being discrete, someone had seen them there together and 'filed' a report. 'Frankly,' the speaker continues, 'if this turns out to be true, and I have no reason to think otherwise, then this is disturbing and dismaying in equal measure.'

Mike sat there as if tied to the chair: hijacked, judged and condemned all at the same time. His uncertain response caused the accuser to take this as a tacit admission of guilt, and so he declared what was evidently a previously determined sentence. 'You will not be allowed to attend church for the next few months. In the meantime, we have asked the pastor to meet and study with you to remind you of the godly standards by which we all must live. This is to be done in the hope that you will repent of your ways. We are of a mind to suggest that once you have repented, you will seek rebaptism to bring cleansing to your life . . . it'll be a fresh start for you.'

Mike wanders away, shell-shocked. It is only as he sits in the quiet of his own bedsit that he realises that, in all the time he was being spoken to, he had barely uttered a single word.

---

[1]As suggested by William G. Kirkwood, 'Storytelling and Self-confrontation: Parables as Communication Strategies', *Quarterly Journal of Speech*, 69.1 (1983).

[2]Richard Shweder et al., 'The "Big Three" of Morality (Autonomy, Community, Divinity) and the "Big Three Explanations of Suffering" ', in: *Morality and Health*, edited by Allan M. Brandt and Paul Rozin (New York, NY: Routledge, 2013), pp. 119-169

[3]Richard A. Shweder, *Why Do Men Barbecue? Recipes for Cultural Psychology* (Harvard University Press, 2003), p. 89

[4]"God Save the Queen'

[5]Psalm 8:5-8 – note that the marginal reading of verse 5 as suggested in the footnotes has been quoted here. The standard reading in the NRSV is: 'You have made them a little lower than God.'

[6]Richard Beck, *Unclean: Meditations on Purity, Hospitality, and Mortality* (Cambridge, UK: Lutterworth Press, 2012), p. 55

[7]Ties, as we know them, were not invented until the eighteenth century. See Francois Chaille, *The Book of Ties*, first edition (Paris: Flammarion, 1994).

[8]For more background, see Frank Viola and George Barna, *Pagan Christianity? Exploring the Roots of Our Church Practices* (Carol Stream, IL: Tyndale House Publishers, Inc., 2010), pp. 145, 146.

[9]Beck suggests that it is a compound metaphor that also includes the concept of purity. See Beck, p. 54.

[10]This is based on Paul Rozin's research referred to in Beck, p. 1.

[11]See also Beck, pp. 21, 22.

[12]Citizens voted to decide whom to exclude through a vote placed by writing on broken pieces of pottery or ostraca, from which the English word 'ostracism' comes.

[13]Susan Bayly, *Caste, Society and Politics in India from the Eighteenth Century to the Modern Age* (Cambridge, UK: Cambridge University Press, 2001), p. 181 – for more on current practices, see Narendra Jadhav, *Untouchables: My Family's Triumphant Escape from India's Caste System* (University of California Press, 2007).

[14]Gareth Stedman Jones, *Outcast London: A Study in the Relationship Between Classes in Victorian Society* (London: Verso Books, 2014)

[15]Willliams suggests that 'the odds are very high that you have experienced episodes of ostracism.' See Kipling D. Williams, *Ostracism: The Power of Silence* (New York, NY: Guilford Press, 2002), p. 2.
[16]Williams, p. 61
[17]Williams, pp. 61, 62
[18]Not his real name

From disgust to mercy

Movement 12

J esus' choice of a Samaritan as His hero was, as we have seen, a radical
one. Jesus often seemed to act in a way that unbalanced people and
forced them to confront their prejudices. In Matthew 9, Jesus upset the
equilibrium by recruiting a traitorous, Roman-collaborating tax collector
to be one of His disciples. Matthew, for it is he, has modestly waited for a
little over eight chapters before he inserts himself into his gospel in a story
that is covered in two scenes found in Matthew 9:9-13.

In the first scene, Matthew is working at his booth, likely collecting road
or poll taxes. Payment of these was mixed with much resentment towards
the occupying power who imposed the taxes, and loathing towards the
person taking the money on their behalf.[1] Seemingly out of the blue, Jesus
walks by and invites Matthew to follow Him, thereby changing Matthew's
life forever. After Matthew accepts the call to discipleship, the story moves
on to the second scene, where he plays host to an infamous gathering of
fellow tax collectors, sinners and Jesus.[2] Somehow, the Pharisees have kept
up to date with developments and approach Jesus' disciples and enquire,
'Why does your teacher eat with tax-collectors and sinners?'[3] What motivates
this question? Most would aver that it's condemnation rather than curiosity.[4]
But what happens if we view it through the lens of the sanctity ethic?

The question reveals much about the way these particular Pharisees
differentiated and ranked different groups of people. It groups despised tax
collectors with sinners . . . and these were no ordinary sinners. They were not
the sort of 'sinners' who merely failed to follow the very strict and long list
of regulations by which the Pharisees lived (for simplicity's sake, we can
refer to these as 'general sinners'). Rather, they were those who had
committed more grievous acts and who were regarded as 'the most criminal
and disreputable types of people in society'.[5] To help distinguish them from
the first group of sinners, we shall call them 'grievous sinners'.

Then there are the disciples to whom the question was posed. They are of
a higher status than sinners and tax collectors, because the Pharisees do not
ask, 'Why is Jesus eating with *you*?' but, 'Why is He eating with *them*?'
Further, Jesus must have been seen eating with His disciples on many
occasions, and there is no mention of this ever being a problem. Jesus' status
as a teacher sets Him apart from His disciples; and, of course, the question

addresses the issue of whether someone of Jesus' standing should be dining with Matthew's guests.[6] Finally, as to the questioners themselves? Well, the highly regarded Pharisees, the ultimate law-keepers, were seen by many, especially themselves, as a class apart.

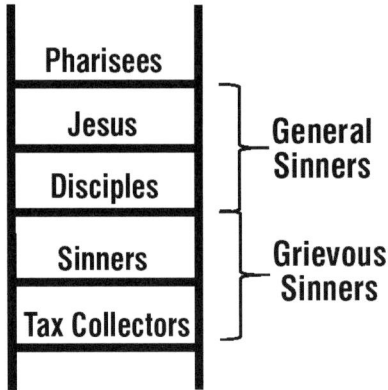

Figure 16: Pharisees and others (according to the Pharisees)

With the natural order of things established, there is just the purity metaphor to add to the mix. Concerns about pollution, impurity and holiness influenced people's thinking in Jesus' day, Pharisee or not.[7] And when you are at the top of the pile and the purity metaphor is applied, it is difficult not to look down upon others and see them as contaminating influences. We can relate to this a bit more easily given the emergence of COVID-19. As I write, the UK and many other countries have gone into lockdown to limit the spread of the virus. It is an uncertain time, and 'hands, face, space' has become a way of life. When out and about, folks are crossing the road to help maintain social distancing. However, it still feels awkward. It seems only polite to exchange smiles and nods to acknowledge that this is nothing personal. But now, where the path narrows, it is not just inconvenient, but potentially perilous, because a 2-metre gap is impossible to maintain. That person you have just encountered could be the one who infects you. And, with the virus potentially spreading through surface contact, will this door handle or that food packaging be the thing that does it for me? Will I, through habit, rub my nose or eyes and allow COVID-19 to enter my system? I wonder how long it will be before we become wary of each other. When will others' humanity start to fade until they are seen as little more than an extension of the virus they may carry? At least for us, the threat to our health and integrity is real. For the Pharisees, it *felt* real, but this was not based on something as tangible as a virus. Rather, their sanctity ethic was working overtime, conjuring up antagonists for them to avoid and malign. The hierarchy that was constructed earlier is partly to blame for this, but its full impact is appreciated only once the purity metaphor is included. This results in the following:

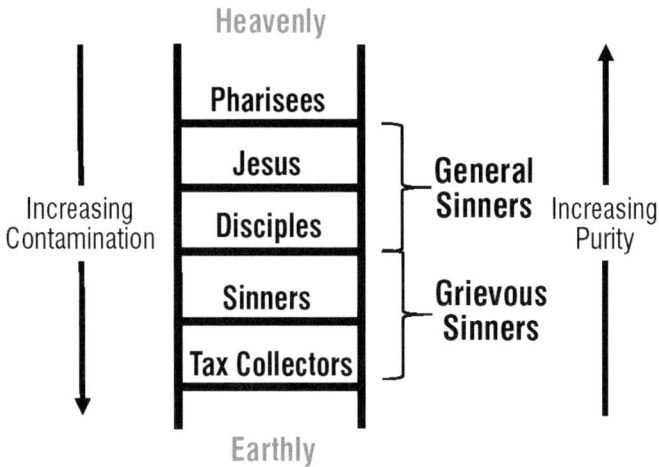

Figure 17: The Pharisees and the others and purity
(according to the Pharisees)

Once the sanctity ethic is allowed to dominate, its purity metaphor becomes concretised. That is, purity is not understood symbolically or metaphorically, but literally. And the greater the distance between you and me on the ladder, the greater the risk of contamination if you are below me. My best option is to avoid you so you will not pollute me. You are no longer a human being to whom I can relate, but a threat. The move towards dehumanisation is inevitable.

Now, avoiding contact is a very physical way of expressing bounded-set thinking: but what is evident in Matthew 9 is not simply a case of 'us' and 'them', the Pharisees and everyone else. The situation is more nuanced than that. In taking Jesus to task for eating the meal at Matthew's house, the Pharisees are trying to maintain a boundary between Jesus and the other guests. But this does not mean that Jesus is part of them. Rather, they are also maintaining a boundary between themselves, Jesus, and tax collectors. This results in the following groups:

Figure 18: The implied boundaries in Matthew 9:9-13

By visualising the social structures, the significance of Jesus reclining at the table and eating a meal comes sharply into focus. Instead of being confined by artificial and damaging boundaries, Jesus breaks them down (see Figure 19). Such an act was laced with meaning at the time. To eat with someone carried with it the significance still seen in Middle-Eastern cultures to this day, where it represents 'the deepest form of social intimacy'.[8] Jesus was, in effect, broadcasting that the lowest of the low in society were part of Him, and He was part of them. Jesus was establishing a boundary-free society even as the Pharisees sought to hide behind their own boundaries.

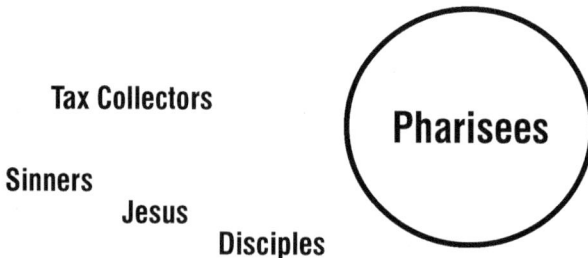

Figure 19: Broken boundaries

By upsetting the natural order, Jesus threatened the very stability of society, because the boundaries He broke through were reinforced by the Pharisees' concept of purity. Rather than a solitary fly landing in Jesus' glass of water, it was as if Jesus had deliberately stepped into a swarm of flies. And, because the sanctity ethic only allows contamination to go in one direction, Jesus was not thought of as cleansing the other guests: they were thought to be polluting Him.[9] Although lost on the Pharisees, the irony is palpable. Even though Scripture proposes that Jesus is the One who brings 'cleansing' to all humanity,[10] the Pharisees cannot see it. Instead of a force for good, holiness and purity are seen as fragile and in need of protection from outside forces. Similarly, it is not thought that jean-wearing teenagers and 'half-dressed' young women are going to be made 'holy' by entering the sanctified space of a church building. Rather, that space is viewed as being threatened by their lack of decorum.

We do not hear the disciples' answer to the Pharisees' question. Instead, Jesus responds by saying, 'Those who are well have no need of a physician, but those who are sick.'[11] There is no doubt that the sinners and tax collectors are the 'sick' in need of healing here. Unlike the Pharisees, they, at least, are the sort of sick people who know they are sick. So what is Jesus to do with Pharisees who are prioritising the sanctity ethic over human dimensions? Rather than providing the solution to them on a plate, Jesus gives the Pharisees some homework to do. 'Go and learn what this means, "I desire mercy, not sacrifice." '[12] Jesus points them to Hosea 6:6, and we are left to wait, wondering if they will take His advice. Will they get around to consulting that familiar text, written down by Hosea centuries before? Will they try and understand what God was telling their ancestors? Will they wrestle and struggle with it to discover the application for themselves and their situation?

Unlike their contemporaries, we modern readers tend not to have high expectations for the Pharisees. Where once they were thought of as the crème de la crème of commandment keepers, to label someone a Pharisee is now an insult. Modern-day Pharisees are legalists, petty and hard to be around. A moment's reflection, however, might reveal an unexpected twist: for now it is we who tend to distance ourselves from Pharisees in the same way they distanced themselves from sinners. Now, the term 'Pharisee' represents the very worst of religious behaviour, but it can also be a dehumanising label used to put others down.

So, if truth be told, we do not assume too much of the Pharisees as we wait on their response. It does not take too long – just three chapters, and our low expectations are realised. It's a fresh encounter, but this time, rather than Jesus, it is the disciples who are the problem. The disciples have the temerity to pluck grain on the Sabbath, thereby (according to some) breaking the Fourth Commandment. The Pharisees emerge from behind sheaves of wheat, accompanied with a police-like attitude, and point out directly to Jesus on this occasion, 'Look, your disciples are doing what is not lawful to do on the sabbath.'[13]

Standard comebacks to such provocative comments are often less than courteous; but Jesus' response to the Pharisees' accusation is considered and densely packed with challenging material. He begins by recounting a story about David. 'Have you not read what David did when he and his companions were hungry? He entered the house of God and ate the bread of the Presence, which it was not lawful for him or his companions to eat, but only for the priests.'[14] The Pharisees, being Pharisees, would have known all about the story found in 1 Samuel 21:1-6. They would also have been aware that Jesus' synopsis of the story only hints at its complexity.

The issue to which Jesus refers arises when David asks the priest Ahimelech, 'Now then, what have you at hand? Give me five loaves of bread. . . .'[15] David is on the run from a murderous Saul, and, being desperate, also adds, '. . . or whatever is here.' The sanctity ethic that prioritises purity, order and holiness is triggered because there is only holy bread available.[16] Also known as the 'bread of presence', it was prepared weekly and taken into the temple on Sabbath, where it was arranged in two rows of six, representing the twelve tribes of Israel and their presence in the covenant. It was holy bread, kept on a holy table in the holy place, and was dedicated to God. After the high priest replaced and removed the loaves from the sanctuary, they were to be eaten only by priests in 'a holy place' – probably within the sanctuary itself.[17] Exclusively apply the sanctity ethic, and Ahimelech must refuse David's request.

But then there is the community ethic, which requires Ahimelech to show hospitality to David. Just as Abraham moves to greet three strangers in Genesis 18, Ahimelech needs to follow through on his 'obligation to nourish and protect travellers who find themselves in a hostile environment'.[18] Exclusively apply the community ethic, and Ahimelech must respond favourably.

And what of the autonomy ethic and its requirement for justice, freedom and liberty? Even as this compels Ahimelech to act to sustain David's life, there is also his own well-being to consider. Standing before Ahimelech is one of the most accomplished and fearsome warriors in the land – one who has not hesitated to use violence to achieve his own ends.[19] Will Ahimelech escape with his life unless he gives David what he wants?[20]

Caught between a rock and hard place, Ahimelech pays lip service to his sanctity ethic by asking whether 'the young men have kept themselves from women'.[21] These are the young men David earlier stated he had arranged to meet in 'such and such a place'.[22] Whether they or the command to refrain from sexual relations he refers to actually exist is far from certain.[23] Even so, that is enough for Ahimelech to accede to David's request; and, with the wiggle room that comes from handing over the priest's bread rather than that on the table, David has his food.[24]

In this story, it can be seen how the sanctity, autonomy and community ethics compete and in this case pull Ahimelech in all directions. Jesus uses the story to highlight how sometimes rules come second to human need. Sometimes, holy bread meant for priests could be eaten by a man on the run from his homicidal father-in-law. 'In this incident, Jesus lays it down that the claim of human need must take precedence over all other claims. The claims of worship, the claims of ritual, the claims of liturgy, are important, but prior to any of them is the claim of human need.'[25] And it is only in Jesus getting the Pharisees to engage with the practical and moral questions, to consider what they would have done in Ahimelech's position, that lessons might hit home. Would they have stuck to the rules and so endangered David's life further, or might they have taken a different path?

Jesus now moves to more directly address the issue of the Sabbath:[26] 'Or have you not read in the law that on the sabbath the priests in the temple break the sabbath and yet are guiltless?'[27] Jesus is referring to instructions about Sabbath sacrifices found in Numbers 28:9, 10. Sabbath was no day of rest for the priests, because of the work involved in sacrificing lambs and preparing grain offerings. Even though the priests are breaking many Pharisaical rules by lighting a fire and preparing the flour and oil on Sabbath, Jesus says they are innocent. It is not so easy to determine how the three categories of ethics are interacting in this scenario. There is an aspect of the community ethic influencing things, because preparing and offering sacrifices on Sabbath is done for the greater good of the society and nation. The purpose of being a priest, after all, is to intercede on behalf of others. But priestly duties, and the sacrificial system as a whole, are heavily influenced by the sanctity ethic. And, if this example is only viewed through the lens of sanctity, then we get a contradiction. No work is to be done on the Sabbath, yet *this* work must be done on the Sabbath. To resolve this inconsistency, the categories that Shweder's model originally proposed need to be revised.

Initially, we need to think about why Jesus uses this example. An authoritarian approach will say that, since God is the One who writes the rules, they can be whatever He wants them to be. Thus, in Matthew 12:8, Jesus says He is the 'Lord of the Sabbath', so He has the authority and right to 'interpret it [the law] in a way which effectively undercuts Pharisaic legalism'.[28] It only needs Jesus' say-so for Sabbath grain-plucking to be permissible. Yet, if we allow this to be our only conclusion, we are perilously close to a 'God says it; just do it' approach.[29] There's more than that, however. Let the sanctity ethic stand alone, and rules, regulations, holiness and order become the ends, and not the means to an end. To counteract this, we need two things: firstly, to ensure that sanctity operates within a living, breathing system that prioritises people. In doing so, we do not eradicate the sanctity ethic, but see it for what it brings. Secondly, we need to account for God, without whom none of this would matter.

And this is where the story of the priests working on Sabbath can help. If the punchline is that 'the worship of God takes precedence over the regulations of the day', Jesus is doing more than providing a legal argument or citing case law to justify His disciples' actions.[30] He is using an example of how we are to prioritise God and our relationship with Him in our decision-making. If we prioritise any of the concepts of community, autonomy or sanctity outside of our worship of and relationship with God, we will run into problems. To fully prioritise the community is to fall into a form of humanism. To fully prioritise autonomy is to buy into the cult of the individual. If the sanctity ethic takes centre stage, dictating forms and establishing traditions, there is the danger of God being pushed into the background, coming second to the forms and traditions themselves. Not only does this mean that human dimensions and, therefore, human beings suffer, but God Himself is diminished.

The original understanding of the three ethics embraced human relationships but neglected explicit reference to God and the relationships we have with Him as individuals and as church communities (see Figure 12). For Christians, if a holistic approach is taken, God will take precedence, but not in an overpowering way. Rather, it is through our relationship with God as our Creator that all other dimensions of life come alive and find their rightful place. It is therefore God who brings balance and stops other dimensions getting out of kilter. This understanding leads to a model that embraces Divinity in its truest Trinitarian sense.[31] The autonomy and community ethics or categories remain intact, and in this life they exist in tension with each other. The sanctity ethic is not discarded, but is instrumental in giving substance to our relationships without dominating in any way. Thus, God is not limited by or to a sanctity ethic. A revised model will look something like this:

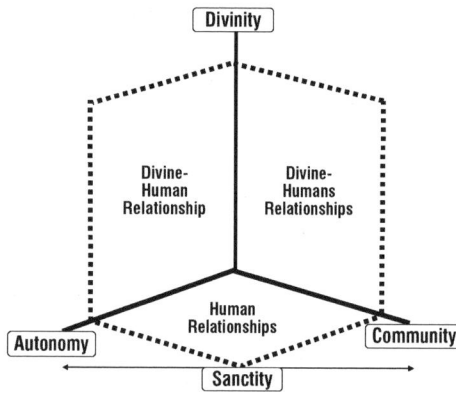

Figure 20: Divinity in relationship with humanity and sanctity

As we noted earlier, Shweder's three categories of ethics are an expression of the things on which we base moral decisions. Now, this revised way of addressing issues emphasises that our decisions are best focused on how they affect our relationships and not sanctity-based constructs. For the Jews, the biggest construct of all was the Jerusalem temple that was the home of the sacrificial system and centre of their life and faith. It loomed large both spiritually and physically, and was described as being 'the most prodigious work that was ever heard of by man'.[32] More than a magnificent building, it

114

was to be the place where God dwelt among His people.[33] Its foundations were not those embedded into rock above the Kidron valley, but the covenant relationship that God established with His chosen people. But, if we allow the sanctity ethic to dominate, the building becomes more important than the people and the reason it was put there in the first place. Keeping the place holy and performing the rituals and the sacrifices in the right way, at the right time, takes priority over the very people the system was set up to serve. So, in His response to the Pharisees, Jesus places this construct in context. He gives a statement realigning their priorities and radically identifies Himself as 'something greater than the temple'.[34] The temple was not an end in itself, but a means to an end in Christ.

So, what about the Sabbath and this alternative model? In Mark's version of this story, the second radical thing that we hear Jesus saying is, 'The sabbath was made for humankind, and not humankind for the sabbath.'[35] In the Pharisees' way of thinking and acting, the seventh day of the week had become a sanctity-driven construct that again had lost sight of people. It is important to note that Jesus is not undermining or doing away with the Sabbath, but pointing out that even something as valuable and as precious as the Sabbath comes second to the people it serves.[36] Admittedly, it is easy to allow the sanctity ethic to dominate because of the language associated with the Sabbath. It is to be kept holy,[37] it can be broken,[38] and it is to be observed.[39] But remove the people context and how it impacts their relationship with God, and it becomes dry and lifeless. Jesus is saying, 'If you get your priorities wrong, religious practices lose their meaning and purpose.'

Jesus has already given the Pharisees much to think about. But, before finishing, He sets the same homework He gave them back in Matthew 9. For a second time, Jesus refers them to Hosea 6:6: but He is a little stronger on this occasion when He says, 'If you had known what this means, "I desire mercy and not sacrifice", you would not have condemned the guiltless.'[40] The Pharisees need to think about what Jesus has said. Will they get it this time? Will they go away and engage at last with the old prophet? Will they absorb the lessons from yesteryear and take them on board? Well, if possible, we now have somewhat lower expectations of them.

We wait for eleven chapters for an answer, arriving at Matthew 23. The opening section of the speech in verses 1 to 36 addresses the scribes' and Pharisees' 'failure to perceive how their religious practice and teaching are in fact inconsistent with their desire to please God'.[41] Jesus is making the same argument as found in Matthew 9 and 12, but now He has to use a sledgehammer to make His point. No other chapter in the Bible so clearly exposes the vacuousness that results from prioritising the sanctity ethic. It is not that the Pharisees are inactive – their religious practices are in many ways exemplary, and include everything from broad phylacteries to diligent tithe paying[42] – but they also 'do not practise what they teach' (verse 3), burden others (verse 4), make a show of their religious practices (verse 5), revel in their elevated status (verses 6 and 7), 'lock people out of the kingdom' (verse 13), corrupt their converts (verse 15), 'are full of greed and self-indulgence' (verse 25), and 'are full of hypocrisy and lawlessness' (verse 28).

As we listen in, the word 'mercy' makes its last appearance in Matthew's gospel: 'Woe to you, scribes and Pharisees, hypocrites! For you tithe mint, dill, and cummin, and have neglected the weightier matters of the law: justice and mercy and faith.'[43] No quotes from Hosea now, as they are beyond that. Where their homework is concerned, they have earnt an 'F'. Jesus gives it to them straight on this final occasion. Mercy is still lacking, and, as a result, so are justice and faith. It is not that what they are doing is wrong. Indeed, Jesus says, 'These [justice, mercy and faith] you ought to have practised *without neglecting the others [tithing conventions]*.'[44] But their religious practices are done without the soul and spirit that come from engaging with God and others. Their sanctity ethic reigns and almost stands alone.

What might the Pharisees have learnt if they had meditated on Hosea 6:6 as Jesus suggested? Initially, it seems as if Hosea is suggesting that God is doing away with religious rituals altogether: 'For I desire steadfast love and not sacrifice, the knowledge of God rather than burnt-offerings.'[45] This is an either/or and not a both/and approach. Given what Jesus says about tithing not being neglected, it appears that Hosea is throwing the baby out with the bathwater. It would have been more comfortable for us if Hosea had said, 'I desire mercy *and* sacrifice.'[46] Then we would get to combine the best of both worlds: the structure that sanctity brings through rituals, combined with the focus on human relations that mercy conveys. But neither Jesus nor Hosea asks for both. So is it a case of choosing one over the other?

If we work a little harder and go back to verse 4 we find God asking, 'What shall I do with you, O Ephraim? What shall I do with you, O Judah? Your love (*hesed*) is like a morning cloud, like the dew that goes away early.' 'Love is present, but it is fragile, and, like dew, does not last very long.'[47] If love is the foundation upon which everything rests, this cannot continue. So *hesed* is called for again in verse 6 where God says that He wants steadfast love (*hesed*) and not sacrifice. *Hesed* is variously rendered as meaning goodness, loving-kindness, faithful love, steadfast love and mercy; but it is one of those words that are so rich and potent that it may be better if it remains untranslated. At its core, *hesed* 'implies a committed love on the basis of a previously established bond, a gratuitous love that goes beyond the call of duty. Love, mercy, and kindness are inadequate translations of *hesed*; it is no one of these virtues, but all of them together.'[48]

Hosea's prophecies have been working towards a dramatic unveiling of God's desires for human beings.[49] At this point in Jewish history, God's spokesmen are moved to declare 'that it is futile to profess love for God in the cult [religious practices] or any other form, if one lacks love for one's neighbour.'[50] And so we come full circle back to the lawyer's answers to his own questions in Luke 10. What God wants is for us to love our neighbours as ourselves. The lawyer knows this, but he has separated love and mercy from righteousness, *hesed* from practice. He does not appear to quite get *hesed*: its intimacy, its commitment, its lack of boundaries. When Hosea says that God desires mercy and not sacrifices, he is not ending religious practice. He is saying that without love, mercy and kindness, religious practice is meaningless.[51] This means that in the book of Hosea God is setting priorities after all. Using hyperbolic language, He is letting us know that *hesed* must come first and take priority to make sense of what follows.

This is not an arbitrary outcome, but is a consequence of God's character, for God is *hesed*. As the psalmist writes, 'The LORD is merciful and gracious, slow to anger and abounding in steadfast love *(hesed)*.'[52] God Himself privileges and prioritises the people dimensions, autonomy and community, because that is where and how *hesed* flourishes. The sanctity ethic has its place, but must never take priority. Therefore, Sabbath is made for human beings, and mercy comes before sacrifice. But the nature of human beings in this fallen world seems to be such that we get these priorities mixed up at times. This is not just a Pharisee problem – this is also our problem.

There are many implications arising out of what has been covered in this chapter, but one stands out for me. There is no more important occasion when mercy is so desperately needed than when someone is caught in a state of shame. It is that terrible topic that is our focus for the next few movements.

Something more to think about along the way

Church bulletins are fascinating documents – not for their prose and literary importance, but because of their social significance. In one church the accuracy of the information in the bulletin became almost a running joke. There, neatly typed out and presented, would be an order of service. Beside each item could be found the name of the person who was to take part in that bit of the service. But, on a very regular basis, the name was wrong – not because of a typographical or administrative error, but because the person hadn't turned up. It was almost routine for announcements to be made from the platform about who was missing and who was taking their place. This was often followed by vigorous shaking of several heads at the lack of organisation and commitment. Frustrations would be expressed, questions raised, people interrogated, competence doubted.

There were so many reasons that folks did not turn up – it was a bit like listening to pupils make their excuses as to why they had not completed their homework. Broadly speaking, they could be grouped into two categories. There were the 'naughty' ones that included those who had simply found something 'better' to do or who had double booked, those who were oblivious to their previously agreed involvement and those who decided that a warm, cosy bed was a more desirable place to be in that morning. In the second category were the ones who were feeling poorly, or there was a situation where a relative had been taken extremely ill and needed a visit, or there was a family crisis of other sorts.

Defending the recalcitrant group was, to be fair, difficult. But even when it was pointed out to the bulletin aficionados that so-and-so was ill, that did not seem to help. It was difficult not to conclude that what was important to them was the accuracy of the text in the bulletin, and not that one of their fellow members was in need. Now, I know these were caring and loving people; but it shows how the language we use can sometimes betray priorities that might not show us in the best light.

[1]For an overview of Roman taxes, see William Barclay, *The Daily Study Bible: The Gospel of Matthew, Volume 1: Chapters 1-10* (Edinburgh: The St Andrew Press), pp. 329, 330.

[2]Matthew does not explicitly identify it as his house; however, Mark and Luke both tell us that it was Levi's house, a name attributed to Matthew: Mark 2:15-22; Luke 5:29-39.

[3]Matthew 9:11

[4]As Weber proposes, 'Their use of the title "teacher" may have been sarcastic. It was generally assumed that such a righteous man as a Jewish teacher would refrain from associating with society's undesirables. Their question was mocking and critical.' See Stu Weber, *Holman New Testament Commentary: Matthew* (Nashville, TN: B&H Publishing Group, 2000), p. 125.

[5]Both groups are discussed in Craig L. Blomberg, *Matthew: An Exegetical and Theological Exposition of Holy Scripture* (Nashville, TN: B&H Publishing Group, 1992), p. 156.

[6]Luke 7:36; 11:37-54; 14:16-24

[7]Yair Furstenberg, Joseph Sievers, and Amy-Jill Levine, 'The Shared Image of Pharasaic Law in the Gospels and Rabbinic Tradition', in: *The Pharisees* (Grand Rapids, MI: William B. Eerdmans Publishing, 2021), pp. 119-219 (p. 205)

[8]Weber, p. 125

[9]As Beck suggests, 'Jesus doesn't purify the sinners. The sinners make Jesus unclean' – Beck, pp. 3, 4.

[10]See 1 John 1:7, for example.

[11]Matthew 9:12

[12]Matthew 9:13

[13]Matthew 12:2

[14]Matthew 12:3, 4

[15]1 Samuel 21:3

[16]This is emphasised twice in verses 4 and 6.

[17]Leviticus 24:5-9; Paul V. M. Flesher, 'Bread of Presence', in: *The Anchor Bible Dictionary, A-J*, edited by David Noel Freedman and Gary A. Herion (New York, NY: Yale University Press, 1992), pp. 780, 781

[18]John Koenig, 'Hospitality', in: *The Anchor Bible Dictionary, A-J*, edited by David Noel Freedman and Gary A. Herion (New York, NY: Yale University Press, 1992), p. 229

[19]By reputation, 'Saul has killed his thousands, and David his tens of thousands.' Foreskins of two hundred dead Philistines provided the dowry for Micah (1 Samuel 18:7, 27, 30).

[20]Space does not allow for all the dynamics in the story to be unpacked – for example, the relevance of the threatening presence of Saul's man Doeg, as recorded in 1 Samuel 21:7. For more, see Keith Bodner, *1 Samuel: A Narrative Commentary* (Sheffield: Sheffield Phoenix Press Limited, 2008), p. 225.

[21]1 Samuel 21:4

[22]1 Samuel 21:2

[23]It is argued that Ahimelech acted as if the young men existed and so needed food – see Craig S. Keener, *Matthew* (Downers Grove, IL: InterVarsity Press, 1997), p. 355.

[24]This is the case because of the reference 'the day it is taken away' in 1 Samuel 21:6 – see Alter, p. 81.

[25]William Barclay, *The Daily Study Bible: The Gospel of Matthew, Volume 2: Chapters 11-25* (Edinburgh: The St Andrew Press), p. 24; see also George R. Knight, *The Abundant Life Bible Amplifier: Matthew* (Boise, ID: Pacific Press Publishing Association), p. 136.

[26]Although the David incident may have occurred on the Sabbath, as that is when the bread was changed.

[27]Matthew 12:5

[28]R. T. France, *The Gospel According to Matthew: An Introduction and Commentary* (William B. Eerdmans Publishing, 1985), p. 204

[29]When we looked at this before, we found this to be unsatisfactory, not least because it turns God into a dictator and us into passive followers – see Movement 2.

[30]Knight, p. 137

[31]Note that this is not the same 'divinity' that Shweder proposed, but God Himself.
[32]Flavius Josephus, *Antiquities, XV.11.3*
[33]Jeremiah 32:37, 38; Zechariah 8:8; Ezekiel 11:20
[34]Matthew 12:6
[35]Mark 2:27
[36]As France writes, this 'is a statement of priority rather than of mutually exclusive options' - R. T. France, *Mark (New International Greek Testament Commentary),* (Grand Rapids, MI/Cambridge, UK: William B. Eerdmans Publishing, 2002), p. 147.
[37]Exodus 20:8-11; Deuteronomy 5:12
[38]Isaiah 58:13
[39]Leviticus 26:2
[40]Matthew 12:7
[41]France, *The Gospel According to Matthew*, p. 326
[42]Matthew 23:5, 15, 23, 25
[43]Matthew 23:23
[44]Matthew 23:23
[45]Hosea 6:6
[46]Beck, p. 83
[47]David Allan Hubbard, *Hosea: An Introduction and Commentary* (InterVarsity Press, 1989), p. 137
[48]Philip J. King, *Amos, Hosea, Micah: An Archaeological Commentary* (Philadelphia, PA: Westminster John Knox Press, 1988), p. 89
[49]'This entire section has been building to this central verse, and much of the next section looks back to it' - Bruce C. Birch, *Hosea, Joel, and Amos* (Louisville, KY: Westminster John Knox Press, 1997), p. 69.
[50]King, p. 90
[51]Note that this 'does not mean that Hosea regarded sacrifice or ritual worship as intrinsically bad, and it should not prompt us to suppose that the path to spirituality is to overthrow all liturgy and formal worship'. See Duane A. Garrett and Paul Ferris, *Hosea, Joel: An Exegetical and Theological Exposition of Holy Scripture* (Nashville, TN: B&H Publishing Group, 1997), p. 161.
[52]Psalm 103:8

From shame to mercy

My first school was secreted away deep in the grim suburbs of 1970s North London. Most of my memories of those days are hazy and fading. Old school photographs help remind me that I was kitted out in a navy-blue jumper; grey, knee-length trousers; white shirt; and blue-and-red tie – but the names of the teachers and fellow pupils are long gone.

There is one episode that remains crystal clear in my mind, however: 'Go and get your PE kit, get changed, and report to Mr Jones.'[1] The instruction from my form teacher that sets things in motion seems to come out of the blue to me. This is to be my first ever physical education lesson. I am bewildered and bamboozled, because I have no idea what a PE class is, or that I am scheduled to have one. I search vainly and frantically through my new school bag for the black shorts, white singlet and cheap plimsolls that are *de rigueur* for school children undertaking physical activities at the time. Returning empty-handed, I have the fearful task of delivering the news to the aforementioned Mr Jones. As he stands over me like a tower block, I suddenly become tongue-tied and hesitant as I inform him, 'I . . . I don't . . . I don't have my kit with me, sir.'

The reactions to such misdemeanours are different now that we are well into the twenty-first century. In this electronic age, texts and emails are sent reminding parents of their duties in making sure their offspring turn up to school with the correct gear. In these more enlightened times, errant children are likely kept back in a classroom as punishment. And, if that classroom has a view of fellow pupils enjoying themselves outside, all the better to hammer home the lesson not to forget your kit next time. But, in the seventies, things were different.

'OK,' comes the response from Mr Jones, 'you'll just have to do the lesson in what you have. Strip down to your pants and vest.'[2] I hesitate, not sure I have heard him correctly. Showing me the way, two other forgetful boys have obediently started to remove their outer clothes, and so, reluctantly, I do the same. To this day, I am thankful that I was not alone in this predicament, and eventually the three of us stand there in our underwear. We are not naked, but it feels like it. Mr Jones proceeds to walk us out through the school and onto the playground. As we march behind him, I am acutely aware of the large windows to my right that offer prime viewing opportunities for any number of staff or pupils who wish to see our humiliation.

Mr Jones stops at a bench at the top end of the playground. I sit at the far left, my fellow 'criminals' to my right. As the others come out in their regulation plimsolls and shorts, the three of us instinctively sit there cross-legged, arms folded, in an anxious attempt to cover ourselves. Some of our classmates consider this a chance to have some fun and make it quite clear that they think it is hilarious that we are being made to sit there in our underwear. As one, our faces turn that little bit more crimson, and we cringe with just a bit more intensity in a fruitless attempt to make ourselves smaller and less of a target. The one moment of slight relief comes when Mr Jones barks an order for our 'admirers' to get on with what they should be doing. At last, we are left in peace to contemplate our plight. How do we feel, sat there on that bench? Uncovered? Yes. Degraded? Absolutely. Ashamed? Of course. Nowadays, there would be an outcry followed by an investigation because children have been treated in this way. But then it was common for shame to be used to control, and for children to be recruited as an example for others. And boy did it work. Never again in that class was a single PE kit missing when required.

Shame does not get talked about much, despite it being part and parcel of everyday existence. No one sits us down and explains what it is, how it will make us feel, and how to deal with it once its terrible effects kick in, even though 'shame is both ubiquitous in its presence (there is no person or experience it does not taint) and infinitely shape-shifting in its presentation.'[3] Shame is not, as some might believe, confined to the weak and susceptible. Rather, to experience shame is to be human.[4]

Shame is easily confused with guilt, which is why they are often discussed together. Simply put, guilt makes it all about what I have done or not done and the person wronged, so directing our attention outward. Shame's gaze is inward, making it all about me.[5]

Suppose little Jimmy steals an apple from Granny Smith. He is feeling guilty, which means he is focused on addressing Granny's loss. He repents of his wrongdoing and makes reparations by replacing the missing fruit. Jimmy turns his life around by vowing never to steal fruit again. Granny forgives him, and they hug. The actions Jimmy needs to take to address his guilt are straightforward and easily understood. More than that, the actions are therapeutic, lead to a resolution and allow him to maintain his sense of self and self-esteem. For these reasons, psychologists prefer guilt to shame.

Christians, too, are fond of guilt. It is the dominant way of addressing the problem of sin that is explored in sermons, songs and prayers. We talk and sing about guilt being carried, brought to Jesus and removed. We are delivered or freed from guilt. Guilty people with guilty consciences bring their guilt to the foot of the cross. Thus, Jesus takes centre stage, standing in for us where we are unable to stand for ourselves so that a renewed life can be ours. And, 'If we confess our sins, he who is faithful and just will forgive us our sins and cleanse us from all unrighteousness.'[6]

However, this way of referring to guilt can be so action-oriented that it can come across as rather mechanical. There is more than a hint of this when parents teach their children to apologise. The offending child is dragged before the person they have wronged and is told, 'Say you're sorry.' Their tone and body language advertise their reluctance, so it is likely that they are just going through the motions. Gritted parental teeth are in view as the familiar follow-ups are uttered: 'Say it like you mean it!' or, 'Look like you mean it!' The message is that it is not enough to be guilty – the child needs to *feel* guilty as well. This may be why some speakers and preachers feel it necessary to attempt to invoke an emotional response in their listeners by using highly manipulative phrases such as, 'Every time you sin, you nail Jesus to the cross.' I remember hearing this for the first time and being frozen to the spot, horrified that I could be party to one of the most sadistic ways of killing a person ever conceived by human beings. The problem is, this does not make people feel guilty. Instead of focusing on the person I have wronged (God) and the things I have done, I look at myself. In turning the focus inward, I start to examine how awful a person I must be to have done this. I am no longer looking to Jesus, who offers the complete solution. I look at myself and I feel ashamed.

So, we may sing, '*God forgave my sin in Jesus' name; I've been born again in Jesus' name*,'[7] but it does not necessarily help those of us who are in a state of shame. And that is because, when it is stated, 'You are forgiven,' you are 'dealing with the act, but not always with the shame that underlies the act'.[8] Look closer and the problem is not that I have done something wrong – it is me telling myself that *I am* something wrong.

Unlike being taught to ask for forgiveness to deal with our guilt, no one talks or walks us through how to deal with shame. Oftentimes we do not know how. In many ways, shame is more animalistic, irrational and invasive than guilt. Shame creeps up on us unannounced, hijacking our emotions and forcing that turn inwards. Shame does this by holding up a mirror for me to evaluate myself – a mirror from which I will do my utmost to escape. Because, like the distorted images in the house of mirrors at a funfair, the picture that shame wants me to see is warped and unflattering. It highlights and amplifies that which I like least about myself. Shame does not want me to see the best of myself. Rather, it wants me to see the worst and to think that is all others see too.

Shame is hard to pin down, but can be grouped into three categories. There is the fleeting sense of shame that brings about a degree of social control. This is the sort of shame that stops people committing incest or indulging in inappropriate displays of nudity, for example. But, despite the positives, it is debatable whether using shame to control in this way is desirable or effective.[9] Then there is shame that is temporary but damaging. It results in unwelcome behaviour and outcomes, and, if it persists, becomes chronic shame. Chronic shame is an ongoing state that 'represents a significant negative condition in our society. It is a condition of polluting, defiling unwantedness that alienates people and groups from themselves and from society.'[10] In attempting to define shame, scholars have come up with a list of descriptive words that brings together the very worst of human experiences.

DIRTY, DEFILED, UNWANTED, DEMEANED, EXPOSED, ON SHOW, FOUND OUT, INSUFFICIENT, SELF-JUDGED, UNDIGNIFIED, REJECTED, INADEQUATE, REPULSED, DEFECTIVE, UNWORTHY, BLAMED, INVALID, LONELY, UNTRUSTED, DESPAIRING, PARALYSIS, CONTEMPT, POWERLESSNESS, IMPOTENT, HELPLESS, NUMBNESS, BURNING, DEFECTIVE, INCOMPETENT, UNDESIRABLE, UNLOVABLE, UNLOVED, ABANDONMENT, DESPICABLE, FAILURE, SCORN[11]

According to the Bible, shame appears early in the story of human beings. It accompanies the serpent as it craftily introduces doubt into the mind of the as-yet-unnamed woman in Genesis 3. 'Did God say, "You shall not eat from any tree in the garden?"'[12] The serpent is not openly challenging the Creator here. On the surface, it is an innocent enquiry. But we know it is dripping with cunning and leading somewhere – indeed, it is the very definition of a leading question. So, when I listen to the serpent, I hear his scepticism loud and clear. His voice is smooth and alluring, but the implied question is, 'Did God *really* say that?' or, 'Is that what God *actually* said?' The woman is being tested on her ability to recall God's words. Is it her memory that is at fault, or is the serpent on to something here? We know what an effective answer should be. It should be a short and to-the-point 'No!' Nowhere does the Bible say that God uttered anything like that. Even though I am tempted each time I read the story to shout at the page, 'Say no, and walk away,' it will do no good. She has been drawn into a conversation and chooses to engage. 'We may eat of the fruit of the trees in the garden; but God said, 'You shall not eat of the fruit of the tree that is in the middle of the garden, nor shall you touch it, or you shall die.'[13] Eagle-eyed readers will have spotted the inclusion of a superfluous 'touch'. We have yet another thing in this conversation that God did not say. God did not ban anything other than eating the fruit of the tree. Touching the fruit has not got a mention. What does this added injunction say about the woman's recall, and what does it say about her relationship with God?

Having reeled the woman in, it is now time for the artful and mischievous serpent to bring shame into play. Now, too, is the snake's rebellion out in the open as God is blatantly contradicted. 'You will not die; for God knows that when you eat of it your eyes will be opened, and you will be like God, knowing good and evil.'[14] When discussing temptation, this is the go-to story. The serpent is dangling before the woman the possibility of gaining opened eyes, being like God and knowing good and evil. He makes it sound exciting.

I will always remember having temptation and sin explained to me at school. This was one of those boys-only lessons that had you questioning what we were going to learn that girls could not. Temptation, we were told, is standing on a street corner on a windy day and noticing that a girl's skirt has blown up around her waist. Sinning is standing on a street corner on a windy day waiting for skirts to flutter and rise. Growing up, it seemed to me that sin was often discussed in a way that made it seem enticing and attractive. After all, temptations are, by definition, tempting. The teacher did try to balance things by delivering stern warnings about giving in to temptation and leading a life of ribaldry, licentiousness and ruin . . . but that did not quite take the shine off. What we needed to hear about was shame. Taking shame into account helps reveal the degrading nature of temptation and evil, and the misery it brings to human existence.

Shame does not want us to focus on what we have, but what we lack. The woman does not have opened eyes, is not like God, and does not know all that she could. Even as the serpent is putting his offers on the table, he is concurrently telling her that she is blind, limited and ignorant. The message is coming through loud and clear that, as she is, she is not good enough. Shame is exceptionally good at this. It gnaws away at our self-esteem and tells us that we are inadequate. Shame is at work in the same unrelenting way to this day. There are so many opportunities to feel deficient and incompetent: not good enough as a parent, a son or daughter, not good enough for someone to love, not good enough at home, at work, at study, at play, and at church. You see, shame wants us to base who we are on what we do, accomplish and have. So we go about doing, accomplishing and having, believing that these actions will at last help us escape our shame.

So now, heavily influenced by shame, the woman starts to base who she is on what she does, so she does something. We know what comes next. We are part of a group that is numbered in the billions who live out the consequences. We know that suffering, pain and tears will become woven into the fabric of life. We know that children will die young and the old will die lonely. So it is painful to watch as she does indeed touch the fruit, which is not prohibited, and eats it, which is. This is not a moment to apportion blame: either to the woman who takes the lead, or to the man 'who was with her' yet does nothing but comply.[15]

Shame gets right down to work now. Eyes that were delighted by the sight of the tree and its enticing fruit are now opened, 'and they knew that they were naked'.[16] Having read Genesis 2:25 means that this is not news for us, but it is news for them. Now they *feel* their nakedness. They are on show and exposed; nothing is hidden; and all that there is about them is ready for scrutiny and judgment. This is like a bad dream, and in response they are inclined to do as we all do on this side of the fateful fruit-eating. There are a few options; but they do not dig a hole and jump into it. Neither do they self-consciously fold their legs and cross their arms, cringing in the hope of making themselves smaller and less conspicuous. On this occasion, they seek to cover their shame with foliage. Yet shame is not so easily overcome. These garments bring little relief, and soon turn out to be inadequate.

God turns up, walking in the cool of the evening breeze. As He does so, shame is investing further time in the couple's case, and they do what countless humans who are ashamed have done ever since – they hide. If an objective of evil is to break relationships apart, then shame is the perfect partner-in-crime. It steps in between us and others, and pushes and pulls until relationships are threatened and eventually start to fracture. Here, shame steps between the Creator God and the son and daughter it seems He has only just brought into being. It can be between any two or more people – shame is not bothered. Shame is promiscuous, indiscriminate and insatiable. In seeing that they are naked, the first couple have looked at themselves, and they do not like what they have become. They do not want others, especially God, to see their shameful state; so they conceal themselves behind yet more foliage. Let this state of affairs continue, and an ongoing situation, where shame is allowed to do its worst, results in social isolation and exclusion. Ultimately, shame desires that we get to a place where we cannot abide the company of others at all. 'It is not good that the man should be alone,'[17] God has declared, but shame has other ideas. It deceives its victims, persuading them that isolation is the only way forward.

But the woman and the man are not quite at that stage, and shame is not yet finished. God calls out with a question that is not so much about geographical location as it is about their state of being. 'Where are you?'[18] They are not in a good place psychologically or spiritually. The man's response is as inadequate and feeble as their attempts to cover themselves: 'I heard the sound of you in the garden, and I was afraid, because I was naked; and I hid myself.'[19] Despite the frantically sewn-together fig leaves they have fashioned, fear lingers and nakedness is still experienced. Shame is generating a feeling of exposure even as the man and woman are apparently covered. Here, then, is a hint at the most terrible aspect of being caught in a state of shame. Try as we might to evade its clutches, when we think we have dodged it, it is right there, hovering over us.

Shame is relentless, and is not letting up quite yet. It produces two common reactions. One response sees us lashing out in anger and fighting back. Shame persuades us to pass on the negative feelings we have about ourselves to others. It assures us that we will feel better about ourselves if others also feel bad. If we feel ashamed that someone has criticised our child's behaviour and, by implication, our parenting, we might be tempted to respond by telling them how terrible a mother or father they are. If someone catches us with our hand in the cookie jar, we can be tempted to remind them of the several occasions we have seen them helping themselves to the contents of the stationery cupboard. But this does not make us feel better. If anything, we feel worse. Lashing out never works, and by the time we work that out, it is too late. Relationships are damaged, sometimes permanently. Shame is getting its way, revelling in the spiralling effect that happens as recrimination and accusations get thrown around.

The other common response is to blame someone else. This is where we avoid taking part or full responsibility for what we have done. The hope is that, by passing on the blame, the accompanying shame will also find a new host. 'To blame another for one's own exposure is a convenient way of avoiding responsibility for one's own actions. It shifts the focus of attention away from the self and the perceived threat to that self, and places it firmly upon the shoulders of another.'[20] This is the method chosen by the man and the woman. The man blames the woman, saying, 'The woman whom you gave to be with me, she gave me fruit from the tree, and I ate.'[21] The woman blames the serpent: 'The serpent tricked me, and I ate.'[22] Shame has flooded their senses and their thinking, overwhelming them so they are in no state to bear responsibility for what they have done. They already feel bad enough about themselves as it is – taking responsibility is too much to ask. To blame another for what we have done never goes down well. Once again, relationships are harmed and damaged. Once again, shame is not so easily avoided or discarded. It wins whichever way we turn. For the woman and the man, this was all brought on by disobeying God's command; but, sometimes, we find ourselves in a state of shame and do not even know why or how. At other times, we find ourselves in such a state through circumstances way beyond our control.

One of my grandfathers was born at the turn of the twentieth century – just a couple of years after Queen Victoria passed away. British society was still dominated by Victorian values and practices that, from a modern perspective, seemed to have people walking around in moral straitjackets. Society as a whole was built upon a class system that kept people in their place and defined appropriate behaviour. So, on the surface, at least, there was a strict code of ethics that preached sexual restraint. His mother, my great-grandmother, was born in the 1880s. One of three children, her younger sister died by the age of six, and both her parents followed soon afterwards, succumbing to all-too-common respiratory diseases. With no one else to look after them, she and her elder brother were placed in rough, tough Victorian orphanages in the Sheffield area. Escaping the orphanage as soon as she came of age, she slowly made her way south, ending up in service in a house in Edgbaston, Birmingham. While there, she gave birth to my grandfather. She named him after her brother, who would go on to die in the trenches in the First World War less than a decade later.

I heard not one bit of this story from Grandpa. He never discussed his roots, his family, or what it was like when he was growing up. As a family, we did not know anything about his background until I undertook some genealogical research. The reason for this is easy to guess. When I got hold of a copy of Grandpa's birth certificate, it had the name of his mother and her occupation, but the spaces for the father's details were blank. My grandfather was conceived out of wedlock, as they used to say, and was the very definition of a bastard. Such children were illegitimate by name and nature, and often unwanted. 'Illegitimacy was a taint that could destroy a woman's life, forever damage her child, wreck her siblings' prospects in marriage, even harm the family business.'[23] At the time, to be born in such circumstances was to have a social stigma cast over you that was never to leave. Grandpa was born into a state of shame and remained there, not just unwilling but unable to even begin to talk about it.

So what could Grandpa have done about his situation? Was there any hope of him overcoming the shame that accompanied him from the moment of his birth? I believe that he did not talk about his background because he could not do anything about it. He could not go back in a time machine and persuade his mother to get married before conceiving him. It was not an option to return to the 1880s, administer antibiotics and other modern drugs to his grandparents so they did not die of consumption, and so allow his mother to benefit from growing up in a more stable and supportive environment. There was nothing he could do about his mother leading what would have been regarded as a promiscuous lifestyle – one that resulted in two children, neither of whom knew their fathers. He was born into shame, and he had to live with that shame.

And this is what shame is brilliant at. It persuades us that there is no hope, because the only way out of shame is for the shame-causing events not to have happened in the first place. The story of my grandfather also demonstrates that we can experience shame without guilt. But guilt rarely, if ever, stands alone, unaccompanied by shame. Little Jimmy does not just feel sorry that he has stolen Granny Smith's apple, which is a guilt-based reaction: Jimmy also feels ashamed for being the sort of person who steals apples from elderly women in the first place. He can repent of his wrongdoing, make reparation and seek forgiveness – but this will not address his shame. It is the same for all of us who 'fall short of the glory of God'.[24] There is the popular forensic or substitutionary model of the atonement that describes how we can make ourselves right with God, but that is only a partial solution. It is because of shame that the simple statement that 'in Christ all is forgiven' is unlikely to resonate. 'Shame does not respond to legal solutions.'[25] Little Jimmy can deal with his guilt, but it seems that his shame will only disappear if it could somehow be arranged that he had not taken that apple in the first place.

My grandfather's situation helps to demonstrate the amorphous nature of shame. Was he guilty of anything? No! He was a victim of circumstance. He had no guilt with which to deal. He had nothing of which to repent, and could not ask for forgiveness. Shame can worm its way into our lives whether we have done anything wrong or not. Even worse, we can feel ashamed and have no idea why.

Sat on that bench in the school playground, dressed only in my underwear, I looked into the distance, praying for this ordeal to be over. But then I spotted someone exiting the school building. She walked with a sense of purpose, and I watched every step she took as it became clear she was headed for my fellow bench-warmers and me. It turned out to be our form teacher. The look in her eyes was so different from the scorn and contempt on the PE teacher's face. Hers was a face full of compassion . . . and something else. It turned out that she had raided the lost property box, and she hurriedly passed a spare pair of shorts to each of us. Just that one item of clothing made the difference. Immediately, our feelings of humiliation and shame at being exposed melted away. We were back to being part of everyone else.

I guess I can understand a little of what Adam and Eve felt in Genesis 3. After the disobedience and the shame come judgment and consequences.[26] I am sure they could not wait for their intense ordeal to be over. But, if we keep reading, we get to the moment when the tension is finally released. It is the most touching scene in the Bible so far – one that reveals so much about God's character. 'And the LORD God made garments of skins for the man and for his wife, and clothed them.'[27] Much is made of the theological significance of God making the first sacrifice so the couple can have clothing. But continue to view this story through the lens of shame, and we get a different perspective. The man and the woman were unable to cover their own shame – their attempts were pitifully inadequate. It turns out that what was needed was what they had been desperately trying to avoid by hiding behind trees. In times of shame, we need someone to be there for us and with us, even as we feel utterly helpless and alone. In my imagination, God puts His arms around them in a moment of compassionate intimacy as He helps them get dressed. They are no longer in the ideal state of being naked and not ashamed – but now they have experienced what I experienced all those years later, because that something else on my form teacher's face was mercy.

Something to think about along the way

Bence Nanay, who lectures at the Universities of Antwerp and Cambridge, tells the story of how one day he is sitting on the subway and observes a female passenger boarding the train.[28] *She has two choices of seat: a spacious one right next to him, or a constricted seat between two women. He cannot help but notice that she chooses the latter. He speculates that the reason she selects that particular seat is because men have a reputation as sexual predators – not least because of the publicity then arising out of the #MeToo movement. His response is to feel shame: not because he is a sexual predator, but because he is a man, and so is viewed as potentially being a sexual predator. His wish is that more men similarly might feel such shame, and so have their behaviour regulated that women are treated appropriately and can feel and be safer. This is, he asserts, an example of positive or healthy shame.*

While applauding his wish to see all men in society treat women appropriately, the issue is one of focus. If I am driven by shame, the right behaviour is brought about because of how I will be affected if I am caught or found out. Isn't a more biblically sound way to approach this to declare, 'I won't sexually abuse women because I have their best interests at heart?'

[1]Not his real name.

[2]Pants as in underwear, not trousers!

[3]Curt Thompson, *The Soul of Shame: Retelling the Stories We Believe About Ourselves* (Downers Grove, IL: InterVarsity Press, 2015), p. 25

[4]Apart from the 1 in 100 who are psychopaths. See Jon Ronson, *The Psychopath Test* (London: Pan Macmillan, 2011).

[5]For more on this, see Helen Block Lewis, *Shame and Guilt in Neurosis* (New York, NY: International Universities Press, 1984), p. 30.

[6]1 John 1:9

[7]From the song, 'God Forgave My Sin (Freely, Freely)', words and music by Carol Owens, copyright © 1974 Bud John Songs/Alliance Media Ltd.

[8]David M. Rhoades and Sandra Roberts Rhoades, 'Justification By Grace: Shame and Acceptance in a County Jail', in: *The Shame Factor: How Shame Shapes Society*, edited by Robert Jewett and Wayne Alloway (Eugene, OR: Wipf and Stock Publishers, 2010), pp. 86-102 (p. 89)

[9]For a discussion on this, see June Price Tangney and Ronda L. Dearing, *Shame and Guilt* (New York; London: Guilford Press, 2002), p. 130ff.

[10]Stephen Pattison, *Shame: Theory, Therapy, Theology* (Cambridge: Cambridge University Press, 2000), p. 186

[11]Taken from the overview given in: Pattison, *Shame*.

[12]Genesis 3:1

[13]Genesis 3:2, 3

[14]Genesis 3:4, 5

[15]Genesis 3:6

[16]Genesis 3:7a

[17]Genesis 2:18

[18]Genesis 3:9

[19]Genesis 3:10

[20]Stockitt, Robin, *Restoring the Shamed: Towards a Theology of Shame* (Cascade Books, an Imprint of Wipf and Stock Publishers, Kindle Edition), loc. 1163

[21]Genesis 3:12

[22]Genesis 3:13

[23]Deborah Cohen, *Family Secrets: The Things We Tried to Hide* (Penguin, 2013)

[24]Romans 3:23

[25]Robin Stockitt, *Restoring the Shamed: Towards a Theology of Shame* (Wipf and Stock Publishers, 2012)

[26]See Genesis 3:14-19.

[27]Genesis 3:21

[28]'#Metoo and the Psychology of Shame', *Psychology Today*: *https://www.psychologytoday.com/blog/psychology-tomorrow/201803/metoo-and-the-psychology-shame* (accessed 1 November 2019)

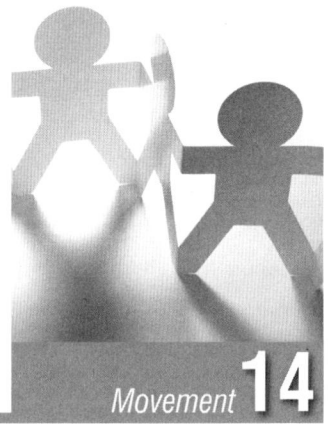

From disgust to shame

Jemima's face had disappointment, discouragement and disillusionment written all over it.[1] She had fallen pregnant. Normally such an event would be cause for rejoicing, but in this case it was a time of uncertainty, as there was a father, but no husband. Eventually she gave birth to a bonny, bouncing baby boy. Eventually she plucked up the courage to attend a church she had been avoiding for several months. She walked in holding the child whose arrival had changed her life forever. Unfortunately, the demands of a newborn baby meant she arrived later than she wanted to – much later. The service was well underway, and the back rows were full, so she was forced to walk to the front like it was a parade. As she did so, heads turned, revealing faces that sported frowns mixed with a hint of contempt. Even now, several months later, Jemima shudders, thinking about how awful it was that members had made their distaste and disapproval so obvious. 'How could they treat me like that?' she laments.

The Pharisees have demonstrated for us how prioritising the sanctity ethic automatically establishes boundaries. They've also shown how the influence of the purity metaphor means that boundaries act as a line of demarcation between what is pure and what is impure (see Figure 21). Once this happens, what is seen as impure is not benign, but is a contaminant that is to be avoided. Finally, if the pure is polluted by the impure, the natural response is disgust; just as if a fly had landed in our soup. So, when trying to make sense of what happened in this story, here is the harsh reality. When the unmarried woman walks into that church building with her newborn child, she is crossing a boundary. As she makes her way down the aisle, she is going deeper into what some think of as holy space. They are unconsciously seeing her as 'defiling' that space merely through her and her baby's presence. Because of this, both the space and the people who fill it are now less than they should be. They are being dragged down the scale and away from the heavenly realm. Hence, they are disgusted.

It is reasonable to suppose the members of that church, of any church, have a closet full of issues they carry with them into the church building and no one utters a word. Baffled by this inconsistency, members and pastors often ask why church communities are so 'hung up' on sexual sins, yet never seem to tackle more widespread issues such as gossip and backbiting. It all

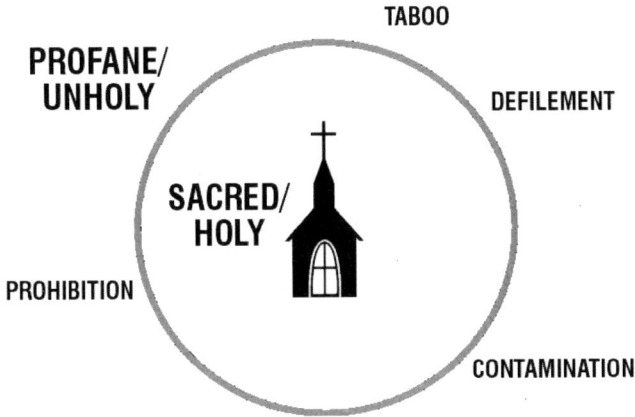

Figure 21: Sacred and profane space

comes down to the sanctity ethic and its associated metaphors. As Beck insightfully suggests, 'Sin categories that are psychologically structured by purity metaphors are experienced as "permanent" and are difficult if not impossible to rehabilitate. For sins of this nature, once purity is "lost" there is no going back. . . . This may be why sexual sins, which are often uniquely structured by the purity metaphor in many churches, elicit more shame and guilt.'[2]

The idea that one is forever tainted because of impurity goes hand-in-hand with shame's standard operating procedure. Shame makes us focus inwards and see ourselves as dirty, unclean and irredeemable. It follows that shame and a dominant sanctity ethic make excellent bedfellows (see Figure 22).

This is a potent mix . . . and not in a good way. In such an environment, shame, which is already bad enough, gets weaponised and is used to control others. It hangs over the whole piece like a malevolent judge waiting to prey on its next victim. It plays on our desire to avoid embarrassment or to be an object of disgust, to be downgraded and degraded. 'It means hiding part of who we are because we are sure we will be rejected for that part.'[3] Church communities are not immune to this, and, arguably, are particularly prone to it. And here's the problem: shame can become so embedded and influential that a shame culture develops.

Shame cultures are found in those groups that 'link what we do or produce to who we are. . . . This produces disengagement, blame, gossip, stagnation, favouritism and a total dearth of creativity and innovation.'[4] In more sinister terms, 'Christianity, like other social institutions, engenders and promotes shame, often to enhance order and control. Shame can be used as a very effective means of manipulating people into obedience and compliance in the interests of the powerful who identify those interests with

Heavenly

UP

Increasing
Contamination

Increasing
Purity

Increasing
Shame

DOWN

Earthly

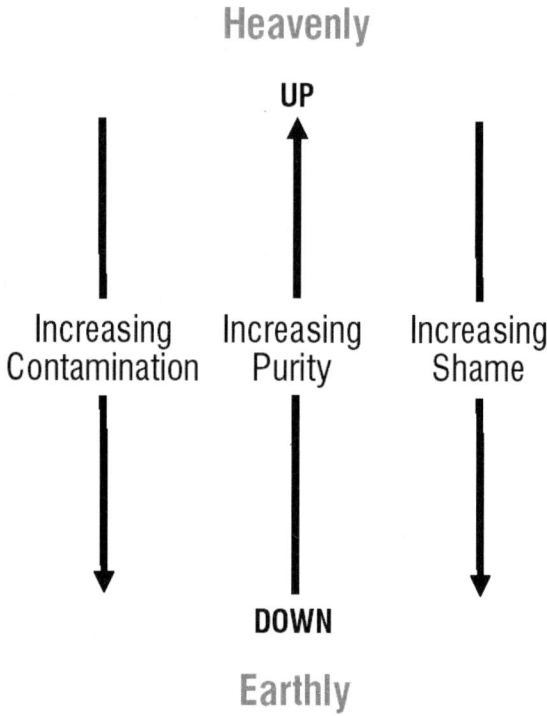

Figure 22: Shame, purity and the up-down scale

the will of God.'[5] Instead of being places where shame is extinguished and fought against, church communities can frequently be places where shame is devastatingly utilised.

Society in the Graeco-Roman world of Jesus' and Paul's day was heavily regulated by honour and shame. It was a complex arrangement that linked who a person was to society's values.[6] In simple terms, honour was all about social status, and a high level of honour could be had simply by being born into the right family and 'through meritorious deeds, or public performance'.[7] How *much* honour a person had was determined not by the person, but by the community that validated a person's societal aspirations. Shame, or dishonour, in this system, was the opposite of this, and in practice meant being 'thwarted or obstructed in one's personal claim to worth or status, along with one's recognition of loss of status involved in this rejection'.[8]

While it is difficult to clearly distinguish between the two, this is a different category of shame to the one that dominates now. In an honour system it is mostly regulated by society at large, whereas in our more individualistic culture it tends towards being private and internalised. Where there is a crossover, however, is where there is external disapproval generated from within a group or community of people . . . for this spawns 'pathogenic' shame.[9]

Pathogenic shame cultures are characterised by blaming, finger-pointing, putdowns, name-calling, favouritism and perfectionism. Shame is used to bring about desired behaviours by making people feel bad about themselves. Such a culture encourages us to base who we are on our performance, and if we do not make the grade then shame is the result.[10] Even as shame gleefully and dreadfully accompanied the entrance of evil into the human story, shame cultures throw the doors wide open and invite the serpent's weapon of choice right into the church community.

My wife recalls being told by one of her ageing relatives when she was barely a teenager, 'If you wear trousers to church, God cannot love you, and you won't get to heaven.' Apart from clearly being spiritual abuse, some assumptions are being made to underpin this statement. Firstly, the person assumes they know what God's will is regarding trouser-wearing in the twenty-first century. Secondly, they assume that God's love is contingent upon females not wearing trousers to church services. And, finally, they assume that this is an issue affecting salvation. If this happened to my wife now, I can imagine her forthright response. Back then, she dared not even consider going against what her seniors said for fear of the shame that would be showered upon her.

The issue of female sexuality that is being highlighted in the example above is significant, because shame has been used prodigiously in churches to control women and girls.[11] As it is, both males and females, their bodies and desires, have been regulated, especially in conservative churches, through the use of shame that has resulted in a diminished view of divinely created sexuality. This makes sex and sexuality out to be utilitarian at best, and to be avoided at worst.[12]

What does a church infected by a shame culture look like in practice? It is suggested that at least some of these things apply:
• Keeping human-made rules to be right
• Maintaining an expectation of total transformation, therefore perfection, at the moment of conversion
• Believing that members with known problems are an embarrassment, as faithful Christians should not have problems
• Avoiding intimacy in church relationships
• Emphasising externals: right dress, right Bible translation, right performance
• Working to reveal and rebut sinners
• Promoting the notion that true spirituality is to be equated with attendance at church services and events[13]

At its root, this can be seen to be an 'image of God' problem, because the god that is envisaged is a tyrannical one who bases his approval or disapproval on externals, and not on any worth he bestows upon individuals outside of their performance. It encourages those of us who 'feel we belong to the "normals" . . . to bolster our own fragile self-esteem by holding those who suffer in contempt, and continue to shame those who trigger our own vulnerabilities'.[14] In such a church, shame is working at peak efficiency to distance people and make church about something much less than community.

Something to think about along the way

At the age of 16, I transferred to the local boys' grammar school to study for my A levels. In many ways, it was a huge culture shock, not least because I was no longer attending a faith school. The whole ethos and educational philosophy to which I was now being subjected made it feel like I was on another planet. And, where previously the majority of my class had been attending the same church or at least churches from the same denomination, now I felt like I stood out like a sore thumb as, mercifully just for a short while, I was referred to as 'joey-deacon'.

Being brought up in a conservative Christian home meant I had never set foot inside a pub or off-licence. I, therefore, had no idea about alcoholic drinks, and could not begin to tell the difference between lager and beer, for example. Despite the boys in my class not yet being of an age where drinking was legal, they all seemed to have navigated that particular hurdle with consummate ease. I was frequently on the margins as they discussed drinking exploits that mostly focused on volume and variety. Aware of my ignorance in such matters, I just kept my mouth shut for fear that my lack of knowledge and naivety would be exposed.

A few of the boys used to collect beer mats: the coasters made out of card and printed with various drinks manufacturers' logos found in pubs up and down the land. On one occasion, as they discussed and swapped beer mats before class, I felt moved to ask a question. Even as the words left my mouth, I was regretting them. 'Aren't you stealing?' Most looked at me with what can only be described as cruel amusement. A kinder soul let me know this simply was not the case – they were free, almost throw-away items. Realising my mistake, and experiencing what I now understand to be shame, it took all that I had not to run out of the classroom. I was mortified. Now, this may seem to be a trivial occurrence on the surface; something to brush off and then move on. However, my Christian upbringing never made me feel more isolated and out of sync with what felt like the whole of the rest of society as it did at that particular moment in time.

What if the roles were reversed, I wonder?

[1] Not her real name.
[2] Beck, p. 8
[3] David A. deSilva, *Honor, Patronage, Kinship & Purity: Unlocking New Testament Culture* (Downers Grove, IL: InterVarsity Press, 2000), p. 90
[4] Brené Brown, *Daring Greatly: How the Courage to Be Vulnerable Transforms the Way We Live, Love, Parent, and Lead* (London: Penguin Life, 2015), pp. 64, 65
[5] Pattison, p. 229
[6] For a fuller explanation, see particularly chapter 1 in: deSilva, p. 23ff.
[7] Bill Warren, 'Shame and Honour', in: *Holman Illustrated Bible Dictionary*, edited by Chad Brand and others (Nashville, TN: B&H Publishing Group, 2015), p. 1443
[8] Betraying the gender-based sensitivities of the day, honourable acts were thought of as masculine, while shameful acts were regarded as feminine in nature. See Malina, p. 50.
[9] DeSilva, p. 90
[10] Brené Brown, pp. 64, 65
[11] Miryam Clough, *Shame, the Church and the Regulation of Female Sexuality* (London; New York: Routledge, 2017)
[12] Tina Schermer Sellers, *Sex, God, and the Conservative Church: Erasing Shame from Sexual Intimacy* (London: Routledge, 2017)
[13] Adapted from Sandra D. Wilson, *Released from Shame: Moving Beyond the Pain of the Past* (InterVarsity Press, 2002), p. 151
[14] Ian Mobsby, *Fresh Expressions of Church and the Kingdom of God* (Norwich, Norfolk: Canterbury Press, 2014)

From shameful me to the image of God

When Jesus and the lawyer cross paths in Luke 10, it is fascinating to compare and contrast the two. The lawyer comes across as a bundle of energy. This is evident in his posture as he stands up. Then there are the questions intended to catch Jesus out, followed by the need to save face and justify himself by testing Jesus further. By comparison, at least in my imagination, Jesus is an island of serenity. The only thing He does is speak as the lawyer frantically buzzes around Him like an irritated wasp.

Even though not all interactions are as confrontational, there is still a degree of measuring each other up when we meet someone for the first time. I was recently attending a Bible conference and experienced, once again, the social dance that takes place when two pastors first cross each other's paths. I started to find it amusing, because I could almost guarantee that the same pastor-specific questions would be asked, each time based on location, number and size of churches, and length of service. There might be other morsels of information passed to and fro, of course; but, by the end of the conversation, each will have been able to understand who the other is enough for social interactions to continue and for identification to be made should we meet again. This is normal. So, for instance, if two mechanics meet, they have their own list of questions, including, presumably, 'What do you work on?' and, 'Where do you stand on hydraulic versus pneumatic systems?' This is because categorising others is how we try to cope with living in a complex and chaotic world. We have to simplify, group and collate the mass of data that comes our way; otherwise we would be overwhelmed with information.

That is the upside. The trouble starts when I start to see my human identity and my sense of self-worth tied up in those categories. For pastors, it is easy to link our value to the location and size of the churches we serve. For others – including pastors, of course – it might be connected to qualifications, income, size of house, physical attributes, talents, gifts, number of children, job title, bank balance and so on. And here is where shame is able to worm its way in. Once our self-worth becomes linked to our actions and the results of those actions, we will never be satisfied. Shame is once again able to reign supreme, because it revels, as we have seen, in us basing who we are on what we do or have done.

It is easy to write about this, but not so easy to counter. For example, in the UK, as in other countries, the idea behind redundancy means it is not the person who is being let go, but the job or role they are doing that ceases to exist. This should enable employees to divorce themselves and their personal identity from their job. However, in reality, there is often the suspicion that there is something else going on, something personal. This results in 'an ingrained sense of shame in the belief that *we* are not wanted'.[1] So shame gets to work, this time in the form of a voice that nags, 'The employer is saying they are making my position redundant . . . but that is just a legal nicety. Everyone knows they are really letting *me* go . . . I am the one who's being rejected.'

No area of life is immune from this way of thinking. If I regard myself as a wit and raconteur and the audience is not amused and enthralled, it is I who am the problem, and not my boring stories or poor jokes. If I think of myself as a wonderful chef and have prepared a cordon bleu meal, pouring my heart and soul into the taste combinations and presentation, but the dinner guests are unimpressed, it is not the menu with which they are struggling, but myself. Fail to separate my sense of worth from what I do and accomplish, and shame is always the winner. There is a terrible inevitability to this. I will never be able to achieve enough to satisfy shame's demands, and eventually my actions will let me down, and that means I will let myself down.

The good news is that the Bible offers a way out of this never-ending downward spiral. As Christians, our sense of identity and self-worth is based on being created in the image of God and the unique place we have in the created order. So important is it to understand this that the very first mention of humans in the Bible is, 'Let us make humankind in our image, according to our likeness; and let them have dominion over the fish of the sea, and over the birds of the air, and over the cattle, and over all the wild animals of the earth, and over every creeping thing that creeps upon the earth.'[2] These verses confirm that we are created as significant and special. No other creature is given the same level of attention and responsibility.

Even so, 'the image of God' is an easy phrase to say, but not so easy to understand. I grew up thinking that it meant having ten fingers and ten toes, two arms and two legs, and so on. This is a biomechanical understanding of the image of God based on having the right amount of flesh and bone in the correct configuration. But some of us have fewer than ten fingers or toes, and some have more. Are they somehow less in the image of God than those of us who can count to twenty on our hands and feet? Does it mean that if I lose a fingernail I am temporarily at a disadvantage? In response, I was informed it was the original design that means we are in God's image, but sin has done its thing so that even the most beautiful and sculptured of us never fully reflects the ideal. But this did not seem to stand up to scrutiny.

Ageing is both a privilege and an ordeal. As we get older, our gums recede, making our teeth unstable and causing them to look as if they have grown longer. Our jaw muscles lose about forty per cent and our jawbones twenty per cent of their mass, meaning our food needs to become softer and less chewy.[3] Particularly of importance for someone as short-sighted as I am, I recently learnt that the jelly-like substance, or vitreous humour, that makes up the majority of our eyeballs starts to thin and collapse away from the retina as we age.[4] Our eyes are amazing instruments, evidence of intelligent design.[5] But the older we get, the less our eyes will reflect that design. So, should I conclude that youngsters possessing vitreous humour with the correct consistency and revelling in 20-20 vision reflect God's image better than I do? Does the same go for those with healthy gums and good muscle mass?

This is not unsatisfactory because it is absurd. It is unsatisfactory because it bases who I am on my body, and shame loves that. We even have a new term for it – 'body-shaming'. It comes in many guises. People have been shamed because they eat too little or too much, are too small or too tall, look too thin or are too fat. If anyone falls outside what society regards as optimal, then, as Tamra Orr writes, 'You are at risk of being called names, having your intelligence and work ethic questioned, and, in general, being shamed for the body that you have.'[6] We see the tragic results of this all around us: depression, anxiety, eating disorders, self-harm and body dysmorphic disorder. The idea of basing our self-worth on our bodies feeds into the narrative where shame always wins. This is not to deny a holistic understanding of human beings – one that includes our 'spirit and soul and body'.[7] Neither is there a desire to downplay God as our Creator and Designer. It does, however, mean that our search for what the image of God represents needs to aim for something deeper.

Creationist or not, humans are seen as special. It is recognised that, of 'all the many millions of species on the planet, only humans have sequenced genomes, invented smartphones and composed moonlight sonatas'.[8] The author of that quote struggles to come up with an evolutionary explanation for this 'uncomfortable observation'. He concludes that, unlike other animals, we can share information accurately and build on others' knowledge, and it is this that allows us to achieve amazing things. His answer highlights three things that make the human race stand out: our disposition to create, communicate and achieve. To this list we also might add the ability to destroy, be curious, question, be aware, love and worship. Other species may show these characteristics in some form, but never to the same extent or with the same complexity. Is this because we are uniquely made in the image of God? It makes sense that God, who in Genesis 1:1 is first introduced as the Creator, would, in turn, create creators if they are to be in His image. It is evident that 'creativity is our birth right. It is an integral part of being human, as basic as walking, talking and thinking.'[9]

This seems to be getting us somewhere, until we remember that to base who we are on what we do is to allow shame to get its way again. If Jill is more creative, communicative and kind than John, does that mean that Jill is more in the image of God than John? If our self-worth is linked to this concept of God's image, then John's way of improving his self-worth is to do more of the right things. But, if he did, John would be playing into shame's hands. He would be doing his best, but, like Sisyphus, would always be required to do more.[10]

In his book on mortality, Atul Gawande throws us out into the road to be confronted by a juggernaut that represents the inevitable death we have no hope of avoiding. Biology and our bodies will let us down unless the Second Coming interrupts the process. In foraging for meaning among all the decay and dying, Gawande concludes that healthcare professionals have it wrong. They are not meant to keep us alive and healthy: rather, their aim should be 'to enable well-being; and well-being is about the reasons one wishes to be alive'.[11] Therein lies a path forward, one away from shame's obsession with well-doing and towards well-being.

Now, design is still important. Hence, we 'are the image of God insofar as we have received, are now fulfilling, and one day will fully actualise a divine design. And this design – God's intent for us – is that we mirror for the sake of creation the nature of the Creator.'[12] But seeking to reflect God's nature moves us away from doing to being, from looking on the outside to focusing on the inside, from the material to the spiritual. It is about who God is in Himself.

John gives a simple, beautiful and comprehensive answer as to who God is when he declares, 'God is love.'[13] Where the Good Samaritan practised *agape* love, now we get to understand that God is *agape* love. This is not in the sense that loving is something that God happens to do. Neither does John mean that 'love is God', resulting in God being some sort of ethereal principle and barely God at all. He is not telling us that God has the potential to love. Rather, John is telling us that God, by and in His very nature, is love. And, if 'God is love' is a foundational aspect of His nature, then there was never, and can never be, a time when God cannot be described as love.

For this to be something more than potential or a principle, God would, through eternity, need someone else to love. Remember, to practise *agape* love is 'to act intentionally, in sympathetic response to others, . . . to promote overall well-being'.[14] If *agape* requires a subject for it to be made real, there 'is a sense in which the fact that God is love requires that He be more than one Person'.[15]

Let us suppose that God is one Person. If so, there would have been a time before creation when God would have been alone. There would have been no one to love apart from Himself. To be and practise *agape*, His only option at this point is to create others to love. But now God is dependent upon His creatures to be who He is in Himself. This would call into question His very divinity, because God cannot depend on someone else to be God. So, what if God is two Persons? Now, God's love is more than potential, because there is Another to love – in fact, there is Another to both love and be loved. But, using a married couple as an analogy, if God were two Persons, this love has the potential to be closed off, out of reach, exclusive and intimate. Again, to open things up, God would have to create others.

However, all such objections and limitations are taken off the table if God is three Persons. The beauty of the doctrine of the Trinity is that God being three Persons in one generates a love that is accessible and available, and which means 'there is a dimension of openness and extension not necessarily found in a love relationship between two persons.'[16] Jesus gives us a glimpse of what this looks like from the inside where He reveals, 'The Father is in me and I am in the Father.'[17] Yes, Their relationship is close, but it is not closed. It is close because love so binds Them together that They are one. It is not closed, because I imagine God's love to be like a deluge of water that cannot be contained. As soon as we think that we have plugged the gap in one place, it bursts out in another, and then another, till it overwhelms us.[18]

This is what I find to be amazing and enlightening. To be in the image of God is not about being in the image of one person, but of a community of persons. Well-being, according to God's design, is to be 'found in living in social/spiritual relationships that are loving, trusting, and submissive to God and our fellow human beings'.[19] The implications of this are transforming. It means I cannot wholly reflect God's image on my own. It says that I am not fully who I can be as an individual on my own. It means that having the capacity and the potential to love is not enough. It tells me that my sense of identity is only capable of being fully expressed in relationship with God and others. It means that the task, or better the status, of image-bearing is not a solitary one.

We often talk about the image that we reflect being flawed, broken or shattered. Now, it follows that the image is damaged because true community is missing in my life: be it communion with God or with others. This concept is right there at the beginning where we are told that the man and the woman became 'one flesh' in the garden – a place where God is to be found walking.[20] Their marriage was about more than the two of them. This is not to deny them intimacy and closeness as a couple, but it does ensure that their love is not selfish.[21] As Ron and Karen Flowers write, 'The perfectly harmonious Trinity, Father, Son, and Holy Spirit, exemplifies the essence of self-giving love that is manifested in the fellowship of persons in relationship. As creatures made in the image of God (Gen. 1:26), the need for harmonious and loving relationships is integral to our very being.'[22] This does not mean that I, as an individual, get lost in the crowd. Rather, I am to relate to others to become fully who I am as an individual. That this continues to be God's ideal for humanity can be seen in the way that community blossoms into being in Revelation 21 as God's purposes are finally realised. In describing God's intentions for us, John does not suggest that our ultimate destination is a timeless, bodiless existence plucking lutes on clouds. No: he reveals that we will live life in a temple city on a newly recreated planet, living together with God and others.[23]

From Genesis to Revelation, the Bible tells a story and provides a view of the world that allows us to find our sense of meaning and purpose. Unlike so many self-help schemes, a biblical approach sees self-worth achieved not by an inward turn, but by an outward one. It is found in reflecting the nature of God by practising *agape*, an other-centred love. This helps explain the apparently contradictory nature of Christ's assertion that 'those who love their life lose it, and those who hate their life in this world will keep it for eternal life,' because it is paradoxically in turning outwards and away from self that true self is found.[24] Who I am is based on who made me and the system of interconnecting relationships within which God has placed me. To be immersed in this network is a state of being, not doing. Thus, we are to 'become a worthy self' rather than 'chase self-worth'.[25] Hence, a satisfactory sense of self is a by-product of this alternative pursuit that is Spirit-powered and not self-generated. It is the Spirit steering us away from pride to the humility necessary to achieve this end. Lastly, as we are made in God's image and are loved by God, we have the right, an obligation even, to love ourselves. We do so because we have extrinsic value, a value that comes from outside of us.

It is worth pausing and reflecting on how releasing this is. My failing an exam, or even failing to get the mark I want in an exam, does not mean I am a failure. It might mean I have failed to study hard enough or do not have a great memory. But this lack of preparation or recall does not diminish who *I* am. If my children misbehave in public and my lack of parenting skills are paraded for all to see, it does not mean that I am a terrible person. It could be that I may need to attend a parenting class, or I might just be having a bad parenting day. Likewise, if I pastor a small district with small congregations in an out-of-the-way place, it does not reflect on who I am as a person called by God.

Carrying around a picture of ourselves as divine-image bearers is one of the profound ways to combat shame in our lives. The challenge is to put it into practice. That is because shame does not let us off the hook so easily. But there is more that we can do to fight it, and that requires us to do the exact opposite of what shame wants us to do . . . but this takes courage and the right environment. This takes community.

Something to reflect upon along the way

Jay Adams tells the story of Midge, a single woman in her twenties who came to her for counselling.[26] *Midge has attended a Bible college and is now working as a secretary. In describing her situation and feelings, Midge says she is depressed, shy and lonely, further adding that 'I'm a nothing,' and 'I feel inferior.'*[27] *Midge's answers to her problems are that other people should be treating her better and nicer, and should make an effort to understand her.*

Adams suggests that her issues are made worse because she is reliant upon other people to provide her with a solution or solutions, rather than seeing a way forward based on her own attitudes. So, instead of waiting on others to put her right and give her what she thinks she wants, 'she must be made aware that she can reach out to others now, developing friendships out of serving others and showing love to them.'[28]*In other words, one way to combat shame is to be a neighbour!*

[1]Laurel Alexander, *Turn Redundancy to Opportunity* (Oxford: How To Books Ltd., 2003), p. 19

[2]Genesis 1:26

[3]For more effects of ageing, see Atul Gawande, *Being Mortal: Illness, Medicine and What Matters in the End* (London: Profile Books, 2014), pp. 29-31.

[4]Severe short-sightedness leads to greater risk of a detached retina.

[5]For example, see William A. Dembski, *Intelligent Design: The Bridge Between Science & Theology* (Downers Grove, IL: InterVarsity Press, 2002), p. 108f.

[6]Tamra B. Orr, *Combatting Body Shaming* (New York, NY: The Rosen Publishing Group, Inc., 2016), p. 6

[7]1 Thessalonians 5:23

[8]Kevin N. Laland, 'These Amazing Creative Animals Show Why Humans Are the Most Innovative Species of All', *The Conversation: http://theconversation.com/these-amazing-creative-animals-show-why-humans-are-the-most-innovative-species-of-all-75515* (accessed 13 April 2020)

[9]John Daido Loori, *The Zen of Creativity: Cultivating Your Artistic Life*, reprint edition (New York: Ballantine Books, 2005)

[10]Sisyphus was punished for being deceitful and proud by being compelled to roll a huge rock up a hill only for it to roll down every time it neared the top.

[11]Gawande, p. 259

[12]Stanley J. Grenz, *Theology for the Community of God* (Grand Rapids, MI: William B. Eerdmans Publishing, 1994), p. 177

[13]1 John 4:8, 16

[14]Oord, p. 47

[15]Millard J. Erickson, *Making Sense of the Trinity: Three Crucial Questions* (Grand Rapids, MI: Baker Academic, 2000), p. 58

[16]Erickson, p. 58

[17]John 10:38

[18]Or, as Gulley puts it, 'By definition the Persons of the relational Trinity have an inner history of reciprocal love for one another – a love that overflows into creation.' See Norman R. Gulley, *Systematic Theology: God as Trinity* (Berrien Springs, MI: Andrews University Press, 2003), p. 4.

[19]Woodrow Wilson Whidden, Jerry Moon, and John W. Reeve, *The Trinity: Understanding God's Love, His Plan of Salvation, and Christian Relationships* (Hagerstown, MD: Review and Herald Publishing Association, 2002), p. 240

[20]Genesis 2:24; 3:8

[21]For more on the Trinitarian basis for marriage, see for example Jack O. Balswick and Judith K. Balswick, *A Model for Marriage: Covenant, Grace, Empowerment and Intimacy* (InterVarsity Press, 2006).

[22]Ron and Karen Flowers, 'Marriage: Twin of the Sabbath, but a Day Older', *Ministry Magazine*, 76.8 (2004), 5-10, 29

[23]Revelation 21:22-26

[24]John 12:25

[25]Jay Edward Adams, *The Biblical View of Self-Esteem, Self-Love, Self-Image*, first edition (Eugene, OR: Harvest House Publishers, 1986), p. 120

[26]Not her real name. See Jay E. Adams, *The Christian Counselor's Casebook* (Grand Rapids, MI: Zondervan, 1986), p. 38.

[27]Jay Edward Adams, p. 40

[28]Jay Edward Adams, p. 122

From shame to vulnerability

I t is one of those prayer meetings where you wish they had given out back support to people of a certain age and cushions to everyone as they stepped through the door. The prayers are lengthy and all-encompassing. No minor concern is left unmentioned, no phrase unrepeated. The ability of some of the saints to pray at length with barely a hint of hesitation is both admirable and soporific. The fight not to nod off takes up the majority of the effort and most of the attention. But, in an instant, the atmosphere noticeably changes. The person praying has moved on to address some of the more personal issues being faced by members of the church community. *'Dear Lord, please help Jessica and Jim through this difficult period in their marriage.'*

Two sets of eyes flash open, instantaneously and simultaneously: Jim's because he has not realised until this very moment that he and his wife are going through a bad patch, and Jessica's because until now she has been completely unaware that the person praying knows about their marital struggles.

Before they have even begun to deal with the shock, the praying church member has moved on with their prayer. *'And, Lord, please help young Timothy, who has hit the bottle once again and rolls around the streets of the city like a ship in the storm. Please lay Your healing hand upon him and guide him back to the safety of Your harbour.'* Several people who thought they knew young Timothy well now realise that they know him just that little bit better.

'And, Lord, please remember our good sister, whose questionable deeds it would not be judicious for me to reveal at this time, but whose decisions leave her standing on the very brink of disaster.' As the speaker rolls the 'r' of the 'brink' for emphasis, single eyelids flutter open, almost in unison, almost involuntarily. And, almost as involuntarily, those unveiled eyes cannot resist the temptation to scan the room, to seek out a flushed face, an uncomfortable shifting in place, anything that means the identity of the good sister can be known – if not, for the moment, the nature of her potentially disastrous deeds.

This description of a prayer meeting is thankfully fictitious, but there is much about it that might seem familiar. The right words are there, mostly in the correct order and accompanied by appropriate sentiments . . . but it does not take an expert of Hercule Poirot's stature to detect that there is something about this that does not sit comfortably. For instance, how often are gossip and judgment about another's failings wrapped up in the nice, neat packaging of apparent Christian concern? Is it right to suspect that there can be a good dose of disapproval present even as words of comfort and care are uttered?

Admittedly, put any group of people together and they – or should that be 'we' – are almost inevitably going to start talking about each other. It often begins as the exchange of useful information, as part of that categorisation process referred to earlier. But gossip is there waiting in the wings, standing by to catch us unawares. Conversations can easily take a downward turn and get seasoned with negativity, salaciousness, even slander.

There is some evidence to suggest that gossip might be beneficial, as in the workplace it can help staff morale by getting people united behind certain 'causes'.[1] This idea has parallels with those who believe there are positive shame experiences. But just because something has a few good effects does not mean it should be given free rein. Permitting 'gossip in the workplace is like encouraging your employees to swim with sharks. . . . Gossip destroys trust, assails credibility, . . . undermines workplace performance, and can be nothing short of disastrous.'[2] These insights resonate with another commentator on the negative power of speech. James writes rather more poetically about 'how great a forest is set ablaze by a small fire! And the tongue is a fire. The tongue is placed among our members as a world of iniquity; it stains the whole body, sets on fire the cycle of nature, and is itself set on fire by hell.'[3] He goes on: 'No one can tame the tongue – a restless evil, full of deadly poison. With it we bless the Lord and Father, and with it we curse those who are made in the likeness of God.'[4]

This is not a modern issue, therefore, but a matter that has infected fallen humanity for millennia. And James's context reminds us that being a Christian does not automatically mean we are gossip-free. Indeed, there is an argument that Christians can be much worse where gossiping is concerned, because we get to add a little spice and heat. You see, Christians have standards against which we measure ourselves. Even then, it is much more comfortable and fun to see how others measure up. It is why Christians are frequently labelled as being hypocritical and judgmental. It is also why an elephant has taken up residence slap-bang in the middle of the room with a poster-sized label that says 'UNSAFE' stuck on its rump; for church communities are often the last place we are free to air our problems, issues and failings. It is that sanctity ethic doing its thing again, telling us that failing people should be kicked out, lest they drag everyone else down with them and contaminate the group. It reminds us that there are standards to maintain, and we can't let one person's downfall create a domino effect.

Sometimes, it seems we are more likely to get a sympathetic hearing in the local pub than in the local pew . . . and this is not limited to any one particular denomination or tradition. Just as I write these words, the Pope is in Bangladesh and has been moved to suggest that 'gossip is terrorism.' He goes on to encourage his church's adherents to 'bite your tongue. You might harm your tongue, but you won't harm your brother or sister.'[5] It is why you can find articles such as '5 Tips for Dealing with Gossip in the Church',[6] or 'The Three Breeds of Gossip' also found in church.[7] It is why there are dozens of books addressing how 'information' is recklessly and irresponsibly mishandled in a church context. In the one place where gossip should not be a problem, it appears to be rampant.

Churches need not be that way, of course. One of the most inspiring passages in the Bible about a church community's potential to offer places where humans flourish rather than being quashed is found in Galatians 6:1-10. It is interesting that such a positive passage is found in this particular letter. Paul is not at all happy with the churches in Galatia – some might say he is grumpy. Unlike in the letter to the Philippians we looked at earlier, for example, he does not feel in the mood to praise them. He has no time for niceties, and by the sixth verse of the first chapter he is berating the Galatian churches, explaining how dismayed he is by their 'turning to a different gospel'.[8] But, once we get to chapter 6, it is as if he has burnt off his frustrations enough to get down to practical matters. In doing so, he paints a beautiful and inspiring picture of a church community: one that is beguiling and transformative, restorative and communal.

For, in Galatians 6:2, he writes: 'Bear one another's burdens, and in this way you will fulfil the law of Christ.' On the face of it, what he is proposing sounds easy enough, even nice enough. *I am right here, we might think, with a whole armoury of tools at the ready to help you carry your burdens. I have an ear that is oh-so-sympathetic, a supportive smile, an arm that is consoling, and a hand that is ready to offer commiserating pats, or at least to reach into a pocket in which some spare change might be found.* And so we might be tempted to move on past this verse without acknowledging the fundamental problem we often have with it. To carry each other's burdens, we have to know what those burdens are in the first place. We have to understand what it is others are carrying around, squashed and pressed down with. We have to know to even begin to start to help. This means getting to a place with each other where we feel safe enough to share our problems.

As I look at the congregation when I speak, I sometimes wonder what burdens are being carried that remain hidden and out of sight. Some of us might carry burdens that seem as big as rocks, and see the local church as being the last place we are going to find burden-bearing assistance. We drag them around with us, every fibre of our being, every muscle and sinew screaming out at us to finally do something about the situation, because we know we are not strong enough to carry them on our own. But we think we have to endure, to continue to hide what's going on in our lives and how we really feel. It can even be the case that people are so used to us carrying our problems, our challenges, our baggage, that the weary, heavy gait we sport as a result is deemed to be simply normal.

Now we spot another elephant hidden behind the first. This time it is labelled 'SUPERFICIALITY'. Attend a church gathering, and you will hear the same exchange happening as if on repeat – I hesitate to call them conversations. They are short but not necessarily sweet, and consist of a question: 'How are you?' and a standard response: 'I'm fine, thank you.' Even as we utter the words and play our part in the performance, we are aware of the trivialness of it all. 'Fine' is so much simpler, less complicated, less risky to say than: 'I've had a terrible night's sleep because I am worried about my son shooting up ketamine. I now have a thumping headache and don't know where to turn to next.' Therein lies the challenge: to move beyond such banalities, to take risks, to take time, to assume that the person who is asking after our welfare is interested in the answer – the unedited, messy answer.

'Fake it till you make it,' they say, so there is often an extra accessory to acquire and utilise. As we have seen, there are those official and unofficial dress codes, but no one mentions that sometimes a mask is also required. It is the mask that backs up our assertion that we are just fine. It is possible to distract people with our masks, you see. It is our masks that allow us to perform and to conform to the expectations we inflict upon ourselves and our perception of what others require of us.

'Mask'
In my bedroom drawer, neatly tucked away,
What mask to church will I wear today?
There are four from which I have to choose,
But today I'll wear the one that hides the blues.
My smiley mask I've nearly worn out:
It hides so well my fears and doubts.

My spiritual mask works like a jewel:
It hides me when I've been mean and cruel;
The mask I call my 'ace in the hole'
Hides me when my heart is cold.
Sometimes I wish others could see
Right past the mask and into me.

And help me find my way back home
To God's dear arms from whence I've roamed –
But others seem to do so well,
My failures I wouldn't dare to tell.
Then the question to myself I ask:
I wonder if they too wear a mask?

by Cheryl A. Mariano (also known as 'Cheremiah')[9]

We are well into shame territory, of course. Shame loves it when we think we need to wear masks. Then we are saying to ourselves that as we are, as we really are, we are not good enough; so we attempt to hide our shame-filled selves, even as our troubles bubble away beneath the surface. Once again, we are basing who we are on what we do and have achieved. Such masks are one of the factors in making Paul's advice in Galatians 6:2 redundant. They prevent burden-sharing; *in extremis,* they prevent any sharing at all.

The burdens Paul is writing about in Galatians 6:2 have been assumed to this point. But what did he have in mind? There is a suggestion that Paul is referring only to financial burdens.[10] Using money to solve all our problems is a clean-cut solution, as our involvement can be at a distance and transactional. But it seems somewhat limiting for Paul to be suggesting that only the burdens that can be relieved by cold, hard cash are of concern here. If someone approaches us for help about a non-financial matter, are we supposed to turn them away? An alternative and more rounded approach is to view him as talking about 'the life I now live in the flesh' through having been crucified with Christ[11] – in other words, the burdens that naturally arise out of living life as a Christian on this planet in this age, including, but not limited to, 'food, clothing, shelter, the threats of violence and disease, the debilitating effects of poverty, and the fear of loss, isolation, and death'.[12] Thus, the burdens Paul was referring to are 'any oppressive ordeal or hardship that is difficult to bear'.[13]

There is also a time factor in play here. The Greek word translated 'burden' is *baros,* and it refers to the carrying of a heavy weight or stone a long way.[14] These are not short-term issues, therefore. They are ones that are overwhelming in nature. They have the ability over time to grind us down and tire us out. The answer to these sorts of problems is not to grit our teeth and push forwards through the pain barrier, buying into what has been referred to as the 'myth of self-sufficiency'.[15] The answer is to be found in a community – a community whose members take responsibility for themselves and others.

To see what sort of community Paul is imagining, it helps to look at the whole section in which Galatians 6:2 is set.[16] By doing this, we can see that Paul alternates between how the Galatian church members are to behave collectively and as individuals.[17]

Table 4

Verse	Responsibility	Action	Focus
6:1a	Group	Restore one another in a spirit of gentleness.	Transgressions
6:1b	Individual	Watch out that you are not also tempted.	Temptations
6:2	Group	Help carry each other's burdens.	Burdens
6:3-5	Individual	Test your own actions and carry your own load.	Personal loads/burdens
6:6	Group	Share all good things with your instructor.	The word

6:7, 8	Individual	Reap what you sow: how you sow affects how you reap.	Sowing to the Spirit
6:9, 10	Group	Do good to all, especially other Christians.	General good works

Once members of a Christian community, we are therefore responsible for and accountable to one another. What happens to you is as much my concern as what happens to me. What affects you affects me. And, by switching between community and individual roles, Paul ensures that we cannot think we can dump our burdens onto others; nor can we consider going it alone. There are things we need to do on our own behalf, even at the same time as we act responsibly towards others.

That is the ideal, but reality is something else altogether. For example, we will happily ask people to pray for certain situations and issues, but not others. Medical problems are fine, as long as they are not embarrassing like an STD or have anything to do with mental health concerns. Career or educational matters such as interviews or exams are acceptable, but getting demoted or sacked not so much. We will gladly pray for people caught up in natural disasters, but disasters brought on by gambling, alcoholism, abuse and broken homes rarely feature. In Galatians 6, Paul is pushing the boundaries, opening up spaces, breaking into our comfort zones. The whole context encourages us to go into those dark, hidden spaces and bring out things we would instinctively rather keep hidden. Why hidden? Because the suspicion is that, once they are brought out into the light, the responses we receive from others would likely destroy or crush us more than the burdens themselves. Rather than receiving empathetic, burden-bearing help, what we will actually get is judgment, condemnation and punishment.

There once was a man whose slumped shoulders and haunted eyes announced he was close to giving up. He blurted out, 'I am having trouble with alcohol, so do what you need to do: disfellowship me, ban me from church, whatever.'[18] He continued, 'I have a lovely home with three children and a beautiful wife. Yet to keep all that going – to pay for the kids, the mortgage – I have to keep my job. I have no choice but to do everything to keep my job, even though I am beyond stressed. I work and work and work. It's like I'm watching someone else at times, because I know I've had enough. I am beyond being full of responsibility and there are so many things to do. But then my boss asks me to do more, and I'm screaming at myself to say no. But I say, "Yes." I have to say "yes" to keep my job. So I leave home when it's dark, and I get home when it's dark, having worked 15-hour days. And, when I do arrive home, the kids are in bed, my wife is in bed, and dinner is a microwaved, dried-out mess. Even then, I get my laptop out to fire off some last-minute emails. Eventually, I sit and just stare into space, depressed at what my life has become. I can feel myself spiralling out of control. And so sometimes – no, more than sometimes; often – I open a bottle and drink a shot or three and experience at least a moment of escape. There is something releasing about feeling the liquid burn its way down to my stomach. So there it is: that's where I am; do your worst.'

'I can't belong to your church any more!' Upon hearing these words, a whole range of emotions and thoughts kick in. Have they lost their belief in God? Is this a spiritual crisis? Is their faith shaky? Do I need to have all the smart answers that have been built up over time at the ready in case they have a doctrinal issue? They go on, 'I can't be a part of your church any more because I smoke – and it's not just tobacco, if you catch my drift. There: I've said it. I've tried to give up. I know it's damaging me. I know it's not healthy. But when life gets too much, I light up. When I need to relax, I light up. When I need courage to face the day, I light up. So I know I can't be one of you any more.'

There was the man whose face was flushed red with embarrassment. He seemed to be forcing reluctant words out into the sunshine. 'I need to get something off my chest.' (It is difficult not to hold my breath at this point.) 'I can't believe I'm telling you about this. But I need to tell someone for some reason. I just feel so ashamed of myself, and I don't know where to turn.' He pauses and tries to gather himself. After taking a deep breath, he announces, 'You see, I look at stuff on my computer that I know that I shouldn't.' He seems a little lighter now. 'The weird thing is, I can go weeks without giving in, and I think, *Yes! I've conquered it.* But then I find my fingers irresistibly typing on the keyboard, and there I go again. I'm disgusted with myself. My family is dishonoured; but, above all, I feel I am dishonouring God simply by walking into church. So I won't be doing that any more. Sorry.'

There is fear, defiance, despair and surrender. All three of these stories have the same potential ending: exit! They all believe they need to jump before they are pushed. Their only option is to evade the words of censure that will wash them away. This is one of our elephants taking effect. I have been told on many occasions, 'I would like to be honest about my struggles, but I fear being judged and condemned because of that honesty.' So, keeping things to ourselves, we wrestle with our burdens, and at the same time we struggle with the horror of being found out and identified with our behaviour.

Remember that depersonalising tendency we all have? We all know the sort of social commentary that hangs in the atmosphere: *There goes the alcoholic'* – rather than Timothy, who has come to terms with controlling the illness that is alcoholism. *'She's the single mother with the delinquent children'* – as opposed to Mary, who has fought bravely to overcome the consequences of some decisions she might have made differently with hindsight. *'Here comes the divorcee'* – not Carley, who coped well when her husband departed for fields anew without her. We are all living out a life story that makes us unique. We and our narrative cannot be distilled down to soulless classifications. Our antennae should be quivering because, as we have seen, labelling others is the first step towards dehumanising them. Our response, as noted above, should be to re-personalise others. Remove the labels, and see individuals and their stories. However, this will only get us so far.

Real change is possible, but we need to move towards God's ideal for humanity. To understand what that entails, we go back again to the beginning. In Genesis, the first humans are described as being 'naked, and . . . not ashamed'.[19] A moment of clarity made me realise that I had subconsciously been adding to this verse to make it more palatable for someone with a conservative Christian upbringing flavoured with a dash of English reserve. I was reading the verse as saying: '*Although* they were naked, they were not ashamed,' or: '*Despite the fact they were* naked, *they were OK about it,* and so not ashamed.' Instead of seeing a fundamental link between the two, I was using one to excuse the other. Such was my discomfort that there was almost an audible sigh of relief once God got around to dressing them 'properly'.[20] At last, the first couple are in a place where we need not avert our gaze and can move along with the story. This same reticence is seen in the attempts to portray the first man and woman in Edenic splendour. In many works of art, their nakedness is discretely accommodated and certainly not celebrated. A judiciously placed fern here, a lock of hair there, all working together to preserve their modesty and our sensibilities.

Yet 'naked and not ashamed' are the last words we read before things start to go wrong. They are the conclusion to the wonderful, barely imaginable acts of creation that are described in Genesis 1 and 2. Six times God has declared His work to be 'good', and once 'very good'. This world, this garden, and this couple are as they should be. This state of being is not incidental. Now, it could be concluded that this is a call for us all to become naturists. However, it is ridiculous to think we are somehow closer to God's design for us every time we take a shower or a bath. We are missing the point if we understand this as being about Adam and Eve running around in their birthday suits. Admittedly, the Bible appears to move us in that direction by talking about clothes and coverings – but, from within their state of nakedness, there is something weightier to be revealed.

I recently came across the concept of a 'naked cake'. Naked cakes are all about exposed layers and minimal garnishes. With no, or barely-there, icing, the idea is to allow what is normally kept hidden – the cakes and fillings – to be the stars of the show. Then there are also phrases such as 'naked flame' or 'the naked truth'. To be naked in this sense is to be authentic, unshielded, not hidden but completely on show.

It is this aspect of nakedness that is found in Job 26:5-14. Here, Job sings a hymn in which the power and authority God has over His creation are laid out for all to see. Everything pales into comparison with God, including death and the grave, as Job exclaims, 'Sheol is naked before God, and Abaddon has no covering.'[21] The writer of the sermon to the Hebrews, commenting on this verse, says, 'And before him no creature is hidden, but all are naked and laid bare to the eyes of the one to whom we must render an account.'[22] This side of Eden, this is the stuff of nightmares. Every crease and every wrinkle is open to scrutiny. A naked body bears witness to every day spent or missed at the gym, every slice of cake that should have been avoided, every child given birth to, every scar from every accident or operation. To be naked like this is to have our stories on show with nothing held back. Those bits of ourselves that we secrete away in the dark recesses of our lives are now illuminated by a ten-thousand-watt bulb. Every good thing we have done, every sin we have committed, every lapse we have suffered is fetched right out into the open. God's goal for humanity is that we be naked and not ashamed. But this sounds like the exact opposite and far from ideal.

And so shame keeps winning; and we need to keep reminding ourselves that God knows what He is doing and is not out to get us, but is for us. There are positives to be found in this state of being: there are no lies, no subterfuge, no deceit. What you see is what you get, and what you get is everything a person is. The man and the woman hold nothing of themselves back. They are naked in the sense that they are fully known.

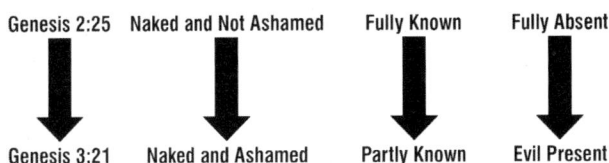

Figure 23: Shame and nakedness

We are only partly known to ourselves and others, but fully to God, of course. Even now, God 'knows us far better than we know ourselves', and knows us completely.[23]

It is unlikely, this side of the Second Coming, that we will ever be fully known by someone else.[24] Even in the most intimate of relationships, both parties hold something of themselves back. But there is a reason that being fully known is God's ideal and is something for which to aim. That is because it realises the God-given potential that lies within the relationships we have with others. In the context of marriage, it is suggested, 'To be loved but not known is comforting but superficial. To be known and not loved is our greatest fear. But to be fully known and truly loved is, well, a lot like being loved by God.'[25]

Herein lies a clue as to how to combat shame. Remember, when shame kicks in, it compels us to run away from people, avoid human contact, refrain from talking about ourselves and our issues. Shame has us deflecting, ducking, resisting and withdrawing. But, if we want to win the war against shame in our lives, then we need to go on the opposite journey to the one Adam and Eve did – to go from being not naked and ashamed to naked and not ashamed, so living up to the Genesis 2:25 ideal. To do that, we need to run towards people, seek human contact, find someone we can trust to talk to, and reveal who we are.

To make this journey to 'knownness' is indeed to feel naked. No wonder that Brené Brown terms the journey away from shame as a voyage towards vulnerability – a practice she characterises as being about uncertainty, risk and emotional exposure.[26] This concept finds biblical support in James's letter, referred to earlier. It is a familiar passage because it gives instructions as to what to do if ill. 'Are any among you sick? They should call for the elders of the church and have them pray over them, anointing them with oil in the name of the Lord.'[27] I have taken part in this service many times; and, apart from on one or two occasions, the person being anointed is at death's door. And it is not just that this biblical practice is left to the last moment. Without exception, the person involved has a physical ailment. As in other walks of life, there seems to be an inevitable privileging of physical illness. However, what about mental or psychological health? What happens if we take into account the Hebrew understanding of a person as a unity of body, soul and spirit?

Illness and suffering came as part of the package when evil took hold in Genesis 3; and, as evil made its inglorious way into the lives of our ancestors, it was accompanied by its handmaiden, shame. Not only do we, as a species, succumb to diseases and a bewildering number of debilitating physical conditions, but we also have to deal with states of shame that cause all sorts of mental anguish and associated physiological issues. Even if it is not the direct cause of our mental health problems, shame exacerbates and worsens their effects because of the shame associated with having the condition in the first place. There is a sea change happening with the rise in education and more people talking openly about their struggles with their mental health. But, in Christian communities, there is still a stigma attached to being depressed, for example, because it's often claimed that Christians should have enough faith not to be in that condition. To suffer a physical injury like a sprained ankle is to be treated with far more compassion.

Bearing this in mind, what if the healing that James is referring to is for more than 'just' physical healing? What if, when he writes, 'Confess your sins to one another, and pray for one another, so that you may be healed,' there is more than guilt being addressed?[28] What if psychological healing can be achieved through the act of confession? What if we expand our understanding of what confession is about to include the sharing, expressing and revealing of personal insights such that we can be made whole? We Protestants have shied away from these verses in case we fall into the trap of confessing our sins to someone other than the God who alone can forgive us – but, in doing so, we may have neglected the therapeutic nature of vulnerability; that, by opening up to each other and praying for one another, we may experience the power of God's healing in our lives as we move towards the ideal of being naked and not ashamed.

A word of caution is appropriate at this point. It is dangerous to think that what is being suggested here is that we should all start counselling each other. Indeed, it is not always safe or appropriate to confess everything to everyone – traumatic experiences being a prime example.[29] But we can encourage a culture of talking and listening that is not about letting it all hang out in public, but about being vulnerable enough to share with people 'with whom we've developed relationships that can bear the weight of our story'.[30] Therefore, this is not about resurrecting the spirit of the *Jeremy Kyle Show* and washing our dirty linen in public. It is about developing authentic, restorative relationships.

This brings us back to Galatians 6: for, if we are to bear one another's burdens, we need to develop relationships that make that possible; to be able to have someone in our lives in front of whom we can take off our masks on the understanding that they have our best interests at heart; to be sure we are in a place where it is safe to begin to make ourselves known to the person, because they do not see our worth in what we do, but in who we are. Such a person is found only by investing in other people ourselves. And, as this is a spiritual enterprise, both parties need to have 'received the Spirit' so they can 'restore such a one in a spirit of gentleness'.[31] What is being asked for here is demanding, but with a Spirit-led heart we can put another's interests first.

To be other-centred is vital in meeting Paul's challenge to be restorers (Galatians 6:1) and bearers (Galatians 6:2). This comes through when considering what Paul means by writing, 'Take care that you yourselves are not tempted' (Galatians 6:1). Tempted by what, exactly? One suggestion is that Paul is warning the restorer not to go the same way of the person being helped, so falling into their sin. But, in the context of other-centredness, how about the temptation to assume a position of superiority – that I am somehow better than you are because you are the one who needs my help? It is only a short step from there to infrahumanising the other person and invoking a sanctity ethic that suggests I am not just better than you, but somehow holier. But Paul cannily warns against this attitude, writing, 'If you think you are too important to help someone, you are only fooling yourself. You are not that important. Pay careful attention to your own work, for then you will get the satisfaction of a job well done, and you won't need to compare yourself to anyone else.'[32] The helper-helped relationship does not result in a ranking system. Vulnerability works both ways. My being vulnerable with you opens up a space for you to be vulnerable with me – in my woundedness I can meet you in yours.[33] I am no longer an expert, but a fellow traveller on a journey to wholeness in a world infected by sin and shame.

I suggested that Galatians 6:1-10 offers an inspiring view of what church can be. I also hope it is an attainable view. I pray for the day when we have communities who actively root out shame and the culture it generates in favour of a culture of vulnerability; that, through the indwelling Spirit, there can be groups of people who are responsibly and carefully going on the journey towards being fully known, and so leaving shame behind.

Something to think about along the way

Some friends and I are away for the weekend and we decide to visit a church none of us has been to before. We turn up fashionably late, but, in our defence, we are on holiday. Much to our surprise, the worship service has yet to start. We hunker down as one announcement follows another, and then another and then another, as each of the dozen or so speakers not only takes their time, but also the opportunity to deliver a mini-sermon.

By the time the service itself starts, we already feel like we have 'done' church, but resist the temptation to leave. After other preliminaries, a time of prayer is announced. In response, many take advantage of the faded, slightly grubby cushions on offer. Failing to secure one of these, one of my accomplices decides he would rather just lean forward in his chair. Just as he has settled, a huge hand gets placed firmly on his shoulder. It comes with just enough pressure to prevent any doubt as to its intended authority. The hand is accompanied by a deep bass voice, a commanding voice, a voice that insists upon and expects obedience. The man to whom both voice and hand belong growls, 'The elder said kneel!' Getting to the 'eel' of 'kneel', the grip on my friend's shoulder becomes vice-like and he is physically forced to the ground.

I have to confess that, at the time, I probably would not have taken this in quite the good grace my friend did. We were well into our twenties. We had driven to this church in our own cars, setting off from houses with mortgages we paid for, so it might be thought that we were long past being treated like children. Worse than that, this person had no idea who we were, where we were from, what we were about. And yet he had taken it upon himself to 'gently restore' my friend.

[1] Guiseppe Labianca, 'Defend Your Research: It's Not "Unprofessional" to Gossip at Work', *Harvard Business Review*, 2010
[2] Mike Myatt, 'The Fastest Way to Kill Corporate Culture', *Forbes*:
https://www.forbes.com/sites/mikemyatt/2012/01/05/the-fastest-way-to-kill-corporate-culture/ (accessed 5 August 2019)
[3] James 3:5b-6
[4] James 3:8, 9
[5] 'Pope Francis: Avoid "Terrorism" of Gossip', *CatholicHerald.Co.Uk*, 2017:
http://www.catholicherald.co.uk/news/2017/12/02/pope-francis-avoid-terrorism-of-gossip/ (accessed 12 January 2018)
[6] Jayson D. Bradley, '5 Tips for Dealing with Gossip in the Church', *Ministry Advice*, 2017:
http://ministryadvice.com/church-gossip/ (accessed 12 January 2018)
[7] 'The Three Breeds of Gossip': *http://www.churchleadership.org/apps/articles/default.asp?articleid=42413&columnid=* (accessed 12 January 2018)
[8] Galatians 1:6
[9] Used with permission.
[10] John G. Strelan, 'Burden-Bearing and the Law of Christ: A Re-Examination of Galatians 6:2', *Journal of Biblical Literature*, 94.2 (1975), 266-276: *https://doi.org/10.2307/3265735*
[11] Galatians 2:20
[12] Martinus C. de Boer, *Galatians: A Commentary* (Louisville, KY: Westminster John Knox Press, 2011), p. 376
[13] 'The word for "burden" (*baros*) means literally "a heavy weight or stone" someone is required to carry for a long distance.' See Timothy George, *Galatians: An Exegetical and Theological Exposition of Holy Scripture* (Nashville, TN: B&H Publishing Group, 1994), p. 413.
[14] George, p. 413
[15] George, p. 414

[16]Rather than a random collection of sayings, it can be seen that in this section of Galatians Paul is alternating between responsibilities a church community has towards its members and how the individual members are to conduct themselves. See Ben Witherington III, *Grace in Galatia: A Commentary on St Paul's Letter to the Galatians* (London, New York: T. & T. Clark Ltd., 2004), p. 419; G. Walter Hansen, *Galatians* (Downers Grove, IL: InterVarsity Press, 1994).

[17]The following is adapted from Hansen, *Galatians*, pp. 182, 183; Ben Witherington III, *Grace in Galatia: A Commentary on Paul's Letter to the Galatians* (London; New York: T. & T. Clark International, 2004), p. 418.

[18]The stories that follow have had the details and situations modified to protect the people involved.

[19]Genesis 2:25

[20]Genesis 3:21

[21]Job 26:6

[22]Hebrews 4:13

[23]Romans 8:27, MSG; 1 Corinthians 13:12

[24]Although viewing being fully known as aspirational, that is not to deny its pursuit, as in Ryan Frederick and Selena Frederick, *See-Through Marriage: Experiencing the Freedom and Joy of Being Fully Known and Fully Loved* (Grand Rapids, MI: Baker Books, 2020).

[25]Timothy Keller, *The Meaning of Marriage: Facing the Complexities of Marriage with the Wisdom of God* (London: Hachette UK, 2011)

[26]Brené Brown, p. 34

[27]James 5:14

[28]James 5:16

[29]'When Not Talking About Past Trauma Is Wise', *Psychology Today*: https://www.psychologytoday.com/blog/the-creativity-cure/201501/when-not-talking-about-past-trauma-is-wise (accessed 5 November 2019)

[30]Brené Brown, p. 46

[31]Galatians 6:1a

[32]Galatians 6:3, 4, NLT

[33]Grant D. Miller and DeWitt C. Baldwin Jr, 'The Implications of the Wounded-Healer Archetype for the Use of Self in Psychotherapy', in: *The Use of Self in Therapy*, edited by Michele Baldwin (New York; London: Routledge, 2013), pp. 81-96

From exclusion to acceptance

D avid M. Brown tells the story of how, when he was at university, he met someone who claimed to be a warlock.[1] They were both attending a party at the time, and the warlock stood out because he was dressed flamboyantly all in black. He was a member of a local coven and had to leave the party because he was on duty that night. Every Thursday he would patrol the streets of the city for four hours in his black car, looking for people who needed help. He asked no questions and did not request to get reimbursed should he assist someone whose car had run out of fuel or who needed a lift because they were hitchhiking. In Brown's experience, this is the only person he ever came across who was a real-life good Samaritan; and so he renames the parable 'The Outsider', and proposes that if Jesus were telling the story today, instead of a Samaritan, He would have an atheist, Muslim or warlock as His hero.[2]

His approach certainly gives the story more of an edge. We might know of the edge between the Jews and the Samaritans, but we do not feel it in the same way as they did. From a distance, the two groups had so much in common that they should have been inseparable. They both believed in the one God, and that they had descended from Abraham, Isaac and Jacob. Their respective priests both came from the tribe of Levi and were from the line that included Aaron, Eleazar and Phineas. It is said that their synagogues were so similar that it was a challenge to tell them apart.[3] The cause of the schism between the two could only have been resolved by modern DNA testing. The Samaritans believed they were the descendants of Ephraim and Manasseh. The Jews thought they were Cutheans, descendants of people from Cuthah who were imported by the all-conquering Assyrians to recolonise Samaria.[4] For a Jew, any similarities were superficial – a Samaritan was an outsider to be rejected.

We Christians would not behave in the same way now, of course? Ask whom we will accept into our church community, and we will quickly answer, 'Everyone!' How could we say anything different? It is the natural and instinctive response, and the opposite would feel wrong; for the opposite of 'accept' is 'reject', and how could any Christian hold their head high having done that?

In practice, it is probably somewhat different. Suppose someone is harassing and stalking one of the other members of the community – would we accept them? How about a person whose sexual predilections mean the children of the church are under threat? What if a person with anger issues disrupts one out of every two meetings? We may like to think that, as Christians, we are accepting of everyone, but, in reality, it is not so easy to be so accommodating. Indeed, we have built quite a different reputation for ourselves. Churches are known to struggle to accept those who identify as LGBTQI, those who are of a different ethnicity to the dominant culture, Christians from differing faith traditions, warlocks and witches. But it goes deeper than that. Even for those who make it 'within the walls of a church', the type of acceptance experienced can leave much to be desired. Instead of it being full and complete, we naturally practise acceptance that is partial, contingent and temporary.

Partial acceptance is what it says on the tin. It is me maintaining that 'I will accept X about you, but not Y.' For example, I accept the Jack who cleans his room, but reject the Jack who makes it untidy in the first place. This is the pick-and-mix version of acceptance, where I accept the things I like, and reject the things I do not. Contingent acceptance occurs when a person is accepted on the understanding that they will change 'for the better'. This is a familiar relationship dynamic seen where a person agrees to marriage thinking that, with a little coaching, their partner will cut out their unacceptable behaviour and turn into the ideal spouse. The vision of the future is a home where the toilet seat is always put down after use, the toothpaste tube is capped, and the bedroom floor is no longer utilised as a two-dimensional wardrobe. All it will take is a few adjustments and some diplomatic, but firm, encouragement. But this is me saying to someone that I will accept them as they are only on the condition they will eventually change to become the person I would like them to be. Finally, there is temporary acceptance. This type of acceptance is related to contingent acceptance, but is time-limited. In effect, this is giving a person a free pass for an amount of time to give them the opportunity to become more acceptable: 'I will "accept" you leaving the toilet seat up for six months, but after that, if you do not change, we're going to have words.'

This is not confined to married couples. Imagine a situation where Johnny turns up to your church services for the first time. Being a church community that values acceptance, you overlook the pungent mix of alcohol and cigarette odour that follows him around as if he is generating his own climate. His clothes are shabby and ill-fitting, and display some disturbing stains. You are fine with this, as the local minister has drilled into the congregation that you need to be accepting of people such as this. A couple of weeks later, he falls asleep and loses control of his bladder. Subsequently, the floor is sanitised. The pew cushions are unceremoniously burnt, as they are way past being rescued. But that is OK, because the church is welcoming to the 'least of these', and that includes Johnny.

In the spirit of good fellowship, there are regular shared lunches where the members bring food for themselves and others. For many, this is the highlight of the month, because, rather than rushing off at the service's conclusion, they get to talk, share and really get to know and support each other. Johnny's introduction to this tradition proves eventful. He has not eaten nutritious food in such quantities in a long while, causing his stomach to violently protest at the sudden intrusion. Most of the lovingly prepared food finds its way back out into the wild, liberally coating the cubicle, cistern, toilet seat and pan that Johnny thankfully made it to before projectile vomiting. The members who are blessed with the spiritual gifts of service and helps spring into action to clean up the facilities and Johnny – all is once again spick and span.

A few weeks later, the preacher has come to a poignant moment in his sermon. Both for effect, and to allow the congregation to contemplate what has been said, he pauses dramatically. Meanwhile, Johnny has had a particularly rough night. The service has acted like anaesthetic, and, combined with comfortable cushions and a warm room, sleep is irresistible. As the speaker looks meaningfully into the congregation's eyes, the silence is shattered with a sonorous snore from Johnny that seems to hit the decibel level of a jet engine. The moment is lost forever. Looks of shock mingle with sniggers. But, in the end, that is fine. Johnny cannot help it.

Fast-forward several months, and Johnny is still providing unwanted sound effects with devastatingly efficient timing. He has deposited the contents of his stomach at various places around the building. He continues to be accompanied by eye-wincing aromas. Plans are hatched to help Johnny out. Clothing is offered, but, alas, is vigorously rebuffed. He is encouraged to enrol in Alcoholics Anonymous to help with his addictions, but after one meeting he declares that it is not for him. Food parcels are accepted, but the suspicion is that they are discarded on the journey home. Johnny is gently encouraged to sit on chairs that are more easily cleaned. During services, sentries are positioned next to him, charged with delivering judicious nudges to help keep Johnny in a conscious, non-snoring state. However, on one occasion this measure backfires as Johnny splutters awake after one particularly firm elbow in the ribs and ejects expletives out into the atmosphere like confetti.

Patience starts to wear thin. Every effort to help Johnny comes to nothing. The chats with him about his behaviour start to get pointed and firm, but prove to be no more effective. The many measures to bring about a reformed, clean-cut Johnny end in abject failure. After months of trying, acceptance has worn thin and reached its expiry date. Finally, it is decided that Johnny should be persuaded he would be better off elsewhere. The people who were so wonderfully accepting at first now find that their acceptance is partial, temporary and contingent. No one should say this acceptance thing is easy.

Partial, contingent and temporary acceptance is driven by our old friend, bounded-set thinking. While Johnny was accepted on one level, he was yet to be accepted as a fully fledged member. Of course, there were good intentions, but the attempts to 'help' Johnny were being driven partly with this aim in mind. There were stated and unstated criteria that Johnny had to meet for the membership boundary to be crossed. The not-so-subtle message is that, to become one of us, Johnny needs to be like us.

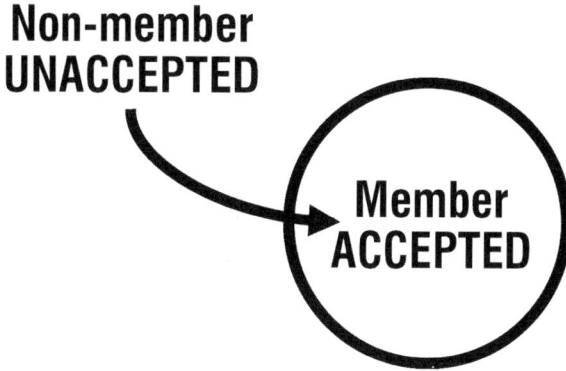

Figure 24: Acceptance and membership

We use language that speaks to this way of thinking by saying that someone has been '*accepted* into membership' and reinforce the concept that acceptance and membership are inextricably linked. Ideally, as the various criteria are met, Johnny would be understood to be on a journey that will see his acceptability grow until he achieves the desired outcomes and occupies a new place within the boundary that encompasses the church community.

So here is the problem. There is a 'difference between accepting someone as he or she is, versus reserving acceptance until that person changes into some image or likeness we might prefer. . . . Underneath that project lurks the reality of conditional acceptance, and that's exactly what weakens and can even destroy a marriage. It prevents love from being fully real.'[5] Even though this is written in the context of marriage, it is relevant in any relationship based on neighbourliness. The implications for reaching out to those outside a church's boundaries are also sobering. 'If a person accepts another on the basis of condition, a message of rejection comes through more strongly than the message of acceptance.'[6] Conditional acceptance is damaging to our relationships, be they inside or outside church communities. For communities who are to be characterised by the *agape* love they have for one another, it is sobering to understand that partial, contingent and temporary acceptance does not qualify as acceptance at all.[7]

This is all related to the subject of personal identity that was raised earlier.[8] As we've seen, to identify someone by the labels we give them depersonalises them and leads to shame. It also makes acceptance difficult. For example, if I see someone covered from head to toe in tattoos, it is easy to mentally label them as 'the tattooed woman' or 'the tattooed man'. Eventually, as they become more and more identified by and with their label, the person disappears and I see only the tattoos. Likewise, when the woman turned up to the funeral in what the elder deemed to be inappropriate clothing, he ceased to see the person and just saw a lack of clothes. If a person turns up to a church service late, rather than someone made in the image of God, we see only a latecomer. We have seen that identifying someone by what they do and achieve leads to shame. It also means that if I disapprove of Johnny's behaviour and actions I will disapprove of Johnny. When I find Johnny's behaviour and actions unacceptable, I will stop accepting Johnny. If I sit down and eat with tax collectors and disreputable sinners and my critics are unable to separate out the person and their actions, they will view my acceptance as tacit approval of others' inappropriate behaviour. In my experience, this is the greatest barrier to overcome in accepting others.

You sometimes bump into Bill and get into a conversation with him over a hot beverage at a local café. He seems a pleasant enough chap to be around. He always has a humorous story to tell, and you gladly have a chat with him whenever you see him. It strikes you one day that you do not know what Bill does for a living. He is evasive when you raise the subject, telling you that he 'does a bit of this and a bit of that'. One day, as you hurry home from work, you catch a glimpse of the local newspaper and stop stock-still in the street. Right on the front page is a picture of Bill. The picture is under the headline, '*Local Car Thief Sentenced to 5 Years in Prison*'. You quickly scan the story and find that Bill has been convicted of stealing over fifty cars in the space of three years – no wonder you have not seen him for a few months, and will certainly not see him for many more.

Bill, once known as a cheeky chappie, now has new labels: thief, criminal, prisoner, inmate. No law-abiding citizen can approve of Bill's behaviour, but can they accept Bill? No, if they think that to accept Bill means to agree with or condone stealing dozens of cars. Yes, if they can separate Bill as a person from his criminal activity. Just because we accept someone does not mean we also have to accept the things they do with which we disagree. And that is why true acceptance is so difficult. Our instinctive way of thinking and behaving undermines our ability to accept others. If I do not care for tattoos, tardiness or a person's sense of fashion, then I might be tempted to reject them as a person.

The greatest exposition on acceptance in the Bible is found in Romans 14:1-15:7. Paul begins and ends this passage with similar instructions.

'**Welcome** those who are weak in faith, but not for the purpose of quarrelling over opinions' (14:1).

'**Welcome** one another, therefore, just as Christ has welcomed you, for the glory of God' (15:7).

The New Revised Standard Version's use of 'welcome' here does not deliver the full force of the word. This is not the sort of welcome that results in being offered a hearty hello, a comfy chair and a slice of cake. Rather, it means 'to incorporate each other into your Christian circle with no inner reservations' or 'to take to oneself'.[9] The King James Version's use of 'receive' moves more towards where we need to be, but arguably those translations, such as the New Living Translation and the New International Version, that translate the original Greek as 'accept' are nearer the mark. Looking at the two verses side by side highlights how Paul develops the concept of acceptance. He begins with a limited view, based on the strong accepting the weak, and concludes by asserting that all should accept all.

In between these two verses, there is a discussion about the behaviour of the weak and the strong, their menu choices and worship practices. Much time has been spent on identifying the two groups.[10] Paul himself categorises 'the weak' as those who 'eat only vegetables' and the strong as those who 'believe in eating anything'.[11] It is noted that no one eats just anything, and at no point since the Flood has a vegetable-only diet been commanded, so Paul may have been exaggerating to make a point. Therefore, ' "eating everything" in the original context means less than everything, and the notion of eating "only vegetables" includes more.'[12] For our purposes, it is not necessary to get involved in identifying the two groups. But we do need to understand that there is one group of people who think, believe and act differently from those of another group. We can then focus on what acceptance is all about according to Paul in these circumstances.

The list of ways to be welcoming or accepting of others is surprisingly short, but demanding:
• Don't argue with people we think are inferior to us (14:1, 2).
• Don't look down on others (14:3).
• Don't condemn others for their actions (14:3).
• Seek to understand others' motives (14:6).[13]
• Don't judge: that is God's job (14:3, 4, 10, 13).
• Get an appropriate sense of perspective (14:16, 17).
• Be other-centred (14:21; 15:1).

What does this sort of acceptance look like in practice? In the passage we examined in Philippians, Paul raised up Christ as our example, and he does so again here by urging the Romans to 'accept each other just as Christ has accepted you so that God will be given glory'.[14] Remember, this is the Christ, who did not cling on to His divinity, but rather took 'the form of a slave, being born in human likeness';[15] Christ – who, as God, is in every possible way superior to us, but did the very opposite of exploiting His position by becoming one of us; Christ – who does not look down on us, but looks us in the eye as a fellow human being; Christ – whom 'God did not send . . . into the world to condemn the world, but in order that the world might be saved through him';[16] Christ – who said, 'I came not to judge the world, but to save the world';[17] Christ – who has the human perspective like no other, such that 'we do not have a high priest who is unable to sympathize with our weaknesses';[18] Christ – who took on the sins of the world in the greatest act of other-centredness that has ever been and ever will be seen, so that you and I might have life.[19] If ever we need to understand what it means to 'take someone to oneself' and be accepting in the ways Paul lists in this passage, we need only look to Jesus.

But is Paul once again setting the standard too high by proposing Christ as our example? More likely, he has more practical outcomes in mind and 'hopes this acceptance will lead to the unity of the weak and the strong, and give the Romans a foretaste of the ultimate unity of Jews and Gentiles in eschatological salvation'.[20] The impact on the purpose of the church is uppermost in Paul's mind. He hopes that, by preaching all-encompassing acceptance, he is preparing 'the Romans for participation in a wider mission because it eliminates prejudice which can hinder the acceptance of the outsider'.[21]

Having thought about this for a while, I am aware that I struggle to fully accept others. I catch myself labelling, infrahumanising and diminishing. I see a politician who is labelled by the media as misogynistic, narcissistic and racist, and those labels dominate the way I view him as a person. I believe that such behaviours are completely unacceptable. And, because I am a sinful human being who struggles to separate the person from what they do, my acceptance is barely even partial. But I have also come to understand that such self-awareness is a crucial first step. Rachel Naomi Remen in her book *Kitchen Table Wisdom* writes about an encounter with psychologist Carl Rogers where he tells her the following: 'Before every session, I take a moment to remember my humanity. There is no experience that this man has that I cannot share with him, no fear that I cannot understand, no suffering that I cannot care about, because I too am human. No matter how deep his wound, he does not need to be ashamed in front of me. I too am vulnerable. And, because of this, I am enough. Whatever his story, he no longer needs to be alone with it. This is what will allow his healing to begin.'[22]

This beautiful quote articulates so much of what acceptance is about and can lead to. It lays out for us the raw power of what it means to 'take someone to oneself' and the healing it brings to others. It challenges the idea that the other is to be set up in opposition by proposing an acceptance that is based on humility, mutuality and identification. As I read that quote, I am reminded of the text from Hebrews 4:15 quoted above. In full, it reads, 'For we do not have a high priest who is unable to sympathize with our weaknesses, but we have one who in every respect has been tested as we are, yet without sin.' Christ's role as our high priest does not see Him elevated and separated; rather, He moves towards us. Peter, in his first letter, takes on the Old Testament concept of a nation of priests and brings it forward into dialogue with the contemporary church whose members are 'like living stones' and so are to let themselves 'be built into a spiritual house, to be a holy priesthood'.[23] In accepting others as Christ accepts us, we too are to be priests who practise acceptance grounded and founded on mutuality, humility and identification.

And here is the deep irony about all of this. It is in accepting others as they are that change happens. Refusal to accept others does not result in them being challenged, but in rejection. If a wife and a husband want to see their relationship grow and deepen, they have to accept each other as they are. If we want to see others deepen their relationship with Christ, we need to accept them as they are. If we come across someone like Bill, we are to accept him as he is. Accept him, in the same way as Jesus accepted a thief He encountered by welcoming him with the words, 'Truly I tell you . . . *you will be with me* in Paradise.'[24]

Acceptance therefore has deep theological significance. What impact might it have on church communities? As daunting as this all is, there are Spirit-filled baby steps we can take to effect change, some of which have been alluded to in the pages above. If acceptance is about taking another to oneself, then it is about reducing the distance between us and them, me and you. This makes sense most within a church community based on centre-set thinking where our inclination to differentiate is downplayed. It makes sense most in a church community that does not operate within boundaries that exclude. This allows us to see every person as on a journey – fellow travellers exploring faith. The alternative 'difference approach' sees a church group acting as a supplier of spiritual goods to the community. An accepting approach would rather see a church community investigate how they fit in as part of their local community. Members of a church that take a 'difference' approach would naturally act as if they are salespeople, rather than accepting that all are on a journey of faith and have something to share with each other.

Often, church communities carry out needs-based surveys in a bid to understand how they can make inroads into their local population. There is, of course, a biblical imperative to meet people's needs – feed the hungry, clothe the naked, shelter the homeless. Identifying the needs in a local community is a compassionate thing to do. However, the 'difference' approach makes it appear as if the needs of the members of the church community are of a different category than those encountered outside in the wider community. A moment's reflection will see us acknowledge that we have much in common: from relationship breakdowns to debts, from loneliness to failing health. An acceptance approach would recognise the commonalities and seek shared solutions. The selling of spiritual goods in a difference approach reinforces the idea that we are to develop 'contacts' and sell a product which, by and large, is based on information and doctrine; but acceptance based on mutuality and humility allows for a dialogue to take place that leads to perspectives being shared and insights exchanged. To achieve this, relationships must be established – and then, as Carl Rogers suggests, the healing can begin.

Table 5

Bounded-set Thinking DIFFERENCE	Centre-set Thinking ACCEPTANCE
Partial-Contingent-Temporary	Humility-Mutuality-Identification
What service(s) can we provide for the community?	What role do we play in our community?
Salesperson selling a product (set of beliefs)	Fellow traveller on a journey of faith
What are the hardships and difficulties, joys and pleasures in people's lives?	What hardships and difficulties, joys and pleasures do we share?
What information do we have to give to others?	What are the different perspectives from which we can learn and understand?
How can we make contacts?	How can we build relationships?
How can we save the neighbourhood?	How can we have a reciprocal relationship with our neighbours?
How can we use resources to build a great church in this location?	How can we use the church's resources to seek a flourishing and great community?
Consumers	Neighbours
Radically different from the community	Radically different from yet radically committed to the community
Passionate disinterest	Passionate identification
People to be won	People to which to be related
Transformed talking to the conformed	Sharing in transformation

[1]David M. Brown, *All the Parables of Jesus: A Guide to Discovery* (Bloomington, IN: WestBow Press, 2012), p. 158
[2]David M. Brown, p. 158
[3]Gary N. Knoppers, *Jews and Samaritans: The Origins and History of Their Early Relations* (Oxford: Oxford University Press, 2013), p. 2
[4]Robert T. Anderson, 'Samaritans', in: *The Anchor Bible Dictionary, A-J*, edited by David Noel Freedman and Gary A. Herion (New York, NY: Yale University Press, 1992), pp. 941-947 (p. 941)
[5]David Michael Thomas, *Christian Marriage: The New Challenge* (Collegeville, MN: Liturgical Press, 2007), p. 109
[6]Marvin Keene Mayers, *Christianity Confronts Culture: A Strategy for Crosscultural Evangelism* (Grand Rapids, MI: Zondervan, 1987), p. 46
[7]I'm thinking of John 13:35 here: 'By this everyone will know that you are my disciples, if you have love for one another.'
[8]See Movements 6 and 15.
[9]The word in the original Greek is Προσλαμβάνω or *proslambano*. See Kittel and Friedrich, *Dictionary,* vol. 4, p. 15.

[10]For a concise summary, see the table in Sigve K. Tonstad, *The Letter to the Romans: Paul Among the Ecologists* (Sheffield: Sheffield Phoenix Press Limited, 2017), p. 339.

[11]Romans 14:2

[12]Tonstad, *Romans*, pp. 334-337

[13]Both groups are looking to honour or please the Lord.

[14]Romans 15:7, NLT

[15]Philippians 2:7

[16]John 3:17

[17]John 12:47

[18]Hebrews 4:15

[19]1 Peter 2:24

[20]Carl N. Toney, *Paul's Inclusive Ethic: Resolving Community Conflicts and Promoting Mission in Romans 14-15* (Mohr Siebeck, 2008), p. 198

[21]Toney, *Paul's Inclusive Ethic*, p. 198

[22]Rachel Naomi Remen, *Kitchen Table Wisdom: Stories that Heal* (New York, NY: Riverhead Books, 1996), pp. 218, 219

[23]1 Peter 2:5; see also Exodus 19:6.

[24]Luke 23:43

Journey's end

When God stated that it 'is not good that the man should be alone' in Genesis 2:18, it was more than a statement affirming the need for a marriage partner to join the man in fulfilling the task of multiplying, filling and subduing, as per Genesis 1:28. It tells us that humans, by divine fiat and by nature, are not solitary creatures, but find completeness in relationships. Hence, 'Isolation is not the divine norm for human beings; community is the creation of God.'[1] But then, with the entrance of evil into the human story, shame inserts itself into relationships and introduces fault lines and fractures. The separation that has occurred because of this is evident immediately in the accusatory statement delivered by the man: 'The woman whom you gave to be with me, she gave me fruit from the tree, and I ate.'[2] No longer unified, 'the man's response to God's interrogation shows that the man and woman are both alone.'[3]

Western societies that are driven by individualism are living demonstrations of the tragic effects of the lack of community. Nowhere is this seen more than in the rise in mental illness. The number of prescriptions for antidepressant medication nearly doubled when comparing 2008 to 2018 in the UK.[4] The strengths and weaknesses of social media are often debated. On a positive note, where young people in particular are concerned, it can be seen to offer a safe space to seek help and advice for issues like mental health. However, the lack of real-world connectivity and community remains a problem. One survey found that young adults and adolescents born after 1995 have shown increased levels of negative psychological symptoms such as psychological distress, major depression and suicidal thoughts. The most noticeable spike in symptoms happened in 2011, which approximately coincides with the emergence of social media.[5] A reticence to talk to someone and seek help when feeling down or depressed means that suicide is the biggest killer of males between the ages of 18 and 49.[6] Half a million people in the UK go five to six days without speaking to or seeing anyone at all.[7] There are 1 million older people in the UK who say they feel lonely all of the time. That loneliness can often be a cause of mental illness is well recognised, and it can be as harmful to health as smoking fifteen cigarettes a day.[8]

The solution is self-evident – social interaction. Aaron Fobian, a clinical psychologist from the University of Alabama, suggests that 'spending time with people face to face is a big protective factor against depression.' Simply talking about issues and having someone listen is greatly therapeutic. It enables us to feel empowered, because we are actively reaching out for connection and our concerns seem less daunting when we talk to others about them.[9] Community is therefore a life-and-death matter. To live apart from others is, with reference to Genesis 2:18, 'not good'. To fail to be in a community, to lack partnerships, to not communicate with another, to go it alone, is far from God's ideal.

While many charities are doing some fantastic things to address these issues, church communities have something more to offer. Churches can be places where humanness can flourish, because they are constituted as the body of the second Adam (that is, Jesus Christ). Churches can offer a space for a person to be a new creation, because they are in Christ. Church communities have the inestimable advantage of embracing as their reference point the *imago Dei*, the image of God Himself – God who is a community of Persons so bound together by love that They are one. A church community can acknowledge and seek the Holy Spirit, His movement, His fruit, His inspiring and empowering presence. And, even as church communities are constantly reminded of their own weaknesses and vulnerabilities, they learn to rely ever more not on their own resources, but on God. If so, church communities can thrive within a framework based on love for God and neighbours: neighbours who are unlimited, unbounded, accepted and seen face to face.

[1]K. A. Mathews, *Genesis* (Nashville, TN: Broadman & Holman Publishers, 1996), 1A, p. 213
[2]Genesis 3:12
[3]Laurence A. Turner, *Genesis* (Sheffield: Sheffield Phoenix Press, 2009), p. 23
[4]36 million increasing to 71 million. There may be other factors such as an over-eagerness to prescribe such medication; however, these factors do not account for the huge uplift in use. Source: NHS Digital.
[5]Jean M. Twenge and others, 'Age, Period, and Cohort Trends in Mood Disorder Indicators and Suicide-Related Outcomes in a Nationally Representative Dataset, 2005-2017', *Journal of Abnormal Psychology*, 128.3 (2019), pp. 185-199
[6]Charlotte Simms and others, *Suicide Statistics Report* (The Samaritans, September 2019)
[7]Age UK 2016, 'No One Should Have No One': *https://www.ageuk.org.uk/globalassets/age-uk/documents/reports-and-publications/reports-and-briefings/health--wellbeing/rb_dec16_no_one_should_have_no_one.pdf*
[8]'Loneliness' (Mind, 2019): *https://www.mind.org.uk/media/34882109/loneliness-2019-pdf-version.pdf* (accessed 17 November 2019); Holt-Lunstad, J., Smith, T. B., Layton, J. B., 'Social relationships and mortality risk: a meta-analytic review', *PLOS Medicine* 2010;7(7)
[9]'The Power of Talking', *Psychology Today*: *https://www.psychologytoday.com/blog/the-chronicles-infertility/201808/the-power-talking* (accessed 17 November 2019)

Appendix

A church that approaches its God-given potential is a community that:

- Prioritises people over rules and regulations;
- Appreciates how commands and commandments are for the benefit of people, and not the other way around;
- Understands the importance of how people are treated in the present because it loves its neighbours;
- Generates communities of neighbourliness;
- Brings the future hope and promise of the Gospel into present reality;
- Sees the greatest commandments not as onerous demands, but as a framework within which to live and thrive;
- Makes the Kingdom of God visible;
- Gets uncomfortable on behalf of and for the benefit of others;
- Expresses *splagchnizomai* compassion;
- Minimises boundaries;
- Has the Father, Son and Spirit at the centre of the life of its community;
- Embraces a dynamic understanding of the Christian journey;
- Understands the importance and primacy of relationships, without neglecting organisational needs;
- Expresses mercy, not disgust; practises mercy; and avoids legalism;
- While maintaining its core relationships and beliefs, adapts to the people whom God sends its way;
- Enhances humanness that is grounded in God's image;
- Values people as persons in their own right;
- Avoids labels and listens to stories;
- Is wary of the dangers and embraces the positives of systems;
- Shuns consumerism;
- Is other-centred and does not think of itself as better than it is;
- Puts others' interests first;
- Adopts an everyone-for-everyone paradigm;
- Does not see others as objects through whom to achieve;
- Does not define people by what they achieve, do, or appear to be, but rather . . .
- Sees others in relationship with and to God;

- Responds to those in a state of shame with mercy;
- Develops trusting relationships that allow for vulnerability and healing;
- Identifies with rather than distances itself from others in a spirit of mutuality;
- Practises acceptance that is unconditional and continuous.

Selected bibliography

Adams, Jay Edward, *The Biblical View of Self-Esteem, Self-Love, Self-Image*, first edition (Eugene, OR: Harvest House Publishers, 1986)

Alter, Robert, *The Art of Biblical Narrative* (Basic Books, 2011)

Beck, Richard, *Unclean: Meditations on Purity, Hospitality, and Mortality* (Cambridge, UK: Lutterworth Press, 2012)

Bosch, David Jacobus, *The Church as the Alternative Community* (Potchefstroom, South Africa: Instituut vir Reformatoriese Studie, 1982)

Brown, Brené, *Daring Greatly: How the Courage to Be Vulnerable Transforms the Way We Live, Love, Parent, and Lead* (London: Penguin Life, 2015)

Brown, David M., *All the Parables of Jesus: A Guide to Discovery* (Bloomington, IN: WestBow Press, 2012)

Clough, Miryam, *Shame, the Church and the Regulation of Female Sexuality* (London; New York: Routledge, 2017)

Cohen, Deborah, *Family Secrets: The Things We Tried to Hide* (Penguin, 2013)

Covey, Stephen R., and Merrill, Rebecca R., *The SPEED of Trust: The One Thing that Changes Everything* (New York, NY: Simon and Schuster, 2008)

Crosby, Robert C., *The Teaming Church: Ministry in the Age of Collaboration* (Nashville, TN: Abingdon Press, 2012)

Dean, Kenda Creasy, *Almost Christian: What the Faith of Our Teenagers Is Telling the American Church* (Oxford University Press, 2010)

DeSilva, David A., *Honor, Patronage, Kinship & Purity: Unlocking New Testament Culture* (Downers Grove, IL: InterVarsity Press, 2000)

Drane, John, *The McDonaldization of the Church: Consumer Culture and the Church's Future* (Macon, GA: Smyth & Helwys Publishing, Incorporated, 2012)

Edwards, Llewellyn, *Values-Led Lives: The Way Jesus Wants Us to Think and Act* (Grantham, UK: The Stanborough Press Limited, 2017)

Ellis, William, *Billy Sunday: The Man and His Message* (Moody Publishers, 2013)

Enns, Peter, *The Bible Tells Me So: Why Defending Scripture Has Made Us Unable to Read It* (London: Hodder & Stoughton, 2020)

Erickson, Millard J., *Making Sense of the Trinity: Three Crucial Questions* (Grand Rapids, MI: Baker Academic, 2000)

Esler, Philip F., *The First Christians in Their Social Worlds: Social-Scientific Approaches to New Testament Interpretation* (London; New York: Routledge, 2002)

Feltman, Charles, *The Thin Book of Trust: An Essential Primer for Building Trust at Work* (Bend, OR: Thin Book Publishing, 2011)

Frederick, Ryan, and Frederick, Selena, *See-Through Marriage: Experiencing the Freedom and Joy of Being Fully Known and Fully Loved* (Grand Rapids, MI: Baker Books, 2020)

Funk, Robert Walter, *Parables and Presence: Forms of the New Testament Tradition* (Phillipsburg, PA: Fortress Press, 1982)

Gawande, Atul, *Being Mortal: Illness, Medicine and What Matters in the End* (London: Profile Books, 2014)

Gowdy, Rick, *Agape-Love: How Important Is It Anyhow?* (Xulon Press, 2007)

Grenz, Stanley J., *Theology for the Community of God* (Grand Rapids, MI: William B. Eerdmans Publishing, 1994)

A Primer on Postmodernism (Grand Rapids, MI: William B. Eerdmans Publishing, 1996)

Gulley, Norman R., *Systematic Theology: God as Trinity* (Berrien Springs, MI: Andrews University Press, 2003)

Harrington, Hannah K., *The Purity and Sanctuary of the Body in Second Temple Judaism* (Göttingen: Vandenhoeck & Ruprecht, 2019)

Hartog, Paul, ' "Work Out Your Salvation": Conduct "Worthy of the Gospel" in a Communal Context', *Themelios*, 33.2 (2008), 19-33

Healy, Nicholas M., *Church, World and the Christian Life: Practical-Prophetic Ecclesiology* (Cambridge, UK: Cambridge University Press, 2000)

Hiebert, Paul G., 'Conversion, Culture and Cognitive Categories', *Gospel in Context*, 1.4 (1978), 24-29

'The Category "Christian" in the Mission Task', *International Review of Mission*, 72.287 (1983), 421-27

Transforming Worldviews: An Anthropological Understanding of How People Change (Baker Academic, 2008)

Jadhav, Narendra, *Untouchables: My Family's Triumphant Escape from India's Caste System* (University of California Press, 2007)

Jeremias, Joachim, *The Parables of Jesus*, translated by S. H. Hooke (London: SCM Press, 1972)

Jones, Gareth Stedman, *Outcast London: A Study in the Relationship Between Classes in Victorian Society* (London: Verso Books, 2014)

Keesmat, Syliva C., 'Strange Neighbours and Risky Care', in: *The Challenge of Jesus' Parables*, edited by Richard N. Longenecker (Grand Rapids, MI: William B. Eerdmans Publishing, 2000)

Kirkwood, William G., 'Storytelling and Self-confrontation: Parables as Communication Strategies', *Quarterly Journal of Speech*, 69.1 (1983)

Knoppers, Gary N., *Jews and Samaritans: The Origins and History of Their Early Relations* (Oxford: Oxford University Press, 2013)

Kumar, Professor Krishan, *The Idea of Englishness: English Culture, National Identity and Social Thought* (Farnham, Surrey: Ashgate Publishing, Ltd., 2015)

Lazić, Tihomir, *Towards an Adventist Version of Communio Ecclesiology: Remnant in Koinonia* (Cham, Switzerland: Springer Publishing Company, 2019)

Lewis, C. S., *The Four Loves* (London: HarperCollins UK, 2010)

Lewis, Helen Block, *Shame and Guilt in Neurosis* (New York, NY: International Universities Press, 1984)

Malina, Bruce J., *The New Testament World: Insights from Cultural Anthropology* (Louisville, KY: Westminster John Knox Press, 2001)

Mayers, Marvin Keene, *Christianity Confronts Culture: A Strategy for Crosscultural Evangelism* (Grand Rapids, MI: Zondervan, 1987)

Mobsby, Ian, *Fresh Expressions of Church and the Kingdom of God* (Norwich, Norfolk: Canterbury Press, 2014)

Morris, Derek J., *The Radical Prayer: Will You Respond to the Appeal of Jesus?* (Hagerstown, MD: Autumn House Publishing, 2008)

Muir-Wood, Robert, *The Cure for Catastrophe* (Oneworld Publications, 2016)

Nario-Redmond, Michelle R., *Ableism: The Causes and Consequences of Disability Prejudice* (Hoboken, NJ: John Wiley & Sons, 2019)

O'Keefe, John J., and Reno, Russell R., *Sanctified Vision: An Introduction to Early Christian Interpretation of the Bible* (Baltimore, MD: JHU Press, 2005)

Oord, Thomas Jay, *Defining Love: A Philosophical, Scientific, and Theological Engagement* (Grand Rapids, MI: Brazos Press, 2010)

Orr, Tamra B., *Combatting Body Shaming* (New York, NY: The Rosen Publishing Group, Inc., 2016)

Pattison, Stephen, *Shame: Theory, Therapy, Theology* (Cambridge: Cambridge University Press, 2000)

Paxman, Jeremy, *The English: A Portrait of a People* (London: Penguin Books, 1999)

Peck, M. Scott, *The Road Less Travelled* (Random House, 2012)

Peckham, John C., *Canonical Theology* (Grand Rapids, MI: William B. Eerdmans Publishing, 2016)

The Love of God: A Canonical Model (InterVarsity Press, 2015)

Percy, Martyn, *Engaging with Contemporary Culture: Christianity, Theology and the Concrete Church* (London; New York: Routledge, 2016)

Peterson, Eugene H., *Working the Angles: The Shape of Pastoral Integrity* (Grand Rapids, MI: William B. Eerdmans Publishing, 1987)

Richards, E. Randolph, and O'Brien, Brandon J., *Misreading Scripture with Western Eyes: Removing Cultural Blinders to Better Understand the Bible* (InterVarsity Press, 2012)

Rogerson, John, 'What Is Holiness?' in: *Holiness: Past and Present*, edited by Stephen C. Barton (London; New York: T. & T. Clark, 2003), pp. 3-21

Sellers, Tina Schermer, *Sex, God, and the Conservative Church: Erasing Shame from*

Sexual Intimacy (London, UK: Routledge, 2017)

Shweder, Richard A., *Why Do Men Barbecue? Recipes for Cultural Psychology* (Harvard University Press, 2003)

Sims, Andrew, *Is Faith Delusion? Why Religion Is Good for Your Health* (Bloomsbury Publishing, 2009)

Smith, David Livingstone, *Less than Human: Why We Demean, Enslave, and Exterminate Others* (New York: St Martin's Press, 2011)

Spicq, Ceslaus, *Agape in the New Testament, Volume 3: Agape in the Gospel, Epistles and Apocalypse of St John* (Eugene, OR: Wipf and Stock Publishers, 2006)

Stein, Robert H., *The Method and Message of Jesus' Teachings* (Louisville, KY, and London, UK: Westminster John Knox Press, 1994)

Stockitt, Robin, *Restoring the Shamed: Towards a Theology of Shame* (Wipf and Stock Publishers, 2012)

Tangney, June Price, and Dearing, Ronda L., *Shame and Guilt* (New York, NY, and London, UK: Guilford Press, 2002)

Thiselton, Anthony C., *Life After Death: A New Approach to the Last Things* (Grand Rapids, MI: William B. Eerdmans Publishing, 2011)

Thompson, Curt, *The Soul of Shame: Retelling the Stories We Believe About Ourselves* (Downers Grove, IL: InterVarsity Press, 2015)

Vanhoozer, Kevin J., *Faith Speaking Understanding: Performing the Drama of Doctrine* (Louisville, KY: Presbyterian Publishing Corporation, 2014)

Vardy, Peter, and Grosch, Paul, *The Puzzle of Ethics* (London: HarperCollins)

Viola, Frank, and Barna, George, *Pagan Christianity? Exploring the Roots of Our Church Practices* (Carol Stream, IL: Tyndale House Publishers, Inc., 2010)

Whidden, Woodrow Wilson, Moon, Jerry, and Reeve, John W., *The Trinity: Understanding God's Love, His Plan of Salvation, and Christian Relationships* (Hagerstown, MD: Review and Herald Publishing Association, 2002)

Wilson, Sandra D., *Released from Shame: Moving Beyond the Pain of the Past* (InterVarsity Press, 2002)

Witherington, Ben, *Making a Meal of It: Rethinking the Theology of the Lord's Supper* (Waco, TX: Baylor University Press, 2007)

Wright, Tom, *Surprised by Hope: Original, Provocative and Practical* (London: SPCK, 2012)

Furstenberg, Yair, Sievers, Joseph, and Levine, Amy-Jill, 'The Shared Image of Pharasaic Law in the Gospels and Rabbinic Tradition', in: *The Pharisees* (Grand Rapids, MI: William B. Eerdmans Publishing, 2021), pp. 119-219 (p. 205)

Zimbardo, Philip, *The Lucifer Effect: How Good People Turn Evil* (London; Sydney; Auckland; Johannesburg: Random House, 2011)